The Project Management A–Z

For Sylvie, Sonia and Paul

With love and countless thanks to
my first and best team.

The Project Management A–Z

A Compendium of Project Management Techniques and How to Use Them

Alan Wren

GOWER

Published by
Gower Publishing Limited
Gower House
Croft Road
Aldershot
Hampshire GU11 3HR
England

Gower Publishing Company
Suite 420
101 Cherry Street
Burlington, VT 05401–4405 USA
USA

Alan Wren has asserted his right under the Copyright, Designs and Patents Act 1988 to be identified as the author of this work.

British Library Cataloguing in Publication Data
Wren, Alan
   The Project Management A-Z: A Compendium of Project Management Techniques and How to Use Them
   1. Project management
   I. Title
   658.4'04

ISBN 0 566 08556 9 (Hardback)
ISBN 0 566 08557 7 (Looseleaf)

Library of Congress Cataloging-in-Publication Data
Wren, Alan
   The Project Management A-Z: A Compendium of Project Management Techniques and How to Use Them / Alan Wren.
      p.   cm.
   Includes bibliographical references.
   1. Project management. I. Title.
   HD69.P75W74 2003
   658.404–dc21   2002043748

Typeset in Bembo by IML Typographers, Birkenhead and printed
in Great Britain by Antony Rowe Ltd, Chippenham, Wiltshire

Contents

Appendix: PRINCE®   365

List of Figures

LIST OF
FIGURES

Background

My journey into project management started in 1969 at Wellworthy Limited in Lymington, Hampshire, then world leaders in the manufacture of diesel engine components. I spent time as a computer operator, then moved into programming and systems analysis, before returning to the Computer Operations Department, which I then managed.

In July 1979, with some trepidation, I moved on to join a team of consultants at John Hoskyns Limited in Bournemouth, initially delivering Operations Management and Systems Analysis training courses. Hoskyns Training was a true pioneer in the field of 'management by projects', with almost every aspect of work conducted using project management principles and techniques. It was an unbelievably stimulating environment, combining the pleasures and rewards of teaching and learning on each new assignment.

Two projects in my later years at Hoskyns were of the life-changing variety. The first followed some well-received training I had conducted for Mobil in Australia over a number of years. The Hoskyns Group decided to establish a project management training business in the region. I agreed to conduct a feasibility study, but, on completion, recommended that the scheme should not go ahead.

On my return, I managed a series of business projects until the second life-changing project arrived unexpectedly, in late 1992. What turned out to be my last assignment for Hoskyns (by then called Cap Gemini), was as the Project Manager of a downsizing and outplacement project in the severe recession that gripped the UK economy by the throat. Many listed for redundancy were senior managers and directors, friends and colleagues. It was a heavy responsibility.

After all the shockwaves settled, the project proceeded smoothly, and by March 1993 I was able to close it and report a high degree of success in helping 'casualties' back into work. Having said that, they were a highly talented and much sought after group of people! I was offered a role in the Management Consultancy Division, but decided to fulfil an ambition and set up my own business, leaving the company in 1993, sad to go, but feeling well equipped to fend for myself. I then launched Alan Wren & Associates, and later incorporated it as AWA Project Management Limited.

Since those early days, assignments have been varied and stimulating, and – as always – provided excellent opportunities to meet new people, learn new approaches and develop skills. I have conducted successful projects and programmes for British American Tobacco, Cap Gemini, The British Council, London Electricity, Pfizer, Anglian Water, Glaxo Wellcome, Charles Schwab, Pirelli Construction, The Public Trust Office, The Official Solicitor's Office and The Public Guardianship Office. Some lasted a few months, some lasted years.

You may find little new or unique in this book other than its direct-access format and presentation. Initially, I was keen to write a series of checklists, but this evolved into an 'instant' reference text, with the topics supplemented by checklists where appropriate. It is difficult to identify many precise sources of information. Much is generic and in the public domain. In many cases, my learning was by doing – admiring the theories often came later! However, it is important to acknowledge the authors who have influenced my thinking. Fred Brook's *Mythical Man Month* (1975) first fired my imagination. I believe that his question, 'How does a project get to be a year late?' might usefully be tattooed on the back of a prospective project manager's left hand, with the answer, 'One day at a time' tattooed on the right hand. This question and its answer may well be the most important things to remember in our projects business.

Project managers will find a good selection of useful textbooks listed in the Bibliography. Over the years, I have made good use of Robert Buttrick's *The Project Workout* (Prentice-Hall, 2000), Anderson, Grude and Haug's *Goal Directed Project Management* (Kogan Page, 1995) and J. Davidson Frame's *Managing Projects in Organizations* (Jossey-Bass, 1995). My personal favourite is probably James Taylor's *A Survival Guide for Project Managers* (Amacom, 1998). To all these authors and many others, I offer thanks for their contribution to my education, and hope that I have not inadvertently broken any rules when writing on topics that they have covered previously.

For project management consultancy services and training, please contact <enquiries@awa-projects.co.uk>.

Acknowledgements

I would like to express my thanks to all those who have contributed to the evolution and publication of *The Project Management A–Z*. This venture started informally, and with entirely different aims. Does this sound like any project that you have seen? Over some years, I had written checklists, prompts and methods for my own work, and had implemented variations in client sites. More in hope than expectation, I sent samples and the outline of a possible book to Jonathan Norman at Gower. Jonathan's early enthusiasm for the proposal was the spur I needed, and as soon as I had completed an existing client assignment, I took a sabbatical to work on the text full time.

It would be wrong to claim this as 'All my own work', similar to a street artist. I did not invent the methods, tools and techniques that appear here, but am simply presenting what I have learned, used and appreciated, in a direct-access format that I hope readers will find useful. I am indebted to the many authors, trainers, colleagues and clients who have influenced my thinking. In particular, my years in Hoskyns Education were inspirational and I am deeply indebted to many in that great team between 1979 and 1993. I was surrounded and awed by an impressively experienced group and absorbed much that has stood me in good stead ever since, greatly influencing the content of this manual. I have also been fortunate in working with, and learning from, many highly professional colleagues on subsequent contracts with Duhig Berry Limited and AMTEC plc.

Some individuals have been particularly significant or influential in my career. Early in the 1970s, Bill Gregory first gave me real responsibility and opportunities in the fledgling computer department at Wellworthy Limited. Later, when I joined Hoskyns, Ken Bowman, as my mentor, first introduced me to real planning. John Lamb was my manager, providing challenges, stimulating opportunities and real responsibilities from the outset.

When I became a freelance project manager in 1993, I worked on assignments with Duhig Berry Limited, another organization full of talented people. On my first project, I teamed-up with Chris Ferguson, now of Novare Consulting (www.novare.com), who introduced me to PRINCE®. Chris kindly reviewed the PRINCE® topics in the book and contributed valuable feedback.

Dennis Lock, himself a project management author and lecturer of many years' standing, reviewed all the non-PRINCE® topics and made thorough, important and encouraging contributions from his encyclopaedic knowledge of the subject and his expertise as an author. Jill Powell of Hildon Associates, an experienced project management practitioner, also reviewed the text and her perceptive feedback persuaded me that I needed to add some topics and expand others. Finally, many thanks to my brother Keith Wren for interrupting his plan to review my budget.

My daughter, Sonia, a relative newcomer to project management, read each topic as the ink dried, asking perceptive and searching questions, and convincing me of the need to amend several drafts. My wife Sylvia and son Paul looked at my drafts from a standpoint detached from the practical aspects of managing projects, helping me to clarify my thinking and my text, removing unnecessary or unhelpful jargon. However, the most important contribution made by all my family was their unreserved belief, lasting enthusiasm and total support, for which I am profoundly grateful.

How You Might Use This Manual

The Project Management A–Z sets out to give you direct access to project management information, on a 'need to know' basis.

During a project, you will undertake some tasks on a daily basis, and others perhaps only once for each project. Whether you are an experienced project manager in need of a reminder about one of the less frequently used techniques, or a relative newcomer in need of advice about how and when to choose and use which technique, you may find the information you are looking for in this manual.

The manual started out as a personal set of checklists and prompts that evolved and expanded into what you now see. It does not set out to teach you how to manage a project, rather concentrating on how you might optimize techniques and ideas along the way, and cut through the jargon and mystery that sometimes inhibits understanding of project work.

You may encounter acronyms or pieces of jargon for the first time and wonder what they mean – there is a glossary of project management terms that you can refer to. This glossary has many cross-references, some of which will point you to topics in the contents list. You can then go directly to detailed accounts of relevant techniques. For example, you might need to know the meaning of the acronym BCWP, find that it belongs within Earned Value Analysis, then put it in context and understand how it applies by going directly to that topic.

The following list gives an indication of when you might consider some of the main techniques and ideas in this manual:

- **Pre-project**
  - Business Case
  - Feasibility Study

- Change Control
- Controlling Against the Schedule
- Decisions in Projects
- Earned Value Analysis
- Filing and Document Management in Projects
- Impact Analysis
- Issue Management
- Lessons Learned
- Project Health Checks
- Quality in Project Work
- Reports in Projects and Programmes
- Request for Change
- Risk Management
- Stages – Start and End Procedures
- Task Checklist

● **Closing a project and post-project**
- Closing a Project
- Handover Options
- Lessons Learned
- Post-project Review

● **Project organization**
- Champion
- Matrix Management
- PRINCE® Project Board
- Project Office
- Responsibility Matrix
- Sponsor
- Steering Group

● **Project finance**
- Authorization
- Budget Control
- Budgets for Project Work
- Earned Value Analysis
- Impact Analysis
- Investment Appraisal for Projects

Introduction

Humans have conducted projects for thousands of years: erecting settlements, villages, towns and cities; building rafts, then boats, then ships for exploration, migration and warfare; building stone circles, pyramids, cathedrals and temples; constructing roads, railways, bridges and factories; assembling printing presses; and even going to the moon. Over those years, we have changed little in our urge to build, change, innovate and develop, though the pace at which things happen today has accelerated beyond the imagination of our ancestors. The human race has acquired millions of person-years of project experience, and developed approaches, techniques and tools that should help us manage our latest projects successfully. So why do projects continue to be so troublesome? Have we forgotten lessons learned from project history, or do we think we have nothing to learn? Do we run into trouble because we fail to recognize the true nature of projects, and the special skills needed to manage them successfully? What is so extraordinary about projects?

British Standard 6079-2:2000 describes a project as:

> a unique process consisting of a set of co-ordinated and controlled activities, with start and finish dates, undertaken to achieve an objective conforming to specific requirements, including constraints of time, cost and resources.

There are many other working definitions, which use different words to say similar things. Several significant words and phrases recur throughout these definitions.

These significant words include *unique*, which usually implies that something is a one-off. While an office software package may have been rolled out thousands of times, this will have taken place at different times, in different organizations, versions, combinations, countries and circumstances, each roll-out a unique venture. This 'uniqueness' differentiates projects from operations, as although each new operational business cycle, such as an accounting period, will bring some variations, the aims will stay the same – process the data for this period and update the year-to-date information. Even at the end of a financial year, the aims and routines will replicate those of previous year-ends.

Entries for *process* in a thesaurus might include such terms as 'course of action', 'development', 'method', 'procedure', 'progression' and 'route', all of which could suggest a methodical approach along a predetermined path between a start and end point. In reality, projects are made up of many linked and often inter-dependent processes, all of which need to contribute to the final outcome. If any process does not advance, protect or otherwise support an enterprise, why do it?

When you *co-ordinate* a series of linked, dependent tasks, you may do one or more of planning, organizing, managing or synchronizing them. If you have a project team, you will find it difficult to direct work effectively any other way. Even when working alone, you should benefit from such an approach. Co-ordination, or planning, is a key factor in distinguishing between the use of the word 'project' in a loose sense, as in 'my next project will be the vegetable garden' and in a more structured and formal sense. The word 'formal' is uncommon in definitions of 'project'. Organizations need to select levels of formality and structure appropriate to size, complexity and risk in each of their projects. Not all projects need the same degree of formality. Proper co-ordination through appropriate planning and control is a fundamental element of professional project management – the essential difference between managed and makeshift projects.

The word *controlled* appears next in the definition and symbolizes the main aim of project management. Other practices are means to ends – delivery of what is needed, when it is needed, at or even below the estimated cost. 'Control' covers all the techniques available to you between the start and finish to help ensure that work is completed accurately, on time and within budget, so that all the ends are achieved.

What marks the *start and finish dates*, the limited and finite duration of a project? End dates tend to be very clear and very public. We often know them long before anyone has given a serious thought to starting. Unfortunately, days and weeks, which are often squandered while deciding when to decide to start a project and spend money, never return. The start date for a project should be confirmed when a project plan and an activity-based project budget have been approved and authorization has been given to implement the plan and spend money from the budget. It is a sad reality of the Project Manager's role that you can wait months for a go-ahead, but woe betide a delivery that is one day late! Do not forget to pay regard to the word *date*. If you are told to finish a project 'by August', 'before the end of the year' or, 'in the third quarter', ask questions that will pin down the requirement. Does 'by 'August' mean by 31 July, or 31 August, or something else? It might not appear to matter much at the start, but might become critical later!

An *objective*, or a defined goal, is vital even before you start a project, which is why pre-project work can make such an important contribution to your eventual success. Not only should your objectives be Specific, but if they are also Measurable, Agreed, Realistic and Time-based (SMART), you will avoid later delays while you try to resolve disagreements and seek clarification, quantification, arbitration and rectification. Note also that a single objective might be somewhat unusual, as they usually appear as part of a set. If this is the case, you would hope that any priorities are clear. You will always need to know what the hierarchy is, particularly if constraints are so tight that you might be unable to deliver everything on time. You can often break objectives down into three groups with a few straightforward questions. These groups should set out priorities in 'Must do', 'Ought to do' and 'Nice to do' ranking.

Specific requirements tend to denote those factors that help ensure that project outputs satisfy the objective(s) and will be acceptable to the customer(s). Various terms are used, such as 'Acceptance Criteria' or 'Quality Criteria'. It is essential that you know whether you are managing a project to deliver a rudimentary or a near-perfect solution, or something in between, as this will have huge influence on plans, risks and budget. When you know, you can use this knowledge to establish a quality strategy for your project and agree specific requirements for all the main outputs.

Project constraints of *time*, *costs* and *resources* are closely linked, and interact throughout projects. A 'triangle' analogy is often used to describe this triple-constraint interaction. For example, if you bring in more resources in an attempt to reduce time, you are likely to increase costs. If your budget is cut, you may have to reduce resources and thus increase the time it will take; alternatively, you might need to seek a reduction in the project's scope.

You manage *time* using a *schedule*, showing who needs to carry out which tasks to deliver outputs by what dates. Any schedule should also indicate the dependencies that exist and the outputs that must be completed before others can be started or completed. It should be the single most important type of document you use to control and communicate about any of your projects. You should always consider starting a project with two working schedules: one in outline for the project, and one in detail for the first stage. You can update the stage plan at suitable intervals as you proceed, and review and update the project plan at the end of stages or when significant variations occur or are forecast. Such major variations are often referred to as *exceptions*. You should also consider saving (baselining) the original approved versions of these two plans so that you can use them as a yardstick for assessing and reporting progress. If you try to track progress against plans that you are changing regularly, how will you ever know where you are in relation to where you should have been on a particular date? For example, if you are part-way through a stage and find that more work needs to be done than has been planned, you might add ten days to the stage duration. If you then finish on that tenth added day, are you on time or ten days late? What if you are working to meet an immovable final delivery date?

Costs are best planned and controlled using a dedicated project budget. Budgets and schedules record different units but tend to be closely related, particularly in projects that incur the majority of their costs because they are people-intensive rather than capital-intensive. You should normally derive your budget from your schedule and any supporting documents, so that your budget is activity-based. Again, it will make sense to use an outline budget for the project and a detailed budget for each stage, tracked with the same frequency as the schedule, and assessed against the baselined originals.

A project is likely to need several different types of *resources*, which term may or may not include capital investment. The single most significant resources are often the people who carry out the tasks to deliver the outputs. They usually need all sorts of equipment, materials and workspaces, most of which will incur costs. Your estimating and scheduling should reflect varied performance expectations for different team members, taking account of their knowledge, skills and experience, and their availability to undertake the project's work.

So, if you are about to run a project, where will you start? How will organize yourself, and perhaps a team, to deliver a successful outcome? Is there a recipe or a cookbook that might help? Should it be highly regulated, or *laissez-faire*? How will you strike a balance between being prescriptive and being pragmatic?

This manual provides a selection of tried and tested techniques and tools, checklists and hints and tips for those who manage projects or who are about to be initiated into a project management role. It has been written from a belief that all projects are worth doing properly, with 'properly' meaning that levels of formality, structure, organization and pragmatism are appropriate to the size, complexity and risks of the project. This is fully explained under the topic heading 'Tuning or Scaling a Project'. You will also find that all the terms and suggestions in this Introduction are explained in the Glossary and amplified in the main text. The manual is arranged alphabetically by topic name and each topic is cross-referred to related topics.

If any degree of formality is a concept that alienates or unsettles you, then you may find yourself uncomfortable managing projects. You may set out to deliver change or innovation using an approach that is 'unconstrained' by any standards, rules or procedures. You may decide that some short cuts are safe for your project, perhaps 'just this once'. If you do cut a corner or two in the perceived interest of making rapid progress, be aware that many who have tried this have found that a project can take control of them, rather than they taking control of the project! In Germany, there is a particularly apt saying: 'He who has burnt his mouth blows on his soup.' Most of these standards, rules, methods and procedures were developed in and graduated from the 'school of hard knocks' and, if used well, are assets rather than constraints. Choosing and using the right technique or tool is fundamental to success. This manual provides a 'toolkit', but you will need to choose and use those that best meet your specific needs.

THE PROJECT MANAGER

As organizations face pressures for continual change and innovation, they need to plan and control projects properly and professionally in order to pursue cost-effective success. This is why there is such demand for skilled Project Managers. There is little room for casual change in modern government, commerce and industry: the stakes are usually too high. So what exactly is a Project Manager, and what does one do? Naturally, this will vary across projects and organizations, but in most cases he or she will be responsible for delivering what is needed, when it is needed, and within an approved budget.

Figure 1 shows a typical mix of tasks – though readers might feel tempted to add 'walking on water' and 'doing the impossible'!

One of the difficulties often faced by Project Managers is that of not having a level of authority to match the level of responsibility that often goes with the job. Whether you are an employee of an organization, or a contractor hired to do a job, you are likely to be engaged to make the right things happen at the right time. You may have heard that there are three basic types of people in workplaces:

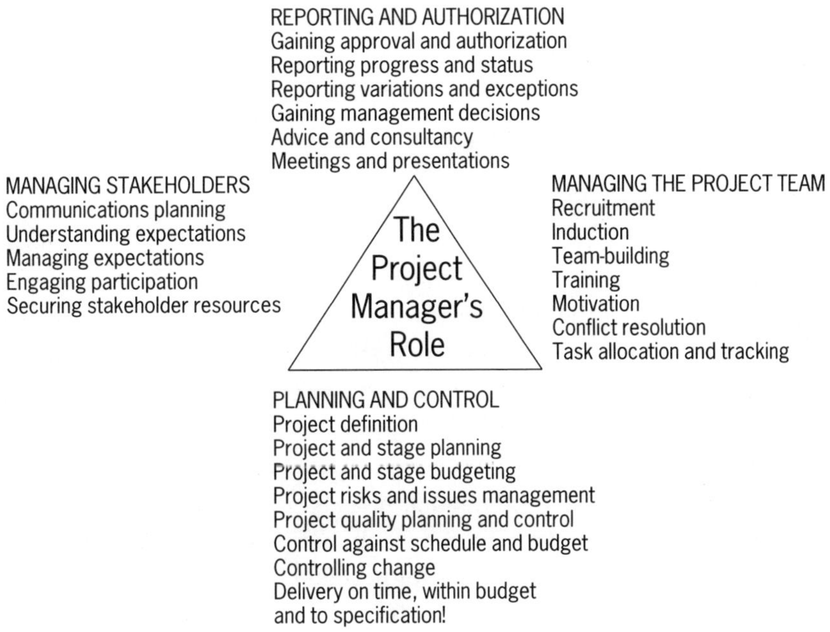

REPORTING AND AUTHORIZATION
Gaining approval and authorization
Reporting progress and status
Reporting variations and exceptions
Gaining management decisions
Advice and consultancy
Meetings and presentations

MANAGING STAKEHOLDERS
Communications planning
Understanding expectations
Managing expectations
Engaging participation
Securing stakeholder resources

The
Project
Manager's
Role

MANAGING THE PROJECT TEAM
Recruitment
Induction
Team-building
Training
Motivation
Conflict resolution
Task allocation and tracking

PLANNING AND CONTROL
Project definition
Project and stage planning
Project and stage budgeting
Project risks and issues management
Project quality planning and control
Control against schedule and budget
Controlling change
Delivery on time, within budget
and to specification!

Figure 1   Typical tasks a Project Manager might need to perform

1. those who make things happen
2. those who watch things happen
3. those who have neither a clue nor an interest in what is happening.

If you are not predominantly type (1), with a sprinkling of type (2) and a complete absence of type (3), you will have a hard time in the Project Manager's role! Whether pragmatism is a quality, an aptitude or a habit, it is fundamental to your success and will earn you the respect you need to help overcome any authority gap.

Here are some other qualities and abilities that might help:

- ability to listen
- ability to see the big picture
- caring about details
- decisive
- determined
- good communicator, verbally and in writing
- inquiring mind
- integrity
- lead by example
- organized and a good organizer
- open-minded and receptive
- own up to mistakes – admit when you are wrong
- political sensitivity
- positive and enthusiastic (a 'can–do' approach)
- problem–solver

- resilient
- stickability – see it through
- systematic
- thorough
- willing to learn
- willing to take direction.

If you have many or all of the above abilities, you should find that leaping over tall buildings in single bounds should be relatively trouble-free! If you do not, fear not – many are characteristics you can acquire and develop through self-discipline, training, coaching, studying and by learning lessons while you carry out your project management tasks.

Managing change and innovation has become a way of life for many people in government, commerce and industry, and thousands have been thrown in at the project management 'deep end'. Survivors swear by it, though possession of experience and good knowledge of the business area in which a project will take place, or experience and good knowledge of project management techniques and tools, will always give a clear advantage. Possession of both business and project experience, coupled with a good range of the qualities and abilities above, ought to make you unstoppable!

Project management has been called 'structured common sense', and when you read many of the pages in this manual, you will see why. You do not need to be a visionary or a great innovator to manage a successful project. You do need to approach the challenge by gaining an understanding of the unique 'big picture' of a particular project, then by systematically breaking it down into manageable pieces of work, organizing them into a logical sequence, monitoring their progress and managing their risks, as described in this manual. If you have an experienced project management mentor to guide you through this, you are very fortunate – do not pass up the opportunity to ask plenty of 'Why?' and 'How?' questions. If you do not have such a mentor, look for answers in the pages that follow.

Project management has also been referred to as an 'accidental profession' that has either drifted or surged into the lives of many. As organizations have changed over recent years, many thousands of so-called 'middle managers' have been stripped out of organizations and millions of person-years of business experience have been written off in the interests of bottom-line performance. Survivors have seldom had time to feel the guilt that was formerly associated with their situation, simply because they did not then, and do not now, have the luxury of time to think much about it. Many now have the 'day jobs' previously done by two or three, while also making time to implement almost continuous change. Still, there are 24 hours in every day, and then there are the nights! If you have arrived in project management via this route, you may or may not have had time to receive any training. You may therefore have justified concerns about project management techniques and how to choose and use those most appropriate to a particular challenge. If this applies to you, I hope you can make time available to use some of the practical hints and checklists you will find in this manual.

If you are experienced in the ways of projects, you may be very familiar with many of the techniques and tools described in the pages that follow. You may also find some new ideas and perspectives. Even if you are deeply engrossed in a project, it can still be valuable to discuss optional approaches, project problems and opportunities with a project management peer, or with someone who can give you experienced advice. Sometimes this can work out, sometimes not. For the occasions when it does not work out, you might find some of the advice you seek in this manual. It might not give you all the answers, but might prompt you with some useful questions and a few tips.

This manual should also be useful if you are a novice or relative newcomer to project management, which can be very daunting. You may feel vulnerable and somewhat exposed. Large numbers of us are expected to manage projects of all shapes and sizes, with little or no training, few sources of available advice, and minimal or no project management standards. If you are in this category, do not try to read the manual from cover to cover. It was not designed or written for such usage, but as an 'instant' reference by subject name. If you are new to the terminology, browse the Glossary, pick out the subjects that are of immediate interest, and take it gradually from there.

Finally, this manual concentrates on the use of techniques, tools and approaches largely specific to project management. Other than in the following paragraph, it does not attempt to cover 'soft skill' aspects, such as motivation, leadership, team-building, decision-making, interviewing, meetings and presentations, which can all make major contributions to success, but which are very well documented elsewhere.

Whatever other assets and resources are available, there is none more valuable to a Project Manager than a highly motivated team made up of people with an optimum mix of skills, knowledge and experience, 'can-do' attitudes and the willingness and ability to communicate clearly and openly. While you will often have to work with people assigned – sometimes unwillingly – to your team, unable to influence team make-up, your skill as a Project Manager can still have a major influence on a team's ultimate performance. You may already know some well-respected motivation theories, and you can put them to good use in getting the best out of whatever team comes your way.

For example, if you are familiar with Maslow's *Hierarchy of Needs* (Maslow et al., 1987), you may recall that base-level needs are likely include such job-related matters as knowing where the project is heading and what is expected of individuals, having the right tools to do the work, decent and safe working conditions, good policies and work practices, adequate support and supervision, and fair compensation. While you may not have control over some of these, particularly in a matrix management environment, you should have some influence over some factors through persuasion, lobbying, seeking the best for your team, and being seen by the team as someone who cares about their conditions and needs. At Maslow's higher levels, many aspects should be available to you as a Project Manager, such as your efforts to create a good team atmosphere and morale, enabling team participation in decisions, consultation on planning and estimating, allowing some self-direction within the plan, sharing out the interesting and challenging work, help with problem-solving, creating opportunities for development and growth and giving recognition for jobs well done. If you can also have some fun along the way and recognize that people need to 'chill out' occasionally, you will help to develop and sustain one of your greatest assets.

Glossary of Common Project Management Terms

This glossary contains many terms, along with cross-references to related topics, that you may encounter when managing or working on a project. Many cross-references will point you towards the entries for main topics in the manual where you will find a full explanation of a technique and can read about the term in its proper context.

Activity	Work to create or review a project output or deliverable. May also be known as a task in some organizations.
ACWP	Actual Cost of Work Performed – the cost of work done on the project. *See* **Earned Value Analysis**.
AOA	Activity on Arrow network diagram.
AON	Activity on Node network diagram. *See also* **Precedence Diagram**.
Approval	Formal acceptance that a deliverable or output is 'fit for purpose'.
Authorization	Permission to start and incur expense on a project or stage, once you have gained approval for the plan and/or budget.
Back-filling	The provision of one or more temporary staff, normally to cover the work of those seconded to a project.
Back-scheduling	Calculation of latest finish and start dates, working backwards from an end date through latest to earliest tasks. Also referred to as a 'backward pass' through a network.
Baseline	An approved product that is 'frozen' and kept available for comparison with future statuses or positions. For example,

when a Project Plan is baselined, this version should be retained even though the plan may evolve and change, so that you can conduct progress reviews against an approved 'yardstick'.

Benefits

Statements of advantageous project outcomes, such as increased revenues, reduced costs, performance and efficiency improvements. Note that benefits should be quantified where possible, so that they are tangible and provide a basis for measurement. Note that less precise benefits may be intangible, or even indeterminable.

Budget

A budget sets out your plans in cost terms, for either a project (Project Budget) or a stage (Stage Budget), in order to gain authorization for the expenditure and to provide a basis for financial control of that work.

Budgetary Control

Procedures to track 'actual' and 'committed' expenditure against that planned and identify variances, which should trigger both investigation of any significant variances and any subsequent corrective actions.

Budgeted Cost of Work Performed (BCWP)

The extra dimension gained by using Earned Value Analysis, linking your original budget (Budgeted Cost) to actual performance (Work Performed) and expressing the result in currency terms or work hours. *See* **Earned Value Analysis**.

Budgeted Cost of Work Scheduled (BCWS)

The project or stage budget, showing costs and timing. *See* **Earned Value Analysis**.

Business Case

Documented justification for setting up and continuing a project, defining the benefits being sought, the likely investment, the constraints and the timescales to answer the question: 'Why should we do this project?'

Business Case Review

A review, normally at the end of each stage, to maintain the relevance and realism of your Business Case, and to assess its ongoing viability. You should also review it when any exception situation occurs or is forecast.

Champion

This is not a formal project role, but if there is a senior individual prepared to suffer considerable sacrifice to ensure that a cause (in this case, a project or programme) in which he or she fervently believes is communicated, promoted, supported and ultimately successful, you will have a great ally.

Change Control	Control of the status of a project's baselined deliverables, to ensure that change is justified, authorized and recorded.
Change – Request for Change (RFC)	A Request for Change (RFC) is used in PRINCE® and non-PRINCE® environments, when a stakeholder asks for a change to a product, or to one or more of its 'Acceptance Criteria'.
Closure	If your project is a set of co-ordinated activities with definite start and end points, there must come a time when you have to undertake 'close and dispose' tasks and bring it to an orderly end. Closing a project is also known as 'close-out' or 'shutdown'. 'Termination' tends to be used when a project is brought to a premature end, usually by a decision of the Steering Group.
Communications Plan	A scheme, based on the Project or Stage Plan, to help ensure that specified stakeholders know what is going on, when, and why, enabling feedback, questions and input from them.
Configuration Library	A central point for safe storage of baselined project outputs, whatever their form. The role of a Configuration Librarian, or that of the Project Office, might be to add items, make sure they are uniquely identifiable, store them, whether on paper, electronically or otherwise, control access to them, and maintain status records.
Configuration Management	The procedures used to take care of the products or outputs of a project and to ensure that each is uniquely identifiable, protected from harm or loss, that only the most recent approved version can be used, and that any proposed changes are authorized, managed and recorded.
Constraints	Confinements, limits or restrictions that may adversely affect a project.
Contract Management	Management of the external suppliers of products or services to the project. The project manager will also need to ensure that management procedures are established for any contract placed by the project for the operational supply of services or products.
Control	Control in a project is a continuous process which addresses such aspects as timing, spending, quality, project risks and issues.

Control Against Budget	Tracking of 'actual' and 'committed' expenditure against that planned, identifying variances, and triggering both investigation of any significant variances and any subsequent corrective actions.
Control Against Schedule	Control is a term for the collection of tasks that you undertake to help ensure that a project or a stage makes progress in line with its plan, or to spot any variances so that you can take prompt corrective action.
Cost Performance Index (CPI)	How much value you have earned from the amount you have spent. *See* **Earned Value**.
Cost Variance (CV)	The difference between budgeted cost and actual cost of work performed. (BCWP – ACWP). *See* **Earned Value**.
CPM	*See* **Critical Path Method**.
Critical Path	Any route all the way through a network diagram that has the longest duration, and where any delay is likely to extend the project.
Critical Path Method (CPM)	A diagrammatic network technique to enable structured analysis and management of complex projects.
Critical Success Factors	Factors identified to enable tracking of the business value of project or programme outputs, particularly when the benefits are largely intangible or indeterminable.
Earned Value	A generic performance measurement term for the concept of representing physical work accomplished in terms of financial worth accrued. Earned Value is also known as Budgeted Cost of Work Performed (BCWP).
Earned Value Analysis	Earned Value Analysis shows how much of the budget you should have spent to achieve the amount of work done so far, based on the budgeted cost of the task.
Estimate	Preliminary statement of the possible duration or cost of a project, stage or task.
Estimate at Completion (EAC)	Forecast of total project cost at completion. *See* **Earned Value**.
Estimate to Completion (ETC)	Forecast of how much more a project will cost to complete from now. *See* **Earned Value**.

Exception	A variation between 'plan' and 'actual' that goes beyond a level deemed in advance as acceptable (falls outside agreed Tolerance), and which thus needs to be reported to management (escalated) for resolution.
Exception Management	A 'hands-off' management philosophy which allows Project Managers to get on with the work of delivering the project without the need for frequent authorization, provided that any variances being experienced or forecast are within a clear and pre-defined range set by the Project Board, Steering Committee, sponsor or other project authority.
Feasibility Study	An early, high-level assessment of whether it would be practicable, desirable and worthwhile to grasp an opportunity or solve a problem and, if so, how. It should identify and evaluate optional solutions, their viability, and how each might be implemented. The study needs to provide sufficient information to justify recommendations on whether to proceed and, if so, how.
Financial Control	*See* **Control Against Budget**.
Gantt Chart	A bar chart used to develop and illustrate project and stage schedules. Named after Henry Gantt (1861–1919), a pioneer American management consultant.
Gateway Review	An independent assurance review used in UK central government civil procurement projects at pre-identified key points, to help ensure that the procurement is in good order and to make confidential recommendations for any remedial work.
Health Check	Brief examination to determine how 'healthy' a project is, and to prescribe any treatments that might improve or avoid deterioration in its condition.
Impact Analysis	A forecast of the possible effects of risks, issues, events, changes or maintenance of the status quo on a project or stage, so that decision-makers can have the opportunity to consider implications before committing to any course of action.
Implementation	Putting a project's outputs into operation, making them available for whatever use or purpose they are to have.
Investment Appraisal	An estimate of the cost of a project and of the possible future costs and benefits that may flow from operational use of its

outputs, which should enable an organization to determine whether the investment will be worthwhile.

Issue

An existing situation or set of circumstances which is affecting the ability of a project, stage or even programme to arrive at its intended outcome.

Lessons Learned

An exercise to recognize and document any lessons that might help improve the running of future projects. The main users of a 'Lessons Learned' report will include the Steering Group or Project Board and Project Team. Such a report might also be circulated to: the Corporate Standards function, or those responsible for Quality Management Systems and Project Management Standards; the Project Office; and managers of future projects.

Life Cycle

The main stages, phases or steps that a project might progress through, from the time someone has an idea that, if progressed, would need a project to turn it into a reality until that reality has been delivered, the project that delivered it has been closed down, and final reports, disposals and evaluations have been completed.

Matrix Management

A term normally used to describe an approach that uses 'borrowed' project team members who report to the Project Manager on project matters, and to their line manager on all other matters, such as 'pay and rations'.

Milestone

A significant, measurable event during a project that can be used to monitor progress or assess status at that point.

Non-conformance

The status of a deliverable that does not meet its specification.

Objectives

Purposes, goals, aims, intentions, intents. Wherever possible, ensure that objectives are Specific, Measurable, Agreed, Realistic and Time-based (SMART).

Off Specification

A PRINCE® term used to describe a product that does not, or is forecast not to, match its specification, or that should have been, but has not been, produced and is not forecast to be produced.

Opportunity

A situation where a project might benefit from favourable consequences of future events, affecting one or more of costs, timescales, benefits and quality, if the opportunity is recognized and acted upon.

PBS	*See* **Product Breakdown Structure**.
PERT	*See* **Programme (or Project) Evaluation Review Technique**.
PFD	*See* **Product Flow Diagram**.
Phase	*See* **Stage**.
PMBOK	The Project Management Body of Knowledge.
Post-project Review	An appraisal to determine whether the expected benefits, as documented in the Business Case, have been achieved or are being achieved, normally planned after a settling-in period during which the achievement of benefits would be expected to become measurable.
Precedence Diagram	Activity on Node (AON) network diagram.
PRINCE®	A project management method, **PR**ojects **IN C**ontrolled **E**nvironments, established in 1989 by the Central Computer and Telecommunications Agency for Government projects. Because it concentrates on project management 'best practice', it is widely used on many different types of projects, both in the UK and abroad. PRINCE® is a registered trademark and all references to PRINCE® throughout this text acknowledge this trademark.
PRINCE® Project Initiation	At the end of the PRINCE® Process 'Initiating a Project' (IP) you will need to have drafted a vital product (document) known as a Project Initiation Document (PID), which will form the foundations on which you will gain authorization to develop and manage the remainder of the project.
Procurement	The purchasing of goods or services to satisfy a defined requirement that might include quality, quantity, availability and price, and usually with the aim of achieving best value for money.
Product	'Product' has a specific meaning in PRINCE® terminology, being a generic term for every project and stage input, deliverable, output or outcome.
Product Breakdown Structure (PBS)	A PRINCE® term for a hierarchical list or diagram, showing how the planned outcomes of a project are to be broken down into component products. Likely to be used in

the creation of a Product Flow Diagram, showing sequence and dependencies.

Product Checklist	A list of the products to be delivered during a Stage Plan, showing relevant important dates.
Product Description (PD)	A PRINCE® term for a document that describes a product's 'purpose, composition, derivation and quality criteria'. You produce PDs during the planning process.
Product Flow Diagram (PFD)	A PRINCE® term for a network diagram showing the production sequence and dependencies of the products that you have identified earlier on a hierarchical Product Breakdown Structure (PBS) diagram.
Programme	A co-ordinated portfolio of projects.
Programme (or Project) Evaluation Review Technique (PERT)	A planning technique that uses time-based networks to show the relationships and dependencies between project tasks.
Progress Control	*See* **Control Against Schedule**.
Project	A unique set of co-ordinated activities, with definite start and end points, undertaken by an individual or organization to meet specific objectives within defined schedule, cost and performance parameters.

Project and Programme Reports

There are a number of typical reports and major documents in and around projects, falling into two main categories. Here are some examples.

1. **Action** – to identify the need for and to facilitate decisions:
   - Feasibility Study Report
   - Project Start-up Document (or Project Initiation Document if using PRINCE®), including plans, the Business Case and budgets
   - Exception Report or other report of serious variance from plan or budget
   - Stage End Report.
2. **Information** - to keep stakeholders up to date, reporting progress and status:
   - Progress or Status Report (or Highlight Report if using PRINCE®)
   - Lessons Learned Report, which may need some actions outside the scope of a project
   - End of Project or Project Closure Report.

Project Board	A PRINCE® Project Board has well-defined roles and responsibilities so that its members can represent the managerial interests of the: ● **business**, in ensuring there is a business need to satisfy and that the project will and eventually does satisfy it and provide value for money ● **user**, who represents the ultimate users of the final product in one way or another, who perhaps need the product to achieve a Key Performance Indicator or objective ● **supplier**, who is responsible for creating and/or delivering the final product and who may be internal or external.
Project Brief	A PRINCE® document providing foundation information prior to initiating a project. *See also* **Statement of Work**.
Project Office	A function established to supply project support within a project-based organization, or an organization that regularly runs several projects side by side.
Project Owner (PO)	A role in UK government projects similar to that of a Project Sponsor. *See also* **Senior Responsible Owner (SRO)** and **Sponsor**.
Project Plan	A relatively 'soft' outline plan for the whole project when you start, but which you will firm up with the delivery of outputs and knowledge gained from each stage. Your high-level plan might include the following: ● Work Breakdown Structure or Product Breakdown Structure ● Work or Product Flow Diagram ● Network Diagram with high-level estimates showing overall duration ● summary-level schedule (bar or Gantt Chart) with main milestones ● Budget ● Resource Plan.
Quality	Fitness for purpose (Juran). The totality of characteristics of an entity which bear on its ability to satisfy stated and implied needs. (The author's view is that there should be no room for implied needs in project work.)
Quality Review	A PRINCE® term for 'an inspection with a specific structure, defined roles and procedure, designed to ensure a document's completeness and adherence to standards'.

Request for Change	*See* **Change – The Request for Change (RFC)**.
Request for Proposal (RFP)	Similar to an Invitation to Tender, where your organization formally asks suppliers to submit competitive tenders to meet a requirement.
Responsibility Matrix	A table identifying accountability and responsibility for project tasks.
Risk	A possible future event or situation that, if it happens, may affect the ability of a stage, project or programme to arrive at its intended outcome.
Risk Management	Whenever you are dealing with change or innovation, things may not always turn out as planned and expected. You will use Risk Management to put procedures in place to identify and record those things that might throw your project off course if they happen or fail to happen, and some measures ready to deal with such eventualities.
Scaling (of a Project Management Approach)	This important concept ought to be self-evident, but experience suggests that it is not. Projects of differing size, complexity and risk need different approaches in organization (Who is responsible for what?), structure (How many stages are needed?), planning (How many plans are needed, and at what level of detail?), risk and issue management, change and configuration control, and so on. If you use the same approach on large, complex projects as for small, simple ones, you will either fall dangerously short on some, create unreasonable overheads for others, or both. Scaling, also known as 'tuning', is the process of putting appropriate factors in place for each unique project, according to its importance, size and complexity. Many organizations provide project templates, setting out different approaches for projects of varying size and complexity.
Schedule	A timetable, plan, programme or scheme; an arrangement for something to happen at a specified time, normally presented as a Gantt or bar chart, showing activities on the vertical axis with horizontal bars opposite each, showing start, duration and end, related to dates across the top of the chart.
Schedule Control	*See* **Control Against Schedule**.
Schedule Performance Index (SPI)	Percentage of work complete. *See* **Earned Value**.

Schedule Variance (SV)	The difference between Budgeted Cost of Work Performed and Budgeted Cost of Work Scheduled. (BCWP – BCWS). *See* **Earned Value**.
Scope	The boundary defining the area in which a project or stage has to operate.
Sensitivity Analysis	A 'What if …?' examination in which you analyse the consequences of variations in costs and benefits on the financial viability of a project.
Small Project	An undertaking below the threshold at which your company would usually wish to use formal project procedures, approaches and organization.
SMART Objectives	Acronym to help you remember that objectives should be checked to see that, as far as practicable, they are: ● **S**pecific – clear and unambiguous ● **M**easurable – numbers preferred to adjectives ● **A**greed – all main stakeholders have bought in ● **R**ealistic – achievable given available resources ● **T**ime-based – stated target date(s) for delivery.
Sponsor	A senior individual in the organization, normally a person who will seek investment in a project, contribute to and endorse the Business Case justifying the project, in order for her or his part of the organization to benefit from the project's outputs. This individual is often the customer-in chief, without whose sponsorship there might not be a project.
SRO	Senior Responsible Owner – a role in UK Government projects similar to that of the PRINCE® Senior User. *See also* **Project Owner (PO)** and **Sponsor**.
Stage	A sub-division of a project to aid effective management, also known as a phase in some organizations. Note that technical divisions of a project are often referred to as stages or phases, such as the Analysis Stage or Analysis Phase, and so on.
Stage Plan	A hard and detailed plan for a Project Stage, which might include: ● Work Breakdown Structure or Product Breakdown Structure diagram ● Work or Product Flow Diagram ● Network Diagram with estimates showing duration ● Schedule (bar or Gantt chart)

- specifications or Product Descriptions
- Budget
- Resource Plan.

Stage Start and End

We create a series of opportunities, between stages, where those accountable for steering the project must check two important matters: that work from a previous stage has been satisfactorily completed; that the justification for the project is still valid; and that the plans and budgets for the next stage and for the remainder of the project are complete, clear and realistic.

Stakeholder

Any person or group involved in or likely to be affected by a project or its outcome, or its failure to deliver the required outcome.

Starting a Project

At the end of this stage, you will need to deliver documentation that:
- fully defines the requirements the project must meet, confirms their justification, and sets out a scheme for their delivery; these will normally consist of a Project Start-up or Project Initiation Document (PRINCE®) and a Project Justification or Business Case
- provides a baseline, or yardstick, against which you, as the Project Manager, and the Project Board can monitor progress
- provides an agreed basis for a Post-project Review.

Statement of Work (SOW)

Sets out the objectives, scope, organization, roles and responsibilities of a project, and identifies the constraints it faces, in a similar manner to a Terms of Reference document or a PRINCE® Project Brief.

Steering Group

A Steering Group's usual responsibility is to steer a project to a successful outcome. It needs to have an ultimate authority and decision-maker, who will normally chair any Steering Group meetings and may nominate the members and appoint the Project Manager. Note that terms such as Steering Group, Steering Committee and Project Board are normally synonymous, though Project Board has a specific meaning and make-up under PRINCE®.

Task

A piece of work to produce a pre-defined deliverable or output. May also be known as a task in some organizations.

Task Checklist

A list of the tasks to be completed during a stage, showing relevant important dates.

Terms of Reference	A structured guiding statement that defines the objectives, scope, constraints and reporting requirements of an investigation or assignment. It should also contain any assumptions, until these have been resolved.
Tolerance	A term for the range of permitted deviation from a project or stage plan or budget, without having to seek prior approval.
Tranche (of a Programme)	Usually a group of projects within a programme that will deliver a distinct outcome, capability or benefits to the sponsoring organization or its customers.
Tuning (of a Project Management Approach)	*See* **Scaling (of a Project Management Approach)**.
Two-level Planning	Use of a detailed plan for each stage, and an outline plan for the remaining stages. As you approach the end of a stage, you can plan the next stage in detail, and firm up the outline plan for the remainder of the project. These are known as 'hard' and 'soft' plans. Also known as 'rolling wave' planning.
Variance	Difference between that which a plan intended and an actual situation. Note that variances are almost inevitable in project work, so we need to define points at which variances become unacceptable and require correction.
VFM	Value For Money.
Web Project	Any project which includes the publication of pages on the Internet or an intranet among its outputs.
Work Breakdown Structure (WBS)	A planning structure, usually a list or diagram, showing how work to deliver a project is to be broken down into work packages, tasks and sub-tasks. *See also* Product **Breakdown Structure**.
Work Distribution Model	A high-level estimating model, based on the historical distribution of work across past projects. Used most commonly in organizations that repeat projects broadly similar in characteristics and structure, and which maintain project histories recording the effort and duration of projects and their stages.
Work Package	A group of work activities identified during WBS development in a Phase or Stage Plan, supported by an information set, normally relating to a key deliverable, with a named individual accountable for its delivery.

A–Z

Approval

Approval is formal management recognition that a deliverable or output is 'fit for purpose'. When you have approval, you can update your plan to indicate completion, whether for a task, stage or project. Before presenting any output for management approval, it would be wise to have some form of independent assessment of the deliverable, against a checklist or other form of criteria established for the deliverable at the outset. If you are using PRINCE®, you should be able arrange a Quality Review, using a product description created during 'Defining and Analysing Products' in the planning process.

Where your deliverable is for your 'internal' project use, such as a plan or a status report, you should have standard criteria for its format, medium and content. Where a deliverable is for 'external' use, by the project's customer or customers, you should have arranged for the customer to create and then to use Acceptance Criteria, against which they will be able to assess and approve each deliverable for use.

You may have already experienced an element of 'chicken' and 'egg' between 'approval' and 'authorization', or may have felt that they mean the same. You should find that approval is the acceptance of project outputs, while authorization permits you to execute plans and spend money. For example, your corporate board may have allocated funds for your project in its Business Plan, but you should not be able to start until you have submitted a plan and Business Case, gained approval for both from your project board and received authorization to start work (and incur costs) probably on the first stage only.

You will find that the single most important approval is usually that which initiates a project. It is at this point that an organization ends the process of evaluating various optional ways forward, by approving a plan to deliver the option it has selected. Decisions are needed to set up a Project Board or Steering Group, appoint people to project roles, authorize the forecast expenditure shown in the Business Case, commit resources, and ensure that the project supports and fits in with the overall business programme.

Be aware that verbal approval of project outputs is unsatisfactory and risky. You should seek some sign-off from the individual who is accountable for approving that deliverable and who is independent of the person or group who has created or procured it. While this may appear bureaucratic and time-consuming, it will minimize, and should eliminate, the risks and waste that can occur if things go wrong later, when an individual might think it is politic to forget a verbal approval he or she has given. If one does not already exist, you can easily create a simple, standard 'Approval' form, with space for a signature, to show what was approved, when, and by whom. Like all original project documents, you should keep this in a properly organized and secure Project File, perhaps under the supervision of a Project Office, if you use one. See Figure 2 for a sample approval document.

Project
Stage
Product name
Version number
Location of deliverable/output if not an attached document.
Description of deliverable/output submitted for approval. *Describe here the Deliverable, Product or Work Package, with unique identifier(s) such as Work Breakdown Structure or Product Breakdown Structure reference number(s).* *List all attached component documents.*
The deliverable described above is approved for the intended purpose by Name .... Signature .... Date .... Name .... Signature .... Date .... Name .... Signature .... Date ....

Note: All original signed documents should be securely stored in Project Filing, the Project Office or the Project Library.

Figure 2   Sample approval document

WHY MIGHT IT BE USEFUL?

You need a good understanding of your organization's approvals process to be better able to provide the information you know your Project Board will need, in the appropriate format and detail, at the right time. There is nothing more frustrating than project delays, awaiting management decisions. Some of this is out of your hands, but it is unforgivable for a project manager to cause delays by failing to understand what is needed to enable approvals, and when.

WHEN MIGHT YOU NEED IT?

There are two main levels of approval in project work:

1. **Macro level** – for approval of stage or project completions.
2. **Micro level** – for approval of deliverables along the way.

Macro

You will need approval from your Steering Group that you have completed each stage to their satisfaction, so that you can then ask for authorization to start the next stage, or to close the project. To enable this, they should have a checklist of all the products you planned to complete during the stage, and you should be able to provide evidence that the project team or its suppliers have delivered and gained approval of each one. The Steering Group will not normally want to approve individual deliverables, except where these are business-critical, such as future contracts with third-party suppliers.

You will not normally be able to commence the next stage until all the outputs from the former, including an updated plan and Business Case, have been approved and you have obtained authorization to move ahead. You will see that while approval and authorization often occur very close together, approval is for things you have done, and authorization is for things you still need to do. You would not expect to receive authorization to execute a plan until it had been approved.

At the end of Stage One, you would then seek approval that you have completed it satisfactorily, so that you can seek authorization to start Stage Two. Eventually, you would seek approval of the outputs of the final stage, and authorization to close the project, wind up the project budget, disband the team, and hand over responsibility for operations and maintenance to the appropriate party.

Micro

As you create deliverables along the way, you need some assurance that they are fit for purpose and complete. You will probably not be able to do this yourself, even though you may have that urge. It is probably better that you delegate this responsibility to a person or group independent of the project team, and provide them with the means to do a satisfactory job. Hopefully, your organization will have both the principles and procedures in place for this, similar to those described in PRINCE® Quality Reviews.

Be aware that regular approvals for deliverables throughout a project stage take time, and allow for this when estimating when those deliverables will be completed, particularly when they are on the critical path.

WHAT SHOULD YOU CHECK?

Make sure you know who needs to approve what, and when. Show the 'macro' approval points as milestones on your plan, and consider allowing some contingency time after these milestones, in case approval is delayed for any reason.

- Do you have documented procedures for:
  - quick and simple approval of a brief plan (and budget) for any early initial work that you may need to conduct before a project is initiated?
  - approval of all the deliverables in a stage?
  - signed approval of a stage by your Steering Group, in which they confirm that it has been completed?
  - signed approval of a project by your Steering Group, in which they confirm that it has been completed?
- Do you know what will need to be done next, if whosoever is responsible for an approval declines to sign off a deliverable as fit for purpose and complete? If not, check your standards and procedures. It is possible that you will be required to do some rework and resubmit the output for approval.
- Do you know whether those responsible for approvals are aware of their responsibility, familiar with what is required, and briefed or trained if necessary? Has someone given them specific or standard terms of reference?
- Do you know what information you should provide, and in what format and sequence to ensure that all approvals proceed smoothly?
- Are all deliverables subject to a Quality Review or other independent inspection?
- If only major deliverables need approval, are the criteria for a major deliverable clear and consistent? (Is everyone clear and agreed on which deliverables are 'major'?)
- Does approval automatically lead to baselining (where any future changes are subject to some degree of formal change control)? Do you have and use a Change Control procedure?
- Does sign-off mean what it implies? Do individuals sign a document to show that they approved the deliverable as complete and to requirements?

SEE ALSO

Authorization
Baselines and Baselining
Change Control
Milestones and Milestone Plans
Network Analysis and the Critical Path
Quality Reviews and Product Descriptions
Starting a Project

Authorization

In project work, authorization usually relates to permission to spend money and use resources, once you have gained approval for the plan and budget.

WHY MIGHT IT BE USEFUL?

You need to know how to gain authorization to start work, spend money and use resources. This is particularly important when you will need to procure products and services externally, as mistaken assumptions here could lead to contract disputes and consequent delays.

WHEN MIGHT YOU NEED IT?

You will normally need to seek formal authorization to spend money and apply resources to work on your project. Ideally, you will have created a Business Case, or some similar written justification. Within this, you may (should!) have conducted some form of investment appraisal that conforms to your organization's rules and conventions. Once the Steering Group approves the overall justification, you should seek authorization for the initiation work, when you will produce detailed plans and budgets. You will then need to seek approval of these, followed by authorization to start the project. At the end of each stage, the Steering Group will need to approve its outputs and give authorization for the following stage, or for project closure when this becomes appropriate. You may have noted that authorization is not the same as approval, which is formal confirmation that you, or perhaps someone in your team, have satisfactorily completed a piece of project work. Approval deals with completed outputs, while authorization is for future expenditure and resource commitment.

HOW DO YOU USE IT?

Be aware that verbal authorization is unsatisfactory and risky. You should seek some sign-off from the individual who is accountable for authorizing the expenditure (normally the Chair of the Steering Group, sometimes all the members of such a body). If a form does not already exist, you can quickly create a standard version, with space for signatures, and showing what has been authorized, when, and by whom (see Figure 3 for an example). Like all original project documents, you should keep this in a properly organized and secure Project File.

Authorization

Permission is granted to apply resouces and incur the costs described on this page and in any attached documents.

Project	
Stage	
Product name	Stage or Project Budget unique identifier
Version number	
Product name	Stage or Project Budget unique identifier
Version number	

Attach the plan and/or budget for which authorization is sought.

Summary of Plan
Brief overview of the purpose of the attached plan (what it will deliver, and when)

Summary of Budget
Brief overview of the attached budget (what it will cost who, and when)

Authorization is sought to incur expenditure totaling £....................................

The plan and/or budget described above is/are authorized.

Tolerance is set at ....

Name .... Signature .... Date ....

Name .... Signature .... Date ....

Name .... Signature .... Date ....

Note: All original signed documents should be securely stored in the Project File, the Project Office or the Project Library.

Figure 3   Sample authorization document

WHAT SHOULD YOU CHECK?

- Is everyone clear exactly where authorization is needed in a project's life cycle?
- Do those responsible for authorization know what they have to do at each point and when those points are likely to be (normally before the start of stages)?
- Does any project authorization duplicate other authorizations made by different bodies at different times – for example for a project within a programme?
- Does your project have any long stages where it might make sense to conduct a review and re-authorization part-way through?
- Do you know what information will be needed at each authorization point? Do/will you have the means to provide it? Is the time and effort that will be needed to generate the information included in your plans?
- Is funding for your project included in the organization's current annual budget?
- If your project is likely to continue beyond the duration of the current annual budget, what is your understanding of the availability of funding to continue and complete the project?
- Does the project plan conform to company requirements? Do you need both an outline Project Plan and a detailed Stage Plan (also known as 'soft' and 'hard' plans) to gain authorization?
- Does the project budget conform to company requirements? Do you need both an outline project budget and a detailed stage budget (also known as 'soft' and 'hard' budgets) to gain authorization?.
- Is there any risk that you may experience delays to, or withholding of, authorization for plans or budgets at any time? If so, have you included this on the Project Risk Log with appropriate contingency and counter-measures?
- Do you have and use a standard document that is signed by the individual or group authorizing expenditure and resource commitment?

SEE ALSO

Approval
Business Case
Filing and Document Management in Projects
Investment Appraisal for Plans
Project and Stage Plans

Back-scheduling

Scheduling is normally done by working from the earliest to latest tasks, left to right across some form of calendar. Back-scheduling simply reverses this process, normally working from a deadline and from the latest to earliest tasks, right to left. It involves calculating the latest finish and start dates for the uncompleted portions of all network activities. These are determined by working backwards through the network logic from the project's end date (Project Management Body of Knowledge).

WHY MIGHT IT BE USEFUL?

As a Project Manager, you may sometimes feel that a date by which you are being asked to deliver is 'mission impossible', but are unsure what to do about it. While instincts and feelings are valuable to you, like warning lights as you approach some yet unseen danger, you will not be able to use them as a basis for important project recommendations or decisions. You need some method: first, to check out and validate the concerns for yourself and, second, to demonstrate the consequences to others if your premonitions turn out to be valid. When deadlines look impossible or very risky, you owe it to your management, your team and yourself to identify the risk, so that it can be recorded, owned at a higher level, and countered in some appropriate way. When you face such a situation, back-scheduling can be useful.

WHEN MIGHT YOU NEED IT?

You may already have found that project work with fixed and tight deadlines is a challenge you face on a regular basis. Such situations are quite common, often business-critical, or mandated by legislation. You will need to handle them skilfully.

HOW DO YOU USE IT?

A schedule should show the activities in a project or stage, and the dates on which they should start and end. Before you start scheduling, you should have invested some time in drawing a logical network diagram, showing task sequences and dependencies. By estimating the durations of the tasks, you can then identify the path through the network with the longest overall duration expressed as a number of days, weeks or months – the critical path (see **Network Analysis and the Critical Path**).

A schedule is usually presented in the form of a bar chart, sometimes also called a Gantt chart, in which you change the units from simple numbers of days, weeks or months to reflect calendar realities, with such extravagances as weekends and public holidays. You are likely to develop this in chronological sequence (from first or earliest tasks to last or latest tasks, working from left to right) illustrating task sequence, dependencies and start and end dates. With reasonable duration estimating, this will help you forecast end dates for a stage or project and for milestones and tasks along the way. Figure 4 shows a simplistic schedule which, from its intended start date, looks likely to miss the required deadline, finishing at the end of the 20th, rather than by the 16th as required.

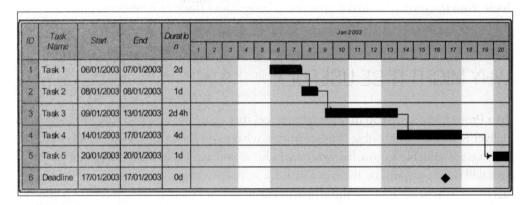

Figure 4   A simple schedule

So instead of working left to right, develop the schedule by working backwards, from the end date towards the start, from last to first tasks. Figure 5 is the same simplistic example as Figure 4, differing only in that the scheduling has started from the deadline, then Task 5, working backwards through Tasks 4, 3, 2 and 1, maintaining the same dependencies and durations as in Figure 4. The example in Figure 5 now shows that the latest you could start and still achieve the deadline is the 1st, not the 6th.

Provided your duration estimating is reasonable, this will help you identify the latest date on which a project, stage or any task should start (or should have started!) if the end date is to be achieved.

If there is a significant disparity between required start dates, first re-check your estimates and the logic of the dependencies. If the end date still appears unachievable with the resources at your disposal and your back-schedule suggests that you should start or should

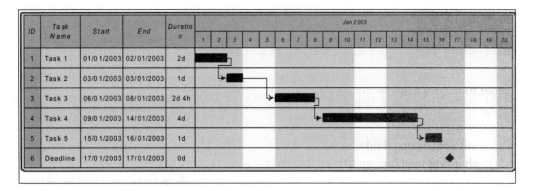

ID	Task Name	Start	End	Duration	Jan 2003																			
					1	2	3	4	5	6	7	8	9	10	11	12	13	14	15	16	17	18	19	20
1	Task 1	01/01/2003	02/01/2003	2d																				
2	Task 2	03/01/2003	03/01/2003	1d																				
3	Task 3	06/01/2003	08/01/2003	2d 4h																				
4	Task 4	09/01/2003	14/01/2003	4d																				
5	Task 5	15/01/2003	16/01/2003	1d																				
6	Deadline	17/01/2003	17/01/2003	0d																				

Figure 5   An example of back-scheduling

have started earlier, conduct and present a risk assessment! Show your Steering Group your findings using simple bar charts and draft Risk Log entries. Do not rely on verbal reporting, and definitely do not rely on a 'corridor conversation'. If your Steering Group insists that you must still achieve the deadline, they must also recognize and own the risks, and you should update the Risk Log to show this. You might be very wise to seek agreement to a reduction in the objectives and scope. This will only work if it reduces overall duration, or enables you to reassign resources made available through any changes you have secured to the objectives and scope.

Back-scheduling may not change the deadline at all, but you will add substance to your assessment of the risks a project faces, identify some clear and important milestones, and provide some protection for you and your team if your predictions turn out to be correct and the deadline is missed.

WHAT SHOULD YOU NEED TO CHECK?

- Do you have a fixed and tight deadline that you believe you are unlikely to achieve based on your planning and estimating?
- Have you identified all the tasks (Work Breakdown Structure) and their required sequence and dependencies (Network Analysis)?
- Have you been able to produce reasonable estimates of the effort needed (person-days/weeks/months)?
- Have you identified the skills you will need and the resources having those skills? Do you know that they are available?
- Have you estimated task durations after considering the skills of the available resources?
- Have you allowed for non-working days, such as holidays, public holidays, training, and management tasks?
- Have you scheduled backwards at least for tasks on the 'critical path'?
- Does the required end date look achievable, or has the required start date already passed?
- If the deadline looks achievable, have you identified key milestones for the start and

35   BACK-
SCHEDULING

end of work on your deliverables, and any 'drop-dead' dates, which if missed will put everything at risk?

● Does the Project Risk Log now reflect findings produced by this approach?

BACK-SCHEDULING WITH MICROSOFT PROJECT®

If you use Microsoft Project®, you will find that it provides a useful facility for back-scheduling. You need to identify tasks, estimate durations and dependencies first, so may have completed a Work Breakdown Structure (WBS), or a Product Breakdown Structure (PBS) and identified its required tasks, and in both cases, drafted a logical network diagram to understand all the dependencies.

Simply click on Project/Project Information and select 'Project Finish Date' rather than 'Project Start Date' in the *Schedule From* dropdown menu. Enter the required finish date, and then enter the tasks and their durations as in Figure 6.

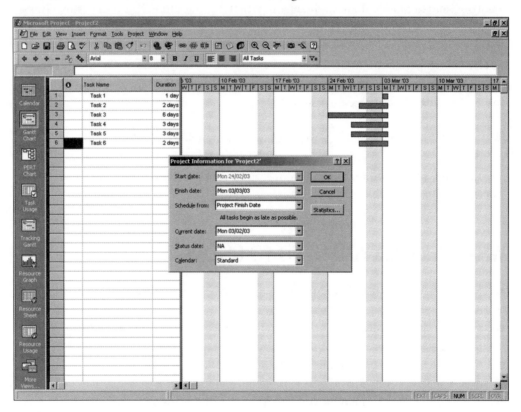

Figure 6   Entering tasks and durations in Microsoft Project®

Then replicate the dependencies, which you can do simply by clicking the cursor on a predecessor task and dragging a line to the successor task. The system will complete a back-schedule for you, and identify the required start date, as in Figure 7.

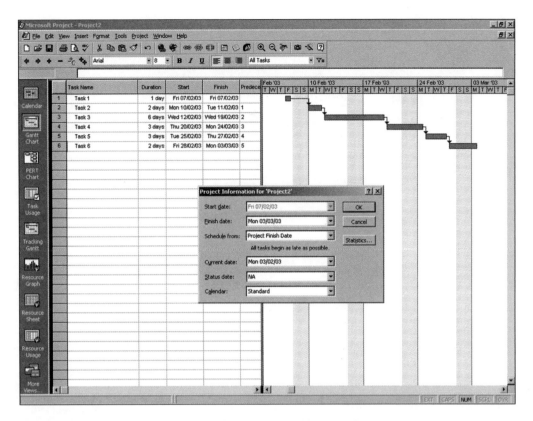

Figure 7   Identifying the start date in Microsoft Project®

SEE ALSO

Network Analysis and the Critical Path
Project and Stage Plans
Risk Management
Scheduling
Work Breakdown Structure

Baselines and Baselining

Baselining provides 'a snapshot – a position or situation which is recorded. Although the position may be updated later, the baseline remains unchanged and available as a reminder of the original state and as a comparison against the current position.' (*Prince® Manual*).

Many organizations choose to baseline the Project Plans and Business Cases they approve at the start of projects. These documents record their original intentions. As projects evolve, plans will change, so you will normally have baselined versions and working versions as a basis for comparison and decision-making. You will also create valuable 'lessons learned' data from these comparisons, which might help improve future project management, particularly in such areas as estimating. If you do not 'baseline' and make periodic changes to your only plan and Business Case, you may lose track of where you ought to have been, and you risk reducing decision-making to tactical or operational levels.

You should only baseline a deliverable after a successful and final test or a Quality Review. This changes its status and 'freezes' its content. You may also store it in a Configuration Library, if you use this service. Note that, once baselined, a product should remain unchanged. You may create a new version of the item at some point, with a new version number and baseline it, but it is always good practice to retain the former version.

WHY MIGHT IT BE USEFUL?

Once a deliverable has been baselined, you can use it with confidence for its intended purpose and as a firm basis for the creation of any dependent deliverable. You should only permit changes to a deliverable that has been baselined after formal justification, an impact analysis on the plan, approval of the revised plan and authorization for any changes to the schedule and budget. This helps you to manage change in a more structured and authorized way, and to avoid delays and overspends resulting from unauthorized and unplanned work. You should always retain any earlier baselined version of a deliverable.

WHEN MIGHT YOU NEED IT?

There are two main situations when you should baseline in project work:
1. **Macro level** – for the documents that provide foundations for projects and stages
2. **Micro level** – for control of deliverables along the way, and for updating plans.

Macro

When your Steering Group has approved your Project Start-up or Initiation Document, or other similar foundation document that includes the initial project plan and authorized budget and resource commitment, this document should be 'baselined'. Whatever changes you make, as reality influences the working version of your plan and the plan changes (as it surely will), you will retain a basis for comparison between 'actual' and 'intention', and for any lessons that can be learned for future projects and planning.

Micro

You should baseline deliverables as soon as they have been assessed as 'fit for purpose', by whatever means is most appropriate. Once you have baselined a deliverable, it should come under the control of your change management procedures. Only then should you show it as 'complete' on your plan.

HOW DO YOU USE IT?

1. Create the deliverable, working to a specification and within a plan.
2. Arrange for the test or review to assess the deliverable against the specification.
3. Correct any flaws or shortcomings, and reassess.
4. When 'fit for purpose', mark the deliverable as 'baselined' and transfer to the control of a librarian.
5. Update the plan to show completion.
6. Do not permit any changes unless justified, authorized, properly planned, and controlled.

WHAT SHOULD YOU CHECK?

- Will the project plan be baselined at initiation, to provide a basis for decision-making during the project, for reviewing the ongoing justification of the project and for identification of subsequent 'lessons learned'?
- Will your project's deliverables be baselined after completion of an assessment of 'fitness for purpose' (such as a Quality Review)?
- Will baselining provide a firm basis for updating the plan to record completion?
- Will baselining enable change and configuration management procedures throughout project and product life cycles?
- Is completion and subsequent baselining the result of some documented and auditable procedure, or is it based on personal opinion or something more whimsical?

- Are project staff allowed to work on, fine-tune, polish or fiddle around with baselined or supposedly completed deliverables without permission, or without authorized changes to the plans and budgets? If so, who will pay for this seemingly unnecessary work, and how will the time thus lost be made up?

SEE ALSO

Business Case
Change Control
Filing and Document Management in Projects
Lessons Learned
Project and Stage Plans
Quality Reviews and Product Descriptions

Benefits

B enefits represent quantified statements of positive project outcomes, such as increased revenues, reduced costs, performance and efficiency improvements.

Do you ever ask 'What's in this for the organization'? Those who finance projects ask similar valid questions when they examine the benefits you claim from a proposed project. You owe it to yourself and your proposal to have done your homework! Make some educated guesses about the costs of delivering, using and maintaining the outputs from your project. You must aim to know whether your project should earn or save money, so you are interested in net benefits – what will be left after all the costs have been met? Finally, you might consider whether and how it will improve the services your organization offers. Do all this work as part of an investment appraisal or feasibility study to attract backing for a proposal – often one of many competing for limited funding.

When Gane and Sarson published *Structured Systems Analysis: Tools and Techniques* in the late 1970s, they included an acronym, IRACIS, with three broad benefit classifications, still of value today when you need to consider the types of benefits that you may pursue:

- **IR**   Improved / Increased Revenues
- **AC**   Avoided Costs (Savings)
- **IS**   Improved Services.

Today, you may also need to consider projects that incur major costs, but do not provide benefits fitting neatly into one of the above pigeonholes. For example:

- You might develop or extend infrastructure to provide essential communications and services to support business operations. The latest expensive technology might not add one penny to the corporate bottom line. You might simply be keeping your organization's modernization options open.

- Many organizations, including public and government bodies, use Key Performance Indicators (KPIs) as part of their objectives/targets/goals. Organizations may quantify their KPIs, which may or may not be financial. They will be crucial factors in the assessment of that organization's success at both departmental and corporate levels.

TANGIBLE BENEFITS

'Tangible' means 'capable of being possessed or realized, material, having physical property'. This often means that we can express benefits *in cash terms*! For example, a downsizing project may deliver a reduction in salary and other employment costs of £10 million per year. A marketing and sales campaign (project) might boost sales by £1 million per year. These benefits will be real, tangible and measurable. Projects that deliver significant tangible benefits are usually easier to justify – provided, of course, the costs are sensible. *Improved Revenues* and *Avoided Costs* mentioned above, both fall into this category.

INTANGIBLE BENEFITS

These benefits are less easy to see, perceive or measure, but are still of some value. For example, when owners sell a firm, they include *goodwill* – an amount of money that values their reputation and relationship with existing customers and which they perceive to have a marketable value. In project terms, *Improved Services* tend to fall into this category. For example, if you install a Contact Management System, you are likely to boost relationships and possibly impress contacts with your efficiency and knowledge. You know this will have some value to your organization, but try quantifying it! Projects based entirely on *Improved Services*, with only these intangible benefits, are traditionally harder to justify. Management Information Systems may not deliver tangible benefits, but consider a situation where your managers are working in the dark, competing against firms that know what is happening and why.

CAN ANY OF YOUR INTANGIBLES BE MADE MORE TANGIBLE?

In the Contact Manager System example, you may not initially claim any tangible benefits. Try your own 'So what?' analysis by asking and answering this question repeatedly until you either come up with something more tangible, or realize that the benefits will always be intangible:

- We can increase contacts by 100 every week!
  - So what?
- Records show that, in the past, ten new contacts can lead to one sale.
  - So what?
- An average sale is worth £1000.
  - So what?
- The project could deliver up to 520 additional sales every year, grossing £520 000!

WHAT SHOULD YOU CHECK?

- What benefits are you claiming for your proposed project?

- Are you clear about which benefits are tangible and intangible?
- Is your project justification dependent only on intangible benefits? Will it just deliver essential infrastructure, or enable achievement of KPIs?
- Can you identify the type(s) of benefits? Can you assign each to an IRACIS category?
- Have you tried your own 'So what?' analysis to firm up your benefits?
- Can you describe each clearly? What is the benefit? When will it be available? Is it one-off or recurring?
- Can you quantify the money value (or range of values, such as 'between £X and £Y') for each?
- Are there any dependencies outside your control that might affect the realization of any of the benefits you are claiming for your project?

Unless you are working on an unusual project, benefits normally only start to appear after the project has been closed and the team disbanded, yet these benefits might be the sole justification. Projects are normally assessed to see whether they were on time and within budget, which can be done as part of the closure process. However, checking to see that the project delivered what the customer needed and that the expected level of benefit is being achieved might be the most important measures of success. It is important to set up this assessment as part of the closure process, even though it might not be conducted for six months or perhaps longer.

FURTHER READING

Gane, Chris P. and Sarson, Trish (1979), *Structured Systems Analysis: Tools and Techniques*, Upper Saddle River, NJ: Prentice-Hall. (This is not a project management text and is now out of print, but is sometimes available second-hand from <http.//www.amazon.com>.)

SEE ALSO

Investment Appraisal for Projects
Post-project Review

Budget Control

Budget control procedures track 'actual' and 'committed' expenditure against that planned, identify variances, and should trigger both investigation of any significant variances and any corrective actions. Do not be too concerned to find budget variances, as the plan on which your budget is based will vary too. Do be concerned about significant variances, and ensure you understand why and how they have occurred. Note that actual expenditure is where payment has been made, whereas committed expenditure is where you have not yet made payment but are contractually committed to do so, such as when you have hired and used the services of a consultant whose company will invoice you in due course.

Note that if you have created a Work Breakdown Structure (WBS), transferred the lowest-level tasks directly into your schedule retaining the unique WBS numbers, calculated the resource needs and costs and fed this information into your budget, you will create a sound and auditable basis for control against your budget and for allocating costs to customers if appropriate.

POTENTIAL DIFFICULTIES

Included in the difficulties you might face, you may encounter:

- reconciling the fixed-cycle accounting period needs of your Accounts Department compared with your need to manage the costs of completing tasks and delivering outputs in line with your project plan

- understanding how and when project costs are accrued, which may be either at the start or end of a task, or in line with the task's percentage completion. If you use percentage completion, you need to be aware that this can be somewhat misleading, as the relationship between progress and cost is very inexact. To illustrate this, Pareto's 80/20 rule suggests that 80 per cent of a requirement might be achieved using 20 per cent of the planned effort, while the remaining 20 per cent of the requirement will consume the remaining 80 per cent of the effort. Fortunately, you should not need to make this decision – just follow the rules

- regular cost overruns, showing variances on the 'wrong' side when comparing actual against plan, particularly likely to hit you when you have had to pare your budget to the bone to get it approved. These overruns will get worse whenever a 'new' requirement is identified, unless your change control process triggers the necessary budget changes

- reconciliation problems through delays while supplier invoices are raised, sent, processed, checked, approved by your organization, and finally posted to your project

- a 'worst case' scenario where your project is behind schedule (late) but over budget, which may mean that both schedule and budget are optimistic, or both started out realistic but suffered cuts to gain approval.

VISIBLE TRACKING

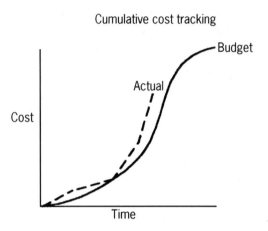

Figure 8 Graph to illustrate actual and budget comparison

You will normally deal with columns of figures, but graphical representation can provide a useful supplementary approach, particularly when you make regular presentations to your Steering Group meetings (see Figures 8 and 9).

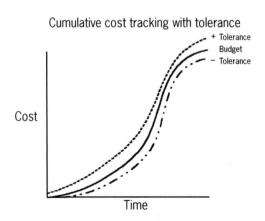

Figure 9 Graph to show allowable tolerance on any variance

As long as the 'Actual' line stays within the lines showing + Tolerance (overspend) and – Tolerance (underspend), the variances will be acceptable. If the 'Actual' line goes out on either side of the tolerance lines, an exception has occurred and you will need to flag this up to your Steering Group. If your organization operates a RAG (Red, Amber, Green) method, this situation is moving into 'red'.

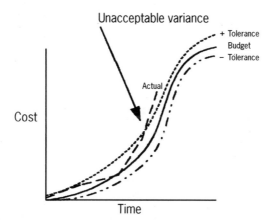

Figure 10   Graph showing an unacceptable variance

In the example in Figure 10 'Actual' has exceeded the '+ Tolerance'. An exception (or red) situation has occurred, and Steering Group decisions will be needed.

Note that you may also need to understand and report on future budget 'commitments', which are sums that you can confidently forecast as committed and which will fall due within a definable period. This may be important when, for example, you are reporting for a period where you have come very close to exceeding your budget tolerance, but escaped an exception or red status because a significant supplier invoice was delayed.

WHAT SHOULD YOU CHECK?

Check your budget against your schedule, using the checklist in Figure 11.

Check that you are comparing 'like with like'. This is particularly important when you may have created your budget in project and stage formats, with little or no regard for corporate accounting periods. When you need to use the schedule as a basis for budgetary control, you may experience conversion and comparison difficulties. You may be able to live with this on projects of modest size, but when a project is large and complex, you may face nightmarish problems and spend most of your time trying to reconcile the irreconcilable.

	Ahead of schedule	*On schedule*	*Behind schedule*
Under budget	• Wow! Re-check your estimates. Could these have been very pessimistic? Is work being delivered faster, with less effort, and thus at lower cost? • Are you sure that completed tasks are complete?	• Has the budget been updated fully? • Looks good on the surface. Check your estimating. • Have you forgotten one or more cost items? Check materials and equipment costs.	• Has the schedule been updated fully? If so, why is work not being completed as planned? • Has the budget been updated fully? • Are you having difficulties finding the right skills for the work? If so, take prompt action. • Are people booking too much 'non-project' time?
On budget	• Are resources working the expected hours, but achieving more? Check your estimating. • Are your sure that completed tasks are complete?	• Be pleased, keep up the good work, and continue to keep things under good control. • Are you sure?	• Has the budget been updated fully? • Are you using resources at the expected rate, but they are achieving less than planned? Check estimates and skill levels.
Over budget	• Are unauthorized resources being used? • Are people working unnecessary overtime? • Have any significant costs been counted twice? • Have costs of other projects been posted to your project in error?	• Have you brought in extra resources to stay 'on schedule'? If so, is it showing? • Have any significant costs been counted twice? • Have costs of other projects been posted to your project in error?	• Has the budget been updated fully? • Was the schedule too optimistic? • Was the budget too optimistic? • Are unauthorized changes being made to specifications or outputs? • Are outputs being 'over-engineered'? • Is the 'error rate' in Quality Reviews too high? If so, is this because work is poor, people do not have the skills, or are reviewers seeking perfection? • Have you allowed 'scope creep'? • Have any significant costs been counted twice? • Have costs of other projects been posted to your project in error?

Figure 11   Budget/schedule checklist

SEE ALSO

Budgets for Project Work
Controlling Against the Schedule
Earned Value Analysis
Project and Stage Planning
Work Breakdown Structure

'I gave Allen an unlimited budget and he still exceeded it.'   Edward Williams

Budgets for Project Work

A budget sets out your plans in terms of cost or work hours, either for a project (Project Budget) or a stage (Stage Budget), in order to gain authorization for the expenditure and to provide a basis for financial control for that work.

Note that you will normally find that developing budgets for project work is one of your key responsibilities. To do it well, you will need a good understanding of your organization's project accounting rules and practices. In particular, gain an understanding of how your organization treats revenue[1] and capital[2] items.

WHY MIGHT IT BE USEFUL?

You will normally need to regard budgets as essential rather than useful items, in order to secure funding for your project. To make the budget doubly useful, ensure that while it provides all the information your accounting functions need, it will also give you a sound basis for control of your project.

WHEN MIGHT YOU NEED IT?

For any project to secure funding, you will need to provide early justification, through a high-level Business Case. You may well look at histories of similar projects and make a top-down assessment of possible benefits and costs. However, to gain authorization for your project, you will need to provide the level of cost detail required by your organization, both for the overall project (probably a 'soft' or outline budget) and for the next stage (a 'hard', detailed budget).

---

1. Revenue items are usually regarded as those products or services with no residual or balance sheet value that are consumed when acquired.
2. Capital items are usually regarded as those that will appear on a balance sheet as assets and will be depreciated over a pre-defined period, in line with corporate accounting policy.

	Cost Type	Cost per day / per unit	Quantity	Initiation Stage	Quantity	Analysis and Design Stage	Quantity	Build and Test stage	Quantity	Install stage	Totals
		Per day	(Days)	Costs	(Days)	Costs	(Days)	Costs	(Days)	Costs	
Direct Labour (DL) costs	Project Manager	£400	10	£4,000	6	£2,400	12	£4,800	15	£6,000	£17,200
	Project Office	£180	10	£1,800	6	£1,080	12	£2,160	10	£1,800	£6,840
	Analyst	£300	0	£0	15	£4,500	0	£0	4	£1,200	£5,700
	Designer	£350	0	£0	15	£5,250	30	£10,500	8	£2,800	£18,550
	User	£250	4	£1,000	12	£3,000	15	£3,750	25	£6,250	£14,000
	Sub Total			£6,800		£16,230		£21,210		£18,050	£62,290
DL Overheads	Overhead %	55		£3,740		£8,927		£11,666		£9,928	£34,260
DL Consumables	Consumables %	5		£340		£812		£1,061		£903	£3,115
	OH & C Sub Total			£4,080		£9,738		£12,726		£10,830	£37,374
	DL & OH&C Sub Total			£10,880		£25,968		£33,936		£28,880	£99,664
Indirect Labour (IL) Costs	Consultant	£750	2	£1,500	0	£0	2	£1,500	5	£3,750	£6,750
	Engineer	£325	0	£0	0	£0	0	£0	15	£4,875	£4,875
	Programmer	£400	0	£0	0	£0	30	£12,000	15	£6,000	£18,000
	IL Sub Total			£1,500		£0		£13,500		£14,625	£29,625
IL Overheads	Overhead %	15		£225		£0		£2,025		£2,194	£4,444
IL Consumables	Consumables %	5		£75		£0		£675		£731	£1,481
	OH & C Sub Total			£300		£0		£2,700		£2,925	£5,925
	IL & OH & C sub total			£1,800		£0		£16,200		£17,550	£35,550
	Total labour			£8,300		£16,230		£34,710		£32,675	£91,915
	Total overhead			£3,965		£8,927		£13,691		£12,121	£38,703
	Total consumables			£415		£812		£1,736		£1,634	£4,596
Stage Total (non-Capital)				£12,680		£25,968		£50,136		£46,430	£135,214
Capital items	Server	£3,000	0	£0	0	0	1	£3,000	0	£0	£3,000
	Printer	£800	0	£0	0	0	1	£800	3	£2,400	£3,200
	PC	£1,250	0	£0	0	0	1	£1,250	14	£17,500	£18,750
	Software licensing	£1,125	0	£0	0	0	1	£1,125	19	£21,375	£22,500
Stage total (Capital)				£0		£0		£6,175		£41,275	£47,450
Totals				£12,680		£25,968		£56,311		£87,705	£182,664

Figure 12   Sample outline budget for a small four-stage project

HOW MIGHT YOU DEVELOP BUDGETS?

Suggested steps:

- Develop and refine your Work Breakdown Structure; retain the WBS numbers throughout the process, so that they appear on the WBS, any flow diagrams and, finally, on the schedule. This will give you a very clear tracking basis and, if you re-charge your project customers, will give a complete audit trail of where the costs were accrued. Note that WBS numbers may not appear on the budget you present. You can record them in an appendix, grouped in line with your standards, or possibly by stage and cost-type, as in Figure 12.
- Create a logical flow diagram to establish sequence and dependencies.
- Estimate the likely effort needed for each task.
- Allocate resources to tasks to estimate durations.
- Use Critical Path Analysis to estimate overall duration.
- Iterate and refine.
- Create a schedule.

- Apply resource (people) costs[3] (known also as 'direct' costs).
- Apply overhead[4] costs.
- Add project-specific costs.[5]
- Add any permitted management reserve[6] and contingency[7] amounts.
- Iterate and refine.
- Format as required.
- Quality Review
- Gain authorization.
- Baseline.
- Implement and use to monitor and control.

WHAT ELSE SHOULD YOU CHECK?

The purpose of your budget

You may be creating a budget for internal use, in which case you may find some of this simply provides checklists and prompts. However, if you work for an organization that is bidding for a contract, you will probably have very detailed guidelines and one serious constraint, which is that whatever you budget turns out to be, it might be cut by a salesperson, in the interests of winning a tender. If this happens, or if your tender is submitted by a sales team member without reference to any project manager and you then become the Project Manager, you will have an uphill battle to make the budget and the schedule work. Your organization will have a contractual obligation to the customer and you will have 'successful delivery' obligation to your management. Projects such as this can result in disputes and litigation and you might find yourself right in the middle. If you are at the opposite end of this and seeking tenders as a customer for project work, be aware of this 'bare-bones' approach, and use your contract terms to discourage it.

Loss factors

There are a number of loss factors that you may overlook at your peril. For example, there are many activities that consume considerable time and costs, which many project managers choose to ignore, or to treat as if any occurrences will always be infrequent, short, effective, one-off and zero-cost. If you know that you will hold weekly checkpoint

---

3. In many information projects, direct costs may well add up to the largest total. Note that while some may be internal costs, others may be external, such as those for contractors.

4. Overhead costs usually include costs of employment such as holidays, National Insurance/Social Security and pensions. They will also probably include office and space costs, power, computer network and other communications. Your organization may require you to treat this as a percentage of your total internal direct costs, with a lower percentage added to external direct costs, where items such as space, power, network and communications will still be needed, but other employment costs will not.

5. Project-specific costs are for products, services or other expenditure items, such as travel, materials, special equipment and possibly consultancy, that will be incurred in a project stage.

6. Management Reserve amounts are sometimes known, perhaps unkindly, as 'fat', or 'fudge factors'. Your experience may tell you that, on all projects, you should make responsible provision for those extra tasks and outputs that you know you will need, but you have not yet been able to identify. Whether your accounting function will see it that way is something you need to find out first! This may be a percentage of total, excluding contingency.

7. You should also consider preparing for the unexpected by adding a contingency amount or percentage. Again, you need to understand your organization's approach.

reviews, project review meetings, quality reviews, management briefings, customer meetings, supplier meetings, these will all consume time and incur costs. How might you allow for these when you do not know when they will occur, or who might attend? If you have access to project histories and these include information on such matters, you may be able to do some analysis and calculate a percentage factor to use. If you have a Project or Programme Office, this information should already be available.

Striking a balance

You may already be aware that the more detailed your plans and budgets, the more time you will need to spend maintaining them, so that you have the control information you need. You need to strike a balance so that you do not have to spend all your time on these tasks, but will be able to keep reasonable track of your expenditure with a proportionate amount of time and effort.

'Budget heads'

You will need to understand the categories within which you will need to accumulate and show cost items, for use by your organization's cost accounting function. These are sometimes called 'budget heads', and though the categories and the names may vary from one organization to the next, the underlying principles will be very similar.

Value Added Tax

Check how your organization deals with Value Added Tax for project budgeting. Find out whether you need to make provision in your budget for external expenditure that will incur VAT, or whether this will be handled by your accounting function.

SEE ALSO

Business Case
Investment Appraisal for Projects
Scheduling
Work Breakdown Structure

'When I was young I thought that money was the most important thing in life; now that I am old I know that it is.'
Oscar Wilde

Business Case

The Business Case is the documented justification for setting up and continuing a project, defining the benefits being sought, the likely investment, the constraints and timescales to answer the question: 'Why should we do this project?'

A Business Case should provide preliminary, then substantive, then ongoing justification for a project. It will be initiated during preliminary work, where benefits may be demonstrable but need further quantification. Costs and duration are often based on analogous project experience (something similar done earlier here or elsewhere).

For project funding to be authorized, the Business Case will normally need to show real and tangible benefits, costs based on a high-level view of resource requirements for activities in the plans, identified fixed costs, known constraints, and risks. The viability of the project should be assessed before any major expenditure is incurred (is it worth doing?). This document should be approved by your Sponsor or Steering Group, and baselined. You should then use it to track the project through its life cycle to determine ongoing viability.

As the project progresses through each stage, the Business Case needs to be updated and checked on an *ongoing* basis, to confirm that the project remains viable and worthwhile. This is normally assessed at each Stage End.

WHAT SHOULD YOU CHECK?

- Is there a Business Case (justification) for the project?
- If the Business Case has been inherited, has it been verified?
- Has the author worked closely with the likely Sponsor and any key stakeholders as the Business Case has been developed?
- Is the Business Case consistent with any corporate and programme strategies? If the project is part of a programme, is the project's Business Case consistent with the programme Business Case? Has double accounting been avoided (project and programme claiming the same benefits for example)?
- Is the content and format consistent with the requirements of the organization?

- Are costs and timescales based on and consistent with any initial project plan?
- Are the benefits justified, clear and quantified? Will they be measurable later. If so, when? Is the measurement process clear and agreed?
- Has the 'as-is' situation been recorded, so that future improvements can be compared properly?
- If the project and benefits realization periods are long, have the cash flows been discounted at sensible rates?
- Is there a complete investment appraisal?
- Have you (or a colleague) checked every item in the Business Case before submitting it for approval and authorization?
- Will all the important stakeholders buy in to this Business Case when it is presented? Have you sounded them out?
- Are there procedures in place to update the Business Case at defined points (for example, at the end of each stage)?
- Are there procedures in place for taking action at any time when the Business Case appears not to be valid or viable? (See **Business Case Review**.)

TYPICAL CONTENT OF A BUSINESS CASE

If you do not have a format in place, the following contents list/format might help:

- **Document objectives** – explaining that it sets out to provide a basis for a management decision on whether a project is likely to be worth doing, by establishing justification for that project based on initial estimates of costs and forecast business benefits.

- **Reasons** – setting out why the project is needed, perhaps including a statement of what the implications of not doing it might be. Note that not all projects are conducted because your organization wants to spend money – an increasing number seem to be needed because there is a legal imperative and deadline.

- **Benefits** – answering the 'What's in it for us?' question. Benefits might include forecasts of improved revenues and avoided costs, both of which will add to the corporate bottom line. Enabling and infrastructure projects may not have clear financial benefits, but may have clear targets – for example, to increase the volume handling characteristics of a computer network or data transmission system. Benefits are tangible, intangible or indeterminable. Only the tangible kind can be quantified and thus made more easily measurable. Note that this is important today in the public sector, too, where Key Performance Indicators (KPIs) may be set for the financial performance of a government organization. Try to show clear justification and quantification for as many claimed benefits as possible. Beware of trying to claim a large number of vague benefits to bolster your case. Note that the benefits of a project should be the domain of the customers and future users of the outputs. Although you may create the Business Case in which they are described and quantified, ownership of these activities should belong elsewhere.

- **Benefits realization** – answering the question, 'When will we recoup the investment and then see some positive returns?' It is also important here to identify how benefits will be measured, so that when any Post-project Review is eventually conducted, there will already be agreement on the key criteria.

- **Timescale** – an initial broad forecast of how long such a project might take so that decision-makers have an indication of how long resources may be committed and thus unable to support other competing projects. You might need to look at project histories for undertakings of similar size and complexity (analogous estimating), but all such forecasts might best be expressed as ranges, such as Optimistic, Expected, Pessimistic, or alternatively as Best, Most Likely, Worst.

- **Costs** – these are usually closely connected to the timescale. Unlike the benefits, which only start after you deliver completed outputs, costs are incurred during the project and during the life of the outputs. Make sure you identify both in their correct category.

- **Investment Appraisal** – when you pull together all the quantified costs, benefits and the benefits realization timescale, make sure you follow your organization's requirements. Note that you should normally use some discounting method to express future income in today's terms, such as Net Present Value (NPV).

SEE ALSO

Baselines and Baselining
Benefits
Business Case Review
Investment Appraisal for Projects
Post-project Review
Starting a Project

Business Case Review

The definition we have used elsewhere for the Business Case is: 'the documented justification for setting up and continuing a project, defining the benefits being sought, the likely investment, the constraints and timescales to answer the question, "Why should we do this project?".' However, the original justification may not last, and you may need to update your Business Case in response to changes as your project evolves.

WHEN MIGHT YOU NEED IT?

You should formally review the Business Case at the end of each stage, maintaining its relevance and realism, and assessing its ongoing viability. You should also review it when any forecast suggests that you might be about to have an exception situation, with potential need for you to create an Exception Plan (a re-plan if a project or stage runs into serious trouble and the existing plan is no longer suitable to get you out of that trouble).

WHAT SHOULD YOU CHECK?

During any such review, you will need to take account of answers to such questions as:

- What circumstances have changed since the Business Case was approved? For example, the forecast duration and costs of the project may have increased (quite commonplace) or decreased (less so). You should revise the Business Case to reflect the most up-to-date information and seek approval from the Steering Group for the revised version. Note that if changed circumstances have a significant effect on costs and/or benefits, the Business Case might no longer be viable, and you will have an 'exception' situation.

- Has the justification for the project changed in any way since the Business Case was originally approved? If so, how, and with what potential effects?

- Will any changes to major milestones affect the costs, benefits or both and, if so, by how much?

- Will changes to any forecast costs significantly affect the cost–benefit analysis? If so, which, and by how much?

- Have any approved Requests for Change significantly affected project costs and/or benefits? If so, which, and by how much?

- Has the supplier situation changed in any way that might affect the costs, benefits or both? If so, what, and by how much?

- Has the environment outside the project changed in any way that might affect the costs, benefits or both? If so, what, and by how much?

- Have project risks, issues or opportunities changed in any way that might affect costs, benefits or both? If so, what, and by how much?

- Does the plan and budget for the next stage (a 'hard' plan) or the Project Plan for the project beyond the next stage (a 'soft' plan) require you to make any changes to the Business Case?

If you conduct such a review and suspect that your project may no longer be viable (no longer capable of delivering required benefits within the established time and costs), your Steering Group may need to decide between options such as:

- continuing the project 'as–is'
- cancelling the project
- suspending the project (perhaps pending further investigation)
- reducing the project's scope
- reducing the project's objectives
- reducing the project's costs.

Note also that changes to a Business Case can be opportunistic and optimistic, embracing such circumstances as good news, lower costs, improved or earlier benefits, or ability to grasp a significant opportunity. Contrary to popular belief, changes are not always of the 'bad news' variety.

INPUTS TO A REVIEW

You may need to make reference to some or all of the following documents:

- existing (baselined) Business Case
- updated plan for current stage
- next Stage Plan ('hard')
- updated Project Plan ('soft')

- updated Project Budget
- Risk Log
- Issues Log
- Opportunities Log
- Change Log
- updated forecast of project benefits
- Project Quality Plan.

SENSITIVITY ANALYSIS

A Sensitivity Analysis uses a range of cost and benefit estimates to help determine whether a project is still likely to be viable, particularly if costs increase and/or benefits diminish. To enable this, the original Business Case must have put a money value on the expected benefits including one or more of the following:

- **IR** – Improved Revenues
- **AC** – Avoided Costs
- **IS** – Improved Services

Improved Revenues and Avoided Costs are usually easier to quantify, but Improved Services or better infrastructure are less tangible ('hard' v. 'soft' benefits). The timing of the realization of benefits should also be taken into account.

You might use a Sensitivity Analysis approach to examine changes through a 'What if …?' approach by asking and attempting to answer questions such as:

- 'What if the expected benefits are 10, 20 or 30 per cent lower? (or such figures as directed by the Steering Group)
- What if the project costs are 10, 20 or 30 per cent higher?
- What are the likely financial implications if the project takes 3, 6 or 9 months longer to complete, with consequent cost increases and benefit delays?
- What if capital costs are 10, 20 or 30 per cent higher?
- Which costs and benefits are most 'fragile' (most likely to deviate from expectations)? What are the contributory factors, and do these costs and benefits need to be reviewed more frequently than at Stage End (say, monthly)?
- Will it be useful to range costs and benefits in 'Best', 'Most Likely' and 'Worst' categories?

If so, the 'Most Likely' figures should be agreed beforehand, probably based on the latest version of your project plan, so that the forecast project duration, timing of the benefits and predicted project costs should be available. If you need it, you should seek accountancy advice on the required approach and method, such as whether to use Net Present Value (NPV), Internal Rate of Return (IRR) or Payback Period (PP). It may be helpful to do calculations for all combinations, with summarized results in NPV, IRR or PP format presented in a table similar to the one shown in Figure 13, where you can show all combinations of costs and benefits, placing the 'most likely' combination at the centre.

		Benefits					
		Best (Highest)		Most Likely		Worst (Lowest)	
Costs	Best (Lowest)						
	Most Likely						
	Worst (Highest)						

Figure 13   Tabulation of possible combinations of factors

You might also wish or need to consult Finance Department specialists to optimize the usefulness of such an analysis and to present findings in line with the organization's financial standards and conventions.

As each stage ends, your Business Case needs to become 'harder'. Project costs tend to accelerate markedly once analysis and design are completed and development or construction starts. Any Business Case needs to be reliable at this point, to enable what will probably be the last real opportunity to make an informed decision before the major investment starts.

OUTPUTS FROM A REVIEW

It is most likely that you will conduct such a review as you approach the end of a project stage and are preparing to gain approval for the closure of the existing stage and authorization for the plan and budget for the next. You would have developed and baselined your Business Case at the start and your Steering Group will understand that, in light of all that you have all learned since, the Business Case may no longer be appropriate. You should therefore consider presenting a report containing your findings and making recommendations to your Steering Group to enable an informed decision. If they decide that the Business Case is no longer valid, you have a Project Issue and a possible 'exception' to resolve.

SEE ALSO

Baselines and Baselining
Business Case
Change Control
Issue Management
Project and Stage Plans
Project Opportunities
Risk Management
Sensitivity Analysis

Champion

This is not a formal project role, but if there is a senior individual prepared to suffer considerable sacrifice to ensure that a cause (in this case a project or programme) in which he or she fervently believes is communicated, promoted, supported and ultimately successful, you will have a great ally! This term comes from history, where it referred to an individual who fought, usually in single combat, on behalf of a cause, such as in the fable of Saint George and the Dragon.

Today's Champions need to have or to be:

- **C**harisma – that 'magnetic' quality that attracts loyalty and commitment
- **H**unger – the ambition and desire that drives people to high levels of achievement
- **A**pplication – 'stickability', to keep things moving, even when the going gets tough
- **M**oney – control or strong influence over the purse strings
- **P**ower – authority to make things happen and overturn any obstacles or dissent
- **I**nspirational – able to rouse people and to pass on to them the Champion's own enthusiasm
- **O**rganizer – the strength of purpose to persuade even the most reluctant stakeholders to get behind the project
- **N**eed – through accountability to Board, Owner or Shareholders, for solving problems or grasping opportunities.

Those who believe that change is not a good thing, or those who believe they have a better approach to a problem or opportunity, often greet project or change proposals with scepticism. Fear of the unknown is a natural phenomenon, and overcoming this needs people of tenacity and courage to lead, promote, persuade, cajole and, if necessary, enforce the vision – the project, programme or change Champion.

Project Champions should communicate the project vision by their words and deeds. They should take a leading role in motivating, inspiring, aligning and energizing all those involved in and affected by the project. They should set an example by minimizing bureaucracy and by taking prompt and effective action to ensure that promised resources are provided when needed.

WHAT SHOULD YOU CHECK?

- Does your project or programme have a Champion who will put his or her reputation on the line to ensure that it succeeds? If not, seek this type of support from the senior customer.
- Do you have access to and support from this individual?
- If not, whose help and support can you call on to overturn major obstacles to the success of your endeavour, particularly those arising through business politics?
- Do you have a Champion with sufficient authority and influence?
- Is the Champion the same individual as the officially appointed Sponsor, if you use this role? If not, is the Champion the Sponsor's delegate, or vice versa? (Both will need to share the vision.)
- Are all the members of your Steering Group likely to act as Champions? If not, what can you do to improve this position?
- If there is no Champion, what risks might this add to your project or programme? Are these recorded in your Risk Log?

SEE ALSO

Sponsor

Change Control

Change Control implies that procedures exist to ensure that all changes to project deliverables are controlled properly, including identification and submission, analysis, decision-making and recording.

Change Control and Change Management differ both in meaning and in level. 'Change Control' is probably best used to describe the micro-level monitoring and regulation of the status of your project's deliverables, while 'Change Management' may be more appropriate at a macro level, describing planned major undertakings, such as a migration from one business or technical state to another through a project or a programme. You will use Change Control, as described here, to help you control authorized changes effectively and to exclude 'informal' and unauthorized alterations or additions to planned or already 'completed' outputs.

You may also use or hear of Configuration Management, which is an extension to Change Control. It provides the procedures and personnel to take care of the products or outputs of a project and to ensure that each is uniquely identifiable and protected from harm or loss, that only the most recent approved version is used and that any proposed changes are authorized, managed and recorded.

WHY MIGHT IT BE USEFUL?

You need to ensure that your Change Control approach will be able to fulfil a dual role in project work. If you use simple and sensible change procedures, you should protect your customers from unauthorized changes by your team and suppliers, and also protect yourself and your team from unofficial 'back-door' customer change requests. Such changes might include one or more of objectives, scope, specifications, costs and scheduling.

If you allow uncontrolled changes to the plans or outputs of your project, you are adding significantly to the risks your project would normally have faced. You may be very familiar with the three main project aims of delivering: (1) that which is needed, (2) when it is needed and (3) within the agreed budget. These three factors are popularly known as the

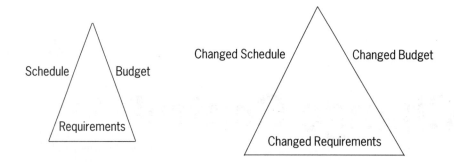

Figure 14   The 'triple constraint', showing the possible impact on budget and schedule of changes to requirements

'triple constraint', and are represented as a triangle, with one side representing each (see Figure 14). It is very difficult to change one without influencing the two others, so if you add to requirements, you are highly likely to increase costs and/or time. If this sort of change is required, it must be managed and under control.

Many of your peers and predecessors in project management have learned too late, that informally relaxing a plan to accommodate new or changed requirements, or allowing unplanned extra work on previously completed outputs looks initially like a recipe for popularity, but instead can leave you with a poisoned chalice and a project that does not deliver that which your customers really needed, and is late and over budget. As the guardian of the plan, you will need to resist temptation to follow the seemingly easy option, and must allow only properly authorized and funded changes.

WHEN MIGHT YOU NEED IT?

You will need agreed procedures in place before the project starts. Everyone should understand that what is specified is what will be delivered, unless any Request for Change (RFC) is made formally. You should analyse the likely impact of a change request, so that the customer members of the Steering Group can decide whether it is worth going ahead with the change if your Impact Analysis identifies any needed revisions to delivery date and cost, or increased risks to the project.

If the change initiative comes from an 'off-specification' report describing an output or product that does not, or is forecast not to, match its specification, or that should have been produced but has not been produced and is not forecast to be, you may need to initiate change to correct or deliver what is needed in line with what was agreed and planned. The key difference in these circumstances is that you should not expect the customers to have to pay for it – they believe they have paid already!

HOW DO YOU USE IT?

You need to ensure that your Change Control approach will fulfil a dual role in all your project work. Stick to simple and sensible change procedures, to protect your customers from unauthorized changes by your team and to protect yourself and your team from unofficial customer change requests. Be on your guard when you hear anything similar to either of these opening gambits:

- 'You know that design I agreed at the end of the last stage? Well, I've just had some new ideas about what we ought to be doing.'
- 'I've been reading a great net magazine. If I could just have a few more days, I could add some great little animations to that intranet page I finished last month.'

A simple 'Request for Change' form should trigger the procedure, which might, for example, be:

- a suggestion for improvement to a deliverable
- identification of an existing or forecast failure or shortcoming in a deliverable
- a question or concern about any of the planned products
- a question or concern about a product that ought to be in the plan but is not, or ought not to be but is
- following discovery of an error in, or mis-specification of a deliverable.

Requests for Change

A Request for Change (RFC) is recommended for use when any stakeholder asks for a change to a project output, or to one or more of its Acceptance Criteria, or details on its specification. It is regarded as good practice for you to enable any such person to raise such a request directly, in which case it should also be recorded as a Project Issue. You may also find that someone has raised a Project Issue, which, after examination, leads to a Request for Change.

Projects stimulate their stakeholders to think about change and innovation, yet many project managers express pained surprise when someone requests even more change than that originally planned, even when the proposed change is relatively minor. You need to anticipate change requests and build in a simple process to handle them as a normal part of your project business. During the life of a project, it is unreasonable and irrational for you to require the rest of the world to stand still until you have finished. Changes will take place in the wider environment, your business organization and its needs. Problems will arise, and opportunities will come and go. You need to provide ways of handling or deferring all these possible change pressures.

Example change process

1. Someone identifies a potential change. Check to see whether it has already been raised and examined, either as a Request for Change or as a Project Issue.

2. If needed, help the individual check raise a Request for Change, and explain the process.

3. Use normal and regular procedures for examining Project Issues. If appropriate, treat any one of these as a 'Request for Change'.

CHANGE
CONTROL

4. If a customer wants to change something that had originally been agreed and planned, or to add to the requirements in any way, he or she needs to understand that as a customer they are likely to need to provide the funding to pay for the change, if the request is accepted.

5. You will need to follow your Change Control procedures and advise the customer of your forecast of any impact on project and stage objectives, scope, time, cost, other products, interfaces and risks.

A Request for Change should include an initial priority rating. Typical ratings are:

- **High** – Must be done, a 'showstopper' situation, otherwise there could be a major business or project failure, or project objectives may be compromised extensively, or the creation or use of one or more major deliverables may fail seriously, or the Business Case benefits may be adversely affected, or one or more businesses critical project milestones may be missed, or the project budget may be exceeded.

- **Medium** – Ought to be done, otherwise the stage could be disrupted, or one or more deliverables may be badly impaired, or agreed stage objectives may be compromised significantly, or one or more stage or project milestones may be missed, or the stage budget may be exceeded.

- **Low** – Nice to do; a useful but non-essential change with little or no perceived impact on any milestone, deliverable or budget.

If using this sort of procedure, you should define and quantify each of the characteristics, using units appropriate to the scale of your projects, but typically expressed in numbers of months, weeks, days; increases in costs or reductions in benefits; or simply in units of currency. (Remember – 'Money talks, I'll not deny, I heard it once, It said "Goodbye." ' Richard Armour.)

Note that you might wish to consider simpler controls for proposed changes of a minor nature that do not affect the Business Case, or the project as defined in the Project Initiation or Start-up Document. You might have authority as Project Manager to approve such minor changes and simply complete an entry in the Change Log, once you have satisfied yourself of the justification and low level of risk involved.

WHAT SHOULD YOU CHECK?

- Do you have existing project change procedures in place?

- Do the procedures contain a Change Request Form, an Impact Analysis form and a Change Log? If not, see the samples in Figures 15, 16 and 17.

Project name:	
Change request log number:	
Date raised:	
Raised by:	

Description of requested change:

Suggested Priority H/M/L:	Suggested Urgency H/M/L:

WBS numbers affected:

Justification and benefits of proposed change:

Implications of not making the change:

Approval sought from:		By date:	

Response:

	Name:
☐ Change approved	
☐ Change approved subject to conditions*	
☐ Change rejected	Date:
Please tick approriate box	

* **Conditions** (Use this section if the approval is subject to any conditions. if so, state what they are; if not, cross through this section.)

Figure 15   Sample Change Request form

Change request log number:	

Potential impact on stage and project completion dates	
H	
M	
L	

Potential impact on Business Case (costs and benefits – quantified)	
H	
M	
L	

Additional/reduced* resource needs

Potential impact on customer's business operations	
H	
M	
L	

Potential impact on other project(s)/programme(s)	
H	
M	
L	

New or changed risks

Impact Analysis completed by:	Date:
Recommendation	Accept/Reject/Defer until dd/mm/yy*

Conditions and comments

* Delete whichever inapplicable.
H = High Impact (or R = Red) – Serious adverse impact on time, cost, quality or risk.
M = Medium Impact (or A = Amber) – Some adverse impact on time, cost, quality or risk.
L = Low Impact (or G = Green) – Acceptable or negligible adverse impact on time, cost, quality or risk.

Figure 16   Sample Impact Analysis form

Change Log no.	Issue Log reference (where appropriate)	Summary of requested change and implications. Include any WBS no(s)	Date raised	Date requested	Initial priority category (H/M/L)	Accepted (A) Rejected (R) Deferred (D)	Date closed	Any new or changed risks? If so, Risk Log references
1								
2								
3								
4								
5								
6								
7								
8								

Figure 17   Sample Change Log

- Do you have priority ratings (High, Medium, Low or Red, Amber, Green)? Do your procedures clearly describe characteristics of each to reduce doubt about which rating to use? If not, and if human nature is a factor, every requested change may be categorized as 'High Priority'.

- Do you have urgency ratings (High, Medium, Low or Red, Amber, Green)? Do your procedures clearly describe the characteristics of each, to reduce doubt about which rating to use? If not, everything may be requested as 'Highly Urgent'.

- Who is going to pay for the change? (This will be very important in both cross-charging and real money invoicing situations.) If the project team requests a change to correct an error, does the customer have to pay? If not, who will? If the customer requests a change because of an oversight or specification error, should the developers have to pay?

- Does the Project Manager have authorization to make or decline to make properly requested small, low-risk changes, where any impact could be met out of contingency time or money?

WHAT SHOULD YOU CHECK ON EACH RFC?

- Is the description of the change clear and complete?
- Is the rationale for the change clear?
- Is the importance of the change clear? Is it a 'must do', 'ought to do' or 'nice to do' type of change?

- Are the implications of not making the change clear?
- Is every factor quantified that can be quantified?
- Is the timing and urgency of the change clear?
- Are the objectives, scope and constraints of the change clear and quantified?
- Do you have enough information to conduct or initiate an Impact Analysis?

SEE ALSO

Business Case
Issue Management
Request for Change
Risk Management
Scheduling
Work Breakdown Structure
PRINCE® 'Off Specification'

'The art of progress is to preserve order amid change and change amid order.'
Alfred North Whitehead, 1861–1947, English mathematician and philosopher

Closing a Project

If your project is a set of co-ordinated activities with definite start and finishing points, there must come a time when you have to undertake 'close and dispose' tasks and bring it to an orderly end. However, this should not be one of those 'Will the last person out please turn off the lights?' situations. Coming to the end of a project involves closing it down professionally, rather than simply 'bailing out', and will mean that the last impression the stakeholders will have is one of a professional and considerate approach. Like all the work earlier in the project, closure requires proper planning, execution and communications. If you close a project and a stakeholder subsequently asks you whether the project is still running, something has not gone as it should.

Any project can close in two very different sets of circumstances: one relatively happy, when it closes because it has delivered all or most of what it was supposed to, and another, potentially traumatic, where, for whatever reason, it has to close before it has delivered. Both types of closure are covered below. It is also important to remember that you should apply the 'scaling' concept to closing a project, so that where it has been large or complex, much will have to be done, and where it has been small or simple, the closure will be relatively short and simple.

25 THINGS YOU MIGHT NEED TO DO OR CHECK

Closure on completion

Have you:

1. completed all the outputs expected at this point in the project?

2. completed internal quality checks to confirm to your satisfaction that all required outputs are complete and fit for purpose?

3. handed over the required outputs to their future 'owners'?

4. confirmed that these outputs meet all the customers' expectations and obtained signed acceptance or approval documents to confirm this?

5. arranged a closure meeting with all the key stakeholders, to confirm closure and advise them of any 'what happens next' information on such aspects as future maintenance of deliverables?

6. formally transferred all responsibilities for use, maintenance and future configuration management of the project's outputs to the new owners?

7. completed all agreed training and documentation where appropriate, to enable the new owners to maximize the benefits from the outputs?

8. transferred any information, documentation and outputs to other projects or programmes if required?

9. written to all suppliers to close down any remaining contracts, to advise them of the procedures you have put in place to receive, check, clear and pay outstanding invoices, and to thank them for their contribution if this is appropriate?

10. shown your appreciation of the team's efforts by thanking them all personally, and perhaps by persuading the Sponsor to fund a party where he or she and the key stakeholders can thank them, too?

11. planned the reassignment of team members with their line managers, and communicated progress and timing to those affected?

12. completed any inputs to performance reviews of matrix team members for whom you are not line manager?

13. kept a close eye on the morale of team members, who may be concerned, apprehensive, insecure or 'demob happy'?

14. closed, or arranged with the Accounts Department to close, all the project's cost centres, and to communicate this closure and any follow-up procedures to all interested parties?

15. collected any outstanding sums owed to the project?

16. wound up the project budget and assessed the total cost once final figures are all in?

17. released other resources that have been used by the team, such as rooms, equipment, computers, printers, network access?

18. returned any unused consumables, where appropriate?

19. tidied and cleared out any office space, and left it as you would like to find it?

20. handed over all remaining and appropriate documentation to the Project Office or Project Librarian, or made arrangements for their distribution or storage?

21. made the necessary updates to complete and close the plans for the project and its final stage?

22. completed reports as needed for the end of the project and the end of the last stage?

23. pulled together all the 'lessons learned' information and completed a Lessons Learned Report for the Project Steering Group and the Project Office or Project Librarian?

24. completed 'what next?' arrangements for yourself?

Premature closure

Why are projects terminated prematurely? There are many possible reasons, but someone will need to explain them to what will probably be a very demoralized team, and it may need to be you. The three main types of closure are precipitated by:

1. project management failures, which are sometimes heralded by an 'exception' situation and Exception Report
2. problems internal to the sponsoring organization;
3. problems external to the organization and beyond its influence.

Depending on the circumstances, such project closures can take place in a number of ways:

- **'Sudden death'** – where the axe falls without warning and the project closes instantly. This could be an internal or external problem. The difficulties here are likely to be shocked disbelief within the team, and maybe among the stakeholders. If you are the Project Manager, you may be left to pack everything up and salvage anything worth salvaging, without anyone to help you.

- **A phased shutdown** – where everyone is told of the decision to close, but time is given to re-deploy team members where possible, cancel orders, negotiate contract terminations, pack everything up in an orderly fashion, document the closure, and hand over any completed outputs that are of value to any stakeholders.

- **'Withering on the vine'** – where closure decisions are deferred or behind-the-scenes political arguments linger over whose responsibility it is to close the project, and no one will grasp the nettle. Support and funding become doubtful, and new expenditure is discouraged or disallowed by implication. There is usually a sharp downturn in morale and motivation, which eventually leads to a non-viable situation, where the team, stakeholders and suppliers are in a state of confusion.

- **Mothballing** – where, perhaps because of current liquidity problems, the organization feels that it is unwise to spend more on the project until the financial pressures ease, but that it will be worth restarting then. Hopefully, there will be enough funding available to close things down professionally, complete documentation, and store everything securely.

Internal project reasons

The Project Manager failed to:

- gain a proper understanding of one or more of the objectives, scope or constraints

- check out one or more significant assumptions and therefore treated it/them as given and factual when this was not the case

- challenge lack of realism in one or more of objectives, scope or constraints and use such techniques as back-scheduling to demonstrate this problem and recommend change

- plan adequately, and the project has turned out to be very different from that planned, usually through significant errors of omission. This could be a consequence of one or more of: not creating a Work Breakdown Structure or similar structured list of deliverables; not considering sequence, dependencies or priorities; poor estimating; no critical path analysis; inappropriate resource allocations; unrealistic team performance expectations; not gaining input to the planning from stakeholders; or not arranging for one or more experienced third-party project managers to review the plan and suggest improvements

- use the plan to exercise adequate control over the project

- respond to the occurrence of small danger signs and problems, allowing them to proliferate and reach an overwhelming mass

- identify risks and issues, or to exercise vigilance in monitoring one or both

- deliver what was needed by agreed dates and to meet the expectations of the stakeholders.

Because of one or more of the above, the project has degenerated into chaos and a decision has been taken by the Sponsor or Steering Group that it will be safer to abandon the current project and take stock before deciding what to do about the problem or opportunity they originally initiated the project to address. In the unlikely event that you were the Project Manager of such a project, there is a real chance that you may not be around to help sort out the situation!

Problems internal to the sponsoring organization

The Sponsor or Steering Group may have:

- appointed a Project Manager with insufficient knowledge, skill or experience in managing projects and failed to provide adequate knowledge, skill or experience to support that individual
- set unrealistic objectives

- failed to gain agreement among the stakeholders about one or more of the objectives, scope, constraints, assumptions, responsibilities, resourcing or funding
- decided that the Business Case is no longer viable, so the justification for the project has disappeared.

Other possible scenarios:

- The Sponsor withdraws support for the project.
- The organization initiates cost-saving measures and is no longer willing to finance the project.
- Politics and infighting over the project among its key stakeholders result in a political situation where the project is unlikely to prosper.
- Your organization withdraws from a joint venture of which your project was a part.

Problems external to the organization and beyond its influence

Your organization might have been:

- ordered by a parent company to cut costs
- taken over by another organization that already has what your project has been set up to deliver
- taken over by another organization that does not want what your project has been set-up to deliver.

On the other hand:

- New laws or regulations may have changed the environment in which your project was conceived, and made it no longer viable.
- A partner organization may have withdrawn support for a joint venture.
- There may be political or economic uncertainty.

ADDITIONAL THINGS YOU MIGHT NEED TO DO OR CHECK

When a project comes to an unplanned end, you may still need to do or arrange many of the tasks on the '25 things to do' list. However, there may be additional burdens for you to bear as Project Manager, including gaining agreement as to the way forward from this point. You need to ensure that the Sponsor or the Chair of your Steering Group explains what is happening, hopefully face to face with the team and stakeholders, rather than by e-mail! On behalf of your team, persuade this individual to meet everyone so that, in making a presentation, the following questions are answered as far as is possible:

- Why has this happened?
- What are the implications for all of us? Do we still have jobs?
- What will happen next, and when will the next important things happen?
- What will happen to the work we have done?
- How can we help to bring the project to a professional close, if this is possible? What do you expect from us?

- Whom should we take our instructions from if we no longer report to the Project Manager?

PROJECT CLOSURE REPORT

The report you produce on closure will vary according to the standards and conventions in your organization. In many organizations, its two main purposes are: (1) to summarize the outcome of the project when compared to what was intended at the outset and documented in your start-up or initiation document, and (2) to make observations and recommendations about the effectiveness, or ineffectiveness, of the project management techniques and tools used. It might usefully summarize such items as:

- what outcomes were planned and delivered, with explanations of any significant variations
- how the project performed against plan and budget
- a high-level summary of lessons learned (perhaps keeping the details in the Lessons Learned Report)
- the impact of authorized changes
- the impact, where significant, of any risks and issues
- any benefits that have already been realized
- any actions recommended for follow-up after project closure
- any arrangements made for a post-project review.

SEE ALSO

Approval
Back-scheduling
Budget Control
Budgets for Project Work
Contract Management
Controlling Against the Schedule
Filing and Document Management in Projects
Issue Management
Lessons Learned
Matrix Management
Project Office
Risk Management
Scheduling
Stakeholders – Identification and Communication
Starting a Project
PRINCE® Project Initiation

Communications Plan

A Communications Plan is a scheme, derived from the Project and Stage Plans, to help ensure that stakeholders know what is going on, when and why, enabling feedback, questions and input from them.

Ineffective communications, both within and around projects, create risks and difficulties that could be avoided if good communications are regarded as a Critical Success Factor (CSF). Time and effort for communications and all communications milestones should be explicit in the Project Plan.

The persons and groups include all those involved in, affected by, supplying to and/or receiving from the project. They need to receive adequate, timely information, using appropriate methods/media, to ensure their understanding and buy-in, and to minimize comments such as:

- 'No one told us …'
- 'I did not expect to have to …'
- 'It's not my fault – I didn't know …'
- 'We're not ready …'
- 'That's not our understanding of …'

WHAT SHOULD YOU CHECK?

- Do you have a Project Communications Plan? Have you assessed the likely administrative workload? Can it be handled?
- Is the Communications Plan based on the Project Plan?
- Have you consulted 'Lessons Learned' reports from other projects, or earlier stages, to identify communications failures?
- Do you have a Project Stakeholder List? Is it prioritized, does it identify specific areas for communication, or is every stakeholder regarded as having the same communications needs?
- Do you specify *who* needs to know *what, why, when, how* and *how much*?
- Do your Work Package specifications state who should be informed and consulted before, during and after the work takes place?

- Do you plan to use an appropriate balance of 'one-to-one', 'one-to-few' and 'one-to-many' communications? Is your need likely to be for thoroughness (one-to-one or one-to-few) or an overview (one-to-many)?
- Do you have a distribution list for all reports?
- Might you be relying too much on chance 'corridor conversation' communications?
- Do you have set times and formats for communications? Do you adhere to both?
- Do you have any ways of checking that outgoing project communications are understood exactly as you intended?
- Do you allow for handling incoming communications and feedback? How?

SEE ALSO

Critical Success Factors
Lessons Learned
Project and Stage Plans
Stakeholders – Identification and Communication
Work Package

'One way communication is not communication at all.'   Milton Mayer

Constraints

If resources are the positive entries on a project's notional 'balance sheet', they will include such assets as adequate money, skilled people, equipment, political will, consensus and the necessary time to help you deliver that project. Constraints make up some of the negative entries – the 'liabilities' – which may be represented by the absence or minimal supply of one or more of those items above that should have been resources. Having insufficient of one or more of these may severely limit your ability to pursue a successful project outcome.

MONEY

Money is often the crucial constraint, in that it limits your ability to seek and pay for the people, skills, materials and equipment you believe are needed to pursue success. When you find yourself appointed to a project with numerous and perhaps diverse objectives, you may quickly develop a Work Breakdown Structure to identify the tasks. You then follow up with a logic flow diagram to try to determine sequence and prerequisites, only to find that there is little logic to be found. However, you keep working and complete a plan, a budget and probably a well-filled Risk Log. Everything goes well until you present the budget to your Steering Group and are instructed to make a 10 per cent cut, which you struggle to achieve, but in doing so find more serious risks for the log. The Steering Group accepts your budget, ignores your Risk Log and takes your budget to the Corporate Board, which requires you to 'trim off' another 10 per cent.

SKILLS, KNOWLEDGE AND EXPERIENCE

Over recent years, many organizations have removed layers of middle managers to save money and, as a result, have sometimes 'thrown the baby out with the bath water'. Thousands of person-years of experience have sometimes been lost to organizations almost overnight. One of the consequences you may encounter during a subsequent project is that when you need to pick the departmental brains, there are either insufficient left to pick, or those still there do not have the knowledge you seek, or are so overworked that they see extra project work as a serious threat and keep it at arm's length. Your organization could buy in interim managers to hold the fort while your chosen resource commits to the project, but only if you have the money and the political will for resources that some may see as a luxury.

POLITICAL WILL

Having mentioned 'political will', have you ever encountered a senior stakeholder who says 'I support you entirely' in front of your Sponsor, but who will always find a good reason not to do so when you need their support? These players at company politics will be well practised at finding a plausible reason to blame you or someone else for their own failure to help. You need to tread warily in these circumstances and must strike a balance between making progress and making an enemy.

The person to sort this out is the Project Sponsor, whose help you will need to enlist in a positive way, rather than by criticizing 'lack of support' or 'negativity' with regard to the person whose help you need. For example, you could write a Project Risk or Issue on the problems that you might encounter or are encountering, which will make your concerns (and implied criticisms) very public. It might be more diplomatic to explain to the stakeholder the vital importance and value of the input you seek from her or him, to help ensure that you can deliver precisely what is needed, and to identify the risks and consequences of this input not being readily available. If this fails, then discreet, positive suggestions to the Project Sponsor might help, and the next step might be to consider an agenda item for the next Steering Group meeting.

Whichever route you take, keep personalities out of the discussion, and stick to the facts. It is safer and more positive to say: 'We need to complete the requirements definition work in Department A by (date), which gives us only x working days. To date we have completed tasks a, b and c, which has taken y working days but represents only 25 per cent of the work required, but has consumed 50 per cent of the time available if the requirements definition is to finish on time. As the requirements definition is on the critical path, the knock-on effect on the design work and the project might mean that we will not implement the project until after the start of the next financial year, which, as we all know, is unacceptable to the company'. Contrast this with the possibly more truthful: 'The lack of co-operation from Mr/Ms Name and his/her staff is putting the whole project at risk.' This is likely to create very difficult working relationships for you and your project team, and is not recommended!

CONSENSUS

Although it is likely to be your Sponsor's role to secure consensus on the vision and objectives of a project, you will need to live with the consequences of any shortcomings here. However, trying to please everyone is often another 'mission impossible'. What you must avoid is completing a project, only to hear that each interest group thinks it has not met their different needs.

TIME

Alongside money, time is one of the more frequent constraints. Organizations often linger over project decisions, and then decide that they needed the outputs yesterday. Other time constraints seem to come about because of external influences such as legislation, but in reality, such a deadline becomes a constraint because organizations often think that there is 'plenty of time for that' until it is almost too late.

EQUIPMENT, FACILITIES, TOOLS AND MATERIALS

When a project team is assembled from those who will be full-time and part-time and with specialists from different disciplines and locations, you may need to co-locate them. For this you will need office space, desks and furniture, network access, telephones, meeting rooms, secretarial services and all those facilities that are regarded as 'normal' in non-project environments. Lack of any these can impair efficiency and effectiveness, while team members spend more of their ingenuity and time trying to solve accommodation problems rather than project problems.

SOLUTIONS RATHER THAN PROBLEMS

It is one thing to recognize constraints, and another to do anything about them. You always risk being stuck with some. You can choose a negative or a positive approach, but most people respond best to a 'can-do' attitude, and as Project Manager you will do a lot to set tones and attitudes. Among the weapons in your armoury, you should be able to use:

- access to, and the ear of, your Sponsor – use this for 'people' problems and to resolve conflicts, to reach consensus and to minimize project politics. If you take this approach, you need to proceed in a positive and sensitive manner, rather than by criticizing fellow managers. Try to talk about opportunities if Department X could free up resources for a defined period, rather than problems because they refuse to do so.
- the Project Risk Log – use this to draw the attention of your Steering Group to threats that the project might face unless avoiding action is taken, or if the threat is unavoidable, identify the need for impact-reduction and contingency measures.
- the Project Issues Log – use this to draw attention to existing difficulties that are impeding progress, and to actions to eliminate or minimize those difficulties.

SEE ALSO

Issue Management
Objectives
Risk Management

Scheduling
Scope
Sponsor
Terms of Reference

Contract Management

You may need to establish or manage external supplier contracts for two different project-related purposes.

PROJECT INPUTS

One or more contractors could be in working on, or supporting a project, or covering work in the customers' areas (back-filling) while a project is under way. The project work or project support role will have to be funded from the project budget. Any work in the customer area to free resources for project work ought to be similarly funded because, if such participation is vital to a successful project, these should be legitimate project costs which would not be incurred if there was no project.

PROJECT OUTPUTS

A contract may be a project deliverable – as, for example, when you tender for a supplier of products or services.

What follows will concentrate on managing the supply of services to a project, though many points will be relevant to the management of operational contracts, too.

WHAT SHOULD YOU CHECK REGARDING 'PROJECT SERVICE' CONTRACTS?

Services to a project might include interim management and resources for operational areas, consultancy, technical skills, trainers, legal advisers, a Project Manager and project support staff such as planners. Note that if the Project Manager is contracted, you will need to provide a senior person from your own organization to oversee that contract and any other contract involving individuals from the same supplier as the Project Manager. This might well be the Project Sponsor or the Chair of a Steering Group, assisted by his or her staff.

- Is the responsibility for managing contracts to supply services to the project owned by a named individual? Is it the Project Manager? If not, why not?
- Is there a nominated deputy to handle urgent situations in the absence of the Contract Manager?
- Did the Contract Manager participate fully in the procurement specification and process?
- Does the specification set out a detailed description of work to be done, any performance requirements, records to be kept and submitted and their frequency, reporting lines, problem resolution, relevant dates, termination rights, breaches, payment terms and rights to vary the agreement?
- Is it your requirement that each supplier nominate a single point of contact? This is recommended.

WHAT SHOULD YOU DO TO ESTABLISH AND MANAGE 'PROJECT SERVICE' CONTRACTS

- Make sure that you have a robust and detailed plan so that you do not underestimate the work required when you intend to procure service supply for a project. If you underestimate and need to negotiate an extension, you may be in a weak position and be unable to tender to replace the established contractor who may see this as an opportunity to recover any revenue shortfall incurred by bidding low to win the original tender.

- Ensure that the specification in your invitation to tender is comprehensive.

- Plan the time you or the nominated Contract Manager will need to manage the contract, so that if they are a project resource, you will take account of their reduced availability.

- Ensure that all specifications provided to supplier staff are clear, complete and accurate and that requirements such as completion dates are explicit.

- Ensure that where specific staff have been offered by the supplier and accepted by the organization, these named staff actually conduct the work.

- Check supplier records, such as timesheets.

- Authorize supplier invoices, having satisfactorily resolved any queries.

- Track invoices against your project budget to make sure that the required work can be completed within budget.

- Check any reports of work that does not meet specification (Off-Specifications) and resolve any re-work requirements with the supplier's named contact.

- Resolve any supplier deviations from your organization's requirements.

- Ensure that the supplier continues to meet all contractual obligations. If you have any areas of concern, check the contract first and, if you are still concerned, it may be wise to consult your own procurement specialists for advice before determining a course of action.

- Ensure that the contractor's staff are provided with all the means needed to perform their duties as required, such as office space, network access, passwords, handbooks of standards, rules and procedures, equipment and supplies.

- Meet with the supplier at agreed intervals to review progress and resolve any significant issues.

- Identify any needs for contract variation that your organization and project have, such as extension, early termination or temporary suspension. Take procurement and legal advice before making recommendations to your Sponsor or Steering Group.

- If the variation appears to require more work from the supplier, first make sure your latest plans and estimates are thorough and have been double-checked. In any case, you will need to assess the impact on your Business Case and gain provisional budgetary approval, and will not want to repeat this process later. Ask the supplier to submit a proposal, and check the costs and other implications before agreeing or negotiating. Issue a formal contract variation, and redouble your monitoring efforts. Make sure that you report this in your Lessons Learned Report, and consider whether any updates are needed for your Risks or Issues Logs.

- Take procurement and legal advice before notifying the supplier if you believe that their organization is not complying with the contract. Advise them of the required remedy and timescale. Take further professional advice if the remedy is not forthcoming.

WHAT SHOULD YOU DO TO ESTABLISH AND MANAGE 'PROJECT SUPPLY' CONTRACTS

If you need new equipment to be in place during a project – for example, a new server and network – bear in mind that you need to plan the installation rigorously, including such aspects as available space for additional cabling, which may sound trivial, but has scuppered some otherwise sound plans. There will need to be installation, testing and commissioning work before your project can continue, so allow good time. You will need a dependable supplier both to ensure a quick handover and for ongoing maintenance. Seek input from your procurement specialists on the use of such items as penalty clauses.

SEE ALSO

Budgets for Project Work

Business Case
Impact Analysis
Issue Management
Lessons Learned
Procurement
Risk Management

Controlling Against the Schedule

Control refers to the collection of tasks you undertake to help ensure that a project or a stage makes progress in line with its plan, or to spot any variances so that you can take prompt corrective action. As Andersen, Grude and Haug point out in *Goal Directed Project Management* (Kogan Page, 1979), monitoring and control are not the same thing. Monitoring simply collects information for analysis. Control involves doing something when that analysis shows that plan and reality are diverging. Control in a project is a continuous process, part of a management cycle, as illustrated in Figure 18.

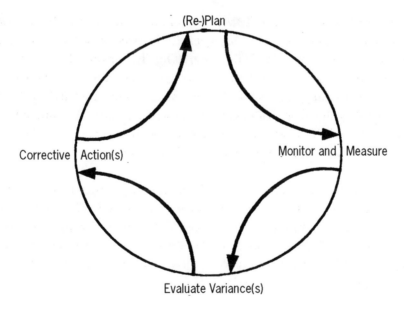

Figure 18   Control in the management cycle

The first purpose of your Project or Stage Plan is for you to set out what will be done, when, by whom, to deliver pre-defined outputs. Therefore, your second purpose is to give yourself a solid basis for tracking and measuring progress, to determine whether what is supposed to happen is happening. The text that follows assumes that your project is large enough to use one or more teams. You should still exercise control on smaller and simpler projects, using a sub-set of the techniques described.

Life and projects face many uncertainties. You need to accept that your plan contains a collection of educated guesses. Some aspects will be good, while some will not work out. You will enhance your reputation as a Project Manager by maximizing those aspects you get right and by your ability to react and recover when things do not go according to plan.

PLAN AND RE-PLAN

At the start of a project, you have a simple choice – you control the project, or you allow it to control you. No planning results in no control. Token planning results in token control. You need to plan, then to make your plan earn its keep by providing you with a basis for ongoing control. Make your plan complete, clear, realistic and 'fit for purpose'. To this end, the bigger your investment in creating a Work Breakdown Structure, building a logical network, estimating likely durations and analysing critical paths, the better the return you will get from your plan. Avoid regarding it as a solid, inflexible entity. Treat it as a dynamic, living asset, on the basis that if you invest further, regular time in maintaining and updating it, it will help you stay in control.

MONITOR AND MEASURE

Fred Brooks, one-time manager of IBM's early and very large System 360 software development project, and author of *The Mythical Man Month*, posed the question, 'How does a project get to be a year late?' His answer? 'One day at a time.' Because this is a fundamental project management truth, it also suggests something about the need for frequency in monitoring progress. You do not have to be immersed in daily detail, but your Team Leaders should be close enough to the action to spot small amounts of slippage or modest increases in 'Estimates to Completion'. On their own, each might be relatively innocuous, but watch out when you add them all together.

If your direct reports monitor on a daily basis and update you weekly (unless, of course, something is going seriously wrong), you should be in a good position to spot variances early. A sample tracking form appears in Figure 19. Responsibilities for monitoring and measuring progress should be defined on a Project Responsibility Matrix, but you must always be accountable for such crucial work. Note that you should normally give priority to monitoring tasks on the critical path.

EVALUATE VARIANCES

You will probably hear regularly about variances between 'plan' and 'actual', and will be running an unusual project if this is not so. You will find two main reasons for the occurrence of variances:

1. Your planning or estimating did not get it right – work is slower (or faster) than you had envisaged.

Project/Stage		Task ID (WBS No.)		Task/Product* Name			Date of Issue	
	Planned Start (dd/mm/yy)	Planned Finish (dd/mm/yy)	Actual Start (dd/mm/yy)	Work done (Hours* Days*)	ETC (Hours* Days*)	Forecast Finish (dd/mm/yy)	Variance Code(s)	Actual Finish (Ready for Review) (dd/mm/yy)
Sub-task A								
Sub-task B								
Sub-task C								

* Delete whichever does not apply.

Figure 19   Sample tracking form

2.   Your planning or estimating got it right – work is slower (or faster) for some other reason(s).

Do not make the mistake of believing that your plan is so good that reality must be wrong.

Be aware that while 'per cent complete' sounds perfectly reasonable and is used in many software tools, clocks and calendars operate in different units. Managing projects is concerned with hours, days, weeks and months. Instead of collecting and evaluating 'per cent complete' information, consider collecting and evaluating information about hours spent on each product and hours (or days or weeks) estimated until it is completed – known as Estimate To Completion (ETC). When ETCs start to grow beyond the remaining scheduled time, you know about a potential problem early on, rather than hearing of an actual problem after it has happened. Your corrective actions might prevent a late delivery. You should only need to fire fight when fire prevention has failed.

Whenever you learn of a variance, you should check whether it falls within a pre-determined range of what is acceptable. If it does, you can decide to let work continue and perhaps ask a Team Leader to monitor more closely or provide any advice or support that might be needed.

You may uncover some variations serious enough to threaten the viability of the current stage, and ultimately the project. This sort of variation is often referred to as an 'exception'. If this occurs, you will have to notify your Steering Group immediately.

CORRECTIVE ACTION

If a variance is outside the acceptable range, you will need to initiate appropriate corrective action in an attempt to get it back on track. For example, you could redirect resources until a problem is resolved, as long as you do not then create an even more serious problem. The first place you should look for resources is tasks that are not on the critical path and therefore have some float time. Alternatively, you might bring in a contractor on a temporary basis if your budget has some contingency reserve. You may also seek authorization to reduce the scope of one or more tasks, or to defer a milestone until an agreed later date.

In an 'exception' situation, you will need to write an Exception Report for the Steering Group, explaining the situation and offering options for the way ahead. It is likely that they will meet and approve one of your options for the way forward, at which point you will need to create and gain authorization for an Exception Plan to replace the existing plan. Note that even though the existing plan may well be flawed, it might better than having no plan at all while you sort out the problems. In an 'exception' situation, you might consider seeking formal approval for its continued use until you can make the revised plan available.

WHAT SHOULD YOU CHECK?

- Have you created a Work Breakdown Structure in partnership with your stakeholders to gain a good understanding of what you need to deliver to the business?
- Did you add in the quality and management tasks, to get a complete picture of the work that everyone would need to do?
- Did you develop a logical network to make sure you know the sequence of events?
- Do your Specifications or Product Descriptions show derivation – that is, the outputs that these items or tasks are dependent upon, otherwise known as prerequisites? If so, did you check these back against your network diagram?
- Are you confident that your estimates are soundly based?
- Did you complete a Critical Path Analysis and establish an overall duration?
- Did you make proper allowances for holidays, training, management time and other loss factors when you finally created a schedule?
- Have you established 'bottom-up' tracking, so that those closest to the work can monitor it daily or at any other required frequency?
- Do you have a process for alerting you immediately when things appear to be about to go off course? To this end, do you always collect Estimate To Completion information?
- Do your Responsibility Matrices make it clear who should monitor what, and with what frequency?
- Do you define what variances are acceptable at task, stage and project levels? If you work in a PRINCE® environment, are you familiar with 'Tolerance' in this context?

SEE ALSO

Network Analysis and the Critical Path
Quality Reviews and Product Descriptions

Quality in Project Work
Responsibility Matrix
Scheduling
Work Breakdown Structure
PRINCE® Product Description
PRINCE® Tolerance

Critical Success Factors

Critical Success Factors are sometimes identified to enable tracking of the business value of project or programme outputs, particularly when the benefits are largely intangible or indeterminable.

This measurement approach can be particularly useful when some of the desired project or programme benefits are difficult to value, or to describe in material terms. Typically, such projects or programmes are 'enabling', related to infrastructure development and improvement, 'mandatory' in response to legislative change, 'public relations' to improve services or perhaps change the corporate logo, or 'management information'. Many of these may lack tangible business benefits, but are regarded as 'must do' changes or innovations by an organization and its advisers.

Critical Success Factors should enable proper assessment of those few fundamental aspects that must still be done well, sometimes also known as 'primary goals' or 'key requirements'. These will often be the main business benefits which, when delivered, will make that undertaking worthwhile for the customers, sponsor and stakeholders. Occasionally, they may also relate to the avoidance of dis-benefits, which, while people are often keen to forecast, they are seldom willing or able to fully define or quantify.

Critical Success Factors can be and often are defined at different levels, usually:

- **Organizational** – direct requirements from corporate strategy
- **Programme** – primary programme goals
- **Project** – key final outputs in either customer or programme terms, or both
- **Phase** – key interim outputs for the customer, project, or both.

Critical Success Factors need supporting units of measure to enable adequate indication of their achievement. These are sometimes referred to as Key Performance Indicators (KPIs), and may need to contain numeric information.

WHAT SHOULD YOU CHECK?

- Is there at least one Critical Success Factor defined for every business benefit that is otherwise intangible or indeterminable?
- Is there at least one Key Performance Indicator that is numeric and will allow tracking and assessment of progress to completion for every Critical Success Factor?
- Is each Critical Success Factor agreed and prioritized?
- Is each Critical Success Factor included in the Business Case or Project/Programme Justification document?

SEE ALSO

Benefits
Business Case

Decisions in Projects

This entry does not set out a decision-making method or system, of which there are a large number. Instead, it concentrates on the recording of decisions, so that everyone involved with and affected by a project can understand what has been decided and why. Some decision points are obvious, and you will show appropriate milestones on your plans, such as those for approval of completion of Project Stages and those that authorize expenditure for following Stages or the Project Closure.

Early in any project, you are likely to face many uncertainties. As you drive the project forward, your Project Sponsor or your Steering Group may need to make decisions that will hopefully reduce uncertainties. Unfortunately, the nature of projects is such that just when you thought every crucial decision has been made, something else happens, or circumstances change. An environment that had seemed settled and predictable becomes fluid, imprecise and in need of yet more decisions. The main difference between routine and non-routine decisions is that for the former, you can place milestones on the plan showing when you need to publish information, such as an End of Stage Report, and when the Steering Group meeting, at which the decisions will be made, is planned. Whatever decision your project needs, decision-makers need information, time to digest it, and perhaps to discuss it and to consider the implications of making, not making, or deferring a decision. You need some form of routine even for non-routine matters.

WHEN MIGHT YOU NEED 'EXTRA' DECISIONS?

Typically, you should have procedures in place for prompting and recording decisions about:

- project start-up or initiation
- stage endings and moving on to the next stage
- closing projects
- avoiding, reducing or accepting Project Risks
- acting on Project Issues
- acting on Project Exceptions.

Decisions that are unpredictable or those that do not fit easily into an established category are naturally more difficult to list, but may be needed for such circumstances as:

- procurement projects, where you have too many top-scoring tenders, or none
- an unpredictable change of corporate circumstances or policy
- an unpredictable change of corporate circumstances for a major supplier
- an unpredictable change or innovation in government policy
- a sudden industrial dispute
- a dispute between key stakeholders.

WHAT SHOULD YOU CHECK?

If a decision is needed that will affect a project:

- Who owns the decision? Is it a corporate decision, or a project decision?
- If it is a project decision, who is accountable (where will the buck stop)?
- What are the implications of making the decision?
- What are the implications of not making it?
- What time constraints are there? Is there a 'drop-dead' decision date? If so, will the needed decision-makers be available? Will the information they need be available?
- What information is known? Is it adequate for the seriousness of the decision? If it is inadequate, what needs to be done?
- What information can the project make available?
- If there is conflict over what decision should be made, who should arbitrate or take control?
- Will the decision be respected, accepted and 'stick', or might it be delayed, modified, sabotaged, or ignored?
- Is the decision confidential, or can it be made in the open? If confidential, who is authorized to know about it now? When will the 'confidential' period end, and what action will be taken then to make the decision and its implications known?
- What are the implications for the Stage Plan until the decision has been made?

DO YOU NEED A PROJECT DECISIONS LOG?

You should have recognized logs for recording Project Risks and Issues. You will create reports at the end of stages and projects, and conduct and minute appropriate meetings that enable related decisions to be made. Little purpose would be served by duplication. However, to record the important additional decisions that may not fit readily into any of the routine categories, you may consider setting up a simple Project Decisions Log. You can create such a log quickly, using any spreadsheet software. Figure 20 shows a public sector example.

No.	Topic	Decision	Date made	Present
1	Fees	Policy change. Fees for work done by the X Division after dd/mm/yy will be on a work-done, not-for-profit but full cost-recovery basis. An examination will be made before dd/mm/yy, to consider fee remissions and the likely size and source of whatever subsidy may be required. The need for this examination and the implications for the project are now recorded as Project Issue 14.	dd/mm/yy	A.N. Other 1 A.N. Other 2 A.N. Other 3 A.N. Other 4 A.N. Other 5
2				
3				
4				
5				
6				
7				
8				

Figure 20   Sample Project Decisions Log

SEE ALSO

Closing a Project
Issue Management
Risk Management
Stages – Start and End Procedures
Starting a Project

Earned Value Analysis

Formal definitions include:

- **Earned Value:** 'A generic performance measurement term for the concept of representing physical work accomplished in terms of financial worth accrued'. *Project Management Body of Knowledge* (PMBOK).
- **Earned Value:** 'The value of useful work done at any given point in a project.'
- **Earned Value Analysis:** 'Technique for assessing whether the earned value in relation to the amount of work completed is ahead, on, or behind plan.' BS 6079:2

When you track progress against a schedule and costs against a budget, you may well identify variances in both cases. Your real difficulties may start when you try to compare your two sets of findings. What really is the status of your project? The earned value approach was developed to help the US military track very large projects with many suppliers, each of which might track and report progress in its own way. After the approach went through a settling-in period, it became mandatory. It has now been widely adopted and adapted by industry and commerce, and is a highly regarded tool in the project management toolkit.

If you use Earned Value Analysis, you measure the *cost* of *work performed*, establishing an immediate link between schedule and budget. You can compare your budget and the cost of work done to date, to determine whether the actual costs incurred are on budget. Earned Value Analysis shows how much of the budget you should have spent to achieve the amount of work done so far, based on the budgeted cost of the task. Earned Value is also known as Budgeted Cost of Work Performed (BCWP), illustrating the link between Budgeted Cost (what you planned to spend on a piece of work) and Work Performed (what has actually been done on that piece of work). Note that Earned Value is commonly expressed in financial terms such as £, $, € or any other currency, but can also be expressed in person-hours, days, weeks or months.

WHAT TERMS MIGHT YOU NEED TO KNOW?

You may find 'Earned Value' terminology and acronyms strange at first, but if you are relatively new, you can get started by understanding just three key terms:

1. **BCWS (Budgeted Cost of Work Scheduled)** – This is the project or stage budget, showing costs and timing, so nothing revolutionary here!
2. **ACWP (Actual Cost of Work Performed)** – You will be familiar with this concept too, as the cost of work done on the project.
3. **BCWP (Budgeted Cost of Work Performed)** – This is the extra dimension you gain by using EVA, because it links your original budget (Budgeted Cost) to actual performance (Work Performed), and expresses the result in currency or work units.

Example

To illustrate this further, let us work through a simple example. Say that you had estimated that Work Breakdown Structure task 1.1.1 (a) would cost £450 to complete (its BCWS) and (b) should be completed on 1 August. On 1 August, your tracking system indicates that the task is 80 per cent complete, so has an earned value (BCWP) of £360 (80 per cent of £450).

If you find that the work to date (ACWP) has cost £400, you can calculate:

- The Cost Variance (CV) using the formula BCWP – ACWP, in this case £360 – £400, with a resulting CV of –£40. A negative result shows 'over budget' status, a negative situation.
- The Schedule Variance (SV) using the formula BCWP – BCWS, in this case £360 – £450, with a resulting SV of –£90. Again, a negative result shows 'behind schedule' status, and again a negative situation.

In both the above examples, a negative outcome means 'over' for budget and 'behind' for schedule, zero means 'on' for both schedule and budget, while a positive outcome means 'under' for budget and 'ahead' for schedule.

Early work

You might wonder how you can arrive at a positive answer, indicating 'ahead of schedule', when calculating Schedule Variance. When using the formula BCWP – BCWS in such circumstances, the BCWP will always be greater than zero for a started task, while the BCWS will always be zero, because the work has been scheduled but not started, hence the 'positive' answer.

WHY MIGHT IT BE USEFUL?

EVA practices were formally introduced by the United States Department of Defense through Department of Defense Instruction (DODI) 7000.2 in 1967, to bring what became compulsory standard methods to large, complex, multi-supplier projects. Since then, the approach has spread to the commercial world, where it is now widely used on projects of all sizes and formats.

Whether you work for a government, commercial or charitable organization, value for money is a universal concept. You can use EVA whenever you need to monitor the progress of a project and determine its status in consistent and tangible terms. You may encounter progress-tracking difficulties with many types of projects. Take, for example, systems and information work. In such cases, tracking is often imprecise because of the intangible nature of deliverables, particularly when they are in the early stages of development. You can use 'per cent complete' figures, but not always with the greatest confidence in their meaning.

Per cent complete

If you collect 'per cent complete' tracking information from several software engineers, you could ask the engineers to report how many lines of code they had written, compare this with estimates of the number of lines each module might need, and record this in percentage terms. However, some lines might be relatively routine and simple, such as report formats, while others might involve complex calculations and algorithms. One engineer might choose to write the simple lines first to get them out of the way. Another might relish the complex part and start there. If they started at the same time and you later took a status check, you might find that one had written 250 lines and the other 50. If both modules were estimated to be of similar size and complexity, you could record statuses of say 25 per cent and 5 per cent complete, when both might be at a similar development stage with regard to the amount of effort still needed.

'Do not put your faith in what statistics say until you have considered what they do not say.'
William W. Watt

The 50:50 Rule

So how can your organization introduce some consistency in these circumstances? Many use a simple approach, known as the 50:50 Rule. This means that at the moment a task starts, it is credited as being 50 per cent complete, and stays this way until it has been completed (100 per cent). For our earlier task (Work Breakdown Structure 1.1.1) with a BCWS of £450, any time you checked status after it had started but before it had been completed, you would record 50 per cent, and a BCWP of £225.

Repeating the earlier calculations, if you found that the work to date has cost £100 (ACWP), you can calculate:

- **The Cost Variance (CV)** using the formula BCWP – ACWP, in this case £225 – £100, with a resulting CV of £125. Do not forget that a positive result shows 'under budget' status – you have £225 earned value, but have only spent £100.
- **The Schedule Variance (SV)** using the formula BCWP – BCWS, in this case £225 – £450, with a resulting SV of –£225. A negative result shows 'behind schedule' status – you should have done enough work to have spent £225 by now.

If you were to take a later status check, when ACWP had risen to, say, £390, you would record:

- **The Cost Variance (CV)**, BCWP – ACWP, in this case £225 – £390, with a resulting CV of –£165. You have overspent, having only 'earned' £225, but having spent £390.
- **The Schedule Variance (SV)**, BCWP – BCWS, still –£225 and staying that way until 100 per cent complete.

While you might have some initial doubts about this 50:50 approach, it is very widely used, and sometimes even mandatory if you are a sub-contractor on a major project where different tracking approaches by different suppliers could cause total confusion. Remember also that you are likely to be assessing many tasks at one time, and that the 'earning' gains you make for every newly started task will be counterbalanced by the lower apparent 'earnings' of tasks that are almost complete. Some organizations use a 20:80 split, and some even use 10:90, but users of the 50:50 approach are probably in a significant majority.

Occasionally, you may also need to use simpler expressions of project performance, such as the following:

Cost Performance Index (CPI)

You will use the same data as those used to calculate Cost Variance:

$$CPI = \frac{BCWP}{ACWP}$$

In our most recent example the figures would be:

$$CPI = \frac{£225}{£390}$$

giving a Cost Performance Index of 0.58. This shows that, for every pound spent, you have earned only £0.58.

Schedule Performance Index

You will use the same data as those used to calculate Schedule Variance:

$$SPI = \frac{BCWP}{BCWS}$$

$$SPI = \frac{£225}{£450}$$

giving a Schedule Performance Index of 0.5. This shows that task 1.1 on the WBS (made up of the five sub-tasks 1.1.1–1.1.5) is 50 per cent complete.

FORECASTING WITH EVA

As a project evolves, you are likely to need to revise both plans and budgets. Each time you check the status of your project, you will have updated information on actual costs (ACWP) against original budget (BCWS). Your Steering Group may also ask you whether the original budget is still valid. You can provide the Steering Group with two pieces of useful information:

1. what you now estimate the final cost of the project to be
2. what costs you estimate you will incur between now and the end of the project.

These are known respectively as:

1. Estimate At Completion (EAC).
2. Estimate To Completion (ETC).

To calculate the former, you need to recall your original budget, known as the Budget At Completion (BAC).

Estimate At Completion

$$EAC = \frac{BAC}{CPI}$$

Let us assume that you had an original project budget of £45 000 and our most recent analysis revealed a cost performance index figure of 0.94. Your calculation is:

$$EAC = \frac{45000}{0.94}$$

which means that you now believe that the final cost of the project will be about £47 900 – an increase of about 6 per cent.

Estimate To Completion

Once you have calculated the EAC, it is a short and simple step to establish the ETC and answer the question, 'How much more do you need to spend to complete the project?' The calculation is:

ETC = EAC − ACWP
(Revised total cost − actual cost of work performed)

If the ACWP was, say, £17 000 the calculation would be:

ETC = £47 900 − £17 000

meaning that you now forecast that you will need £30 900 to finish the project, rather than the £28 000 provisioned in the original budget, an increase of £2900.

SEE ALSO

Budget Control
Budgets for Project Work
Work Breakdown Structure

Estimating

I t's easy when you know how!

There's an easy way to find the weight of a pig without scales! You put a plank across a stool, and then get a two big stones. You balance the plank on top of one of the stones, then sit the pig on one end of the plank, put the second stone on the other end of the plank and shift it until it balances. Then you work out mass and volume to calculate the weight of the stone on the plank and if you know the length of the plank, you can easily estimate the weight of the pig.

In some organizations, task and project estimating has an equally scientific basis. You can do better.

TOPIC NOTES

You may already know that the most frequent questions you are likely to be asked as a Project Manager will be 'When will it be ready?' or 'How long will that take?'. Whether you use science, art or guesswork, you need to be aware that once you have given an answer, it may be taken as a promise. Good estimating is vital to sound planning and control but, with some exceptions, techniques are often vague, and their outputs questionable.

In some industries, where similar tasks are repeated, it is possible to collect and re-use information on how long future tasks are likely to take. Examples might include house-building and other construction, the preparation of the Space Shuttle for launch, or coding and debugging with an established programming language. If you make allowances for variations – for example, different skill levels, fewer or more resources – you have a good basis for estimating. Using project histories and adapting them to your conditions is known as analogous estimating.

You are more likely to encounter difficulties in such projects as research and development – genuine one-offs where no previous related experience is available. You may also encounter difficulties in an organization that does not maintain readily accessible records about what happened on previous projects, including how long tasks took in reality.

Estimating needs to take place at different levels. During a Feasibility Study, you will need to make global estimates of how long each option might take, with very little detailed information. Talk to other project managers and seek their input. Collect whatever information is available from previous similar projects. You should consult specialists on topics such as procurement, where this is part of one or more options. If you are a member or associate of a professional body, ask fellow members when you have a meeting. You will have to make adjustments that reflect such things as resource availability, but should be able to move towards estimating a high-level, relative 'size' for each option. You can also estimate to produce a range of results, from 'optimistic' through 'most likely' to 'pessimistic', also known as 'best', 'likely' and 'worst'.

Note that people who conduct work on a daily basis are often best able to estimate many similar project tasks. You will gain much better buy-in to estimates that your team can influence than if you impose your own without consultation. However, you must be prepared to challenge some estimates and check that individuals are not building in too much 'fat' for their own comfort!

ESTIMATING OPTIONS

Estimating with PERT

During the Cold War Polaris development was in uncharted waters. There were no analogous projects (see below) on which to base estimates, so these were developed using the formula:

$$T_e = \frac{a + 4m + b}{6}$$

where a = most optimistic duration; b = most pessimistic duration; m = most likely duration and T_e = the resulting estimate duration which, statistically, you will have a 50 per cent chance of achieving or beating. You can improve the confidence in such estimates by adding one or more standard deviations. This text is not the place to learn the detailed theory that underlies this approach, but many of you will already be familiar with it.

Let us suppose that our estimates are optimistic 4 days, most likely 6 days, and pessimistic 7 days. Using the formula with the estimates:

$$T_e = \frac{4 + (4 \times 6) + 7}{6}$$

$$T_e = 5.8 \text{ days}$$

Statistically (and assuming that the estimates are sensible!), there is a 50 per cent probability that you will finish the task on or within 5.8 days. To improve confidence in beating or achieving an estimate, you can add one or more standard deviations for which there is another simple formula:

$$\sigma = \frac{b - a}{6}$$

where a and b mean optimistic and pessimistic, as above. So, using the formula and the numbers, calculate one standard deviation (σ):

$$\sigma = \frac{7 - 4}{6}$$

$\sigma = 0.5$ (days)

Statistical theory tells us that if you add:

- one standard deviation (5.8 + 0.5 = 6.3 days), you will now have an 85 per cent chance of beating or achieving the estimate

- two standard deviations (5.8 + 0.5 + 0.5 = 6.8 days), you will now have a 99 per cent chance of beating or achieving the estimate (which degree of accuracy ought to be good enough for most people)

- three standard deviations (5.8 + 0.5 + 0.5 + 0.5 = 7.3 days), you will now have almost 100 per cent chance of beating or achieving the estimate (of course, some might suggest that it would be quicker and easier just to use the worst-case estimate).

You can apply the formula and standard deviations to estimates at any level, project, stage, or task, but beware the 'garbage-in, garbage-out' rule, and be prepared to do the required groundwork first. Some approaches to avoid feeding 'garbage' into your estimates follow.

Analogous estimates

In this context, we use the term 'analogous' to mean 'similar', or bearing resemblance to some other project work. If you have, or can obtain, information about the time and effort needed on previous work of a similar nature, you can use this to provide a guide, or to validate any estimates you make using a different technique. The closer the similarities, the better the value to our estimates. This approach is particularly useful if your projects are repetitious, for example when you analyse, design, write and implement software solutions. You can also adjust your findings to compensate for size and complexity variations. When you close a project, it makes great sense to review actual resource usage, costs and times against original estimates and record 'lessons learned'. It makes even more sense to store this information safely and in a readily accessible format. Good management information has an intrinsic value that should outweigh the time and cost you use to preserve it.

Standard times

In some organizations, it is customary to go a step beyond the analogy approach and use standard times for estimating. If your projects include repetitive work, you can establish a 'standard time' for someone with a defined skill level to do a certain amount of work. For example, if you were in the Polaris Project and needed to employ sub-contract welders to plate a submarine hull, you should know how many square feet each can cover in a day using steel sheets of specified size, and thus be able to estimate how long the entire job should take in person-months. Once your main contractor tells you how many welders it can provide, you can quickly convert your person-month estimate into duration-months, by dividing the surface area by the number of welders. You will also recognize that some tasks cannot be shared between unlimited resources. For example, if the standard time for welding one plate is one hour, you might be able to cut it down to 30 minutes by employing two welders, but not to 10 minutes by using six! You may also need to adjust standard times to allow for such circumstances as people being trained, or training or supervising others (increases on standard times), or those who are experts (reductions on standard times).

Benchmarking: a short story from experience

One January, a Project Manager hired an Assistant Project Manager to help with the planning for a project that was making little headway, but had a deadline of 31 July. The Assistant examined the Gantt chart and asked for the detailed plan, as there were only eight parallel tasks, each stretching from the previous year until the following August, though there were over forty people working on the project. 'This is the detailed plan,' said the Project Manager, 'and the estimates are from my personal experience.'

The Assistant Project Manager sought short-term extra expertise and a PRINCE® specialist developed a Product Breakdown Structure with almost 1300 products. Of these, eight had to be completed for each of 160 territories, varying in size and complexity.

The Assistant Project Manager then allowed work to continue for one month while collecting data from the team, to establish how long each of the eight products took to complete and whether they were simple, moderate or complex and for small, medium or large territories. At the end of that month, these benchmark findings were converted into standard times. The standard times were applied to all the tasks on a network derived from the Product Breakdown Structure and amalgamated into a schedule. This showed that only 25 per cent of the work could be completed by the deadline.

The Project Manager resigned, and the Assistant took over. The newly planned work was delivered late in July, with a few days to spare, achieving completion of all the products in territories assessed by the organization as having the greatest commercial risks.
You may find a similar approach valuable when there is little or no history on which to base your estimates, and may even attempt to do this during a Feasibility Study or other pre-project study.

GROUP ANALYSIS

When there are no readily available sources of input to estimating, no analogous projects and little of any clear value, you may be compelled to fall back on educated guesswork ('guesstimating'). You might have to work alone, but if you can arrange a collective effort, this can be of considerable value. Try to 'borrow' a few experienced Project Managers for a short while. Experience has shown that when intelligent guesses are averaged, you can produce estimates that turn out to be quite reasonable.

To conduct such a session, identify each task you want to guesstimate, one at a time, asking each individual to jot down his or her view and a few words of justification. Poll the group, and collect the input and the justifications. When finished, give the participants the opportunity to modify their estimate using any new ideas from justification that others have suggested. Collect the estimates again and calculate the average (arithmetic mean) as your estimate for that piece of work.

Bottom-up approach

When developing detailed estimates for a project or stage, you will find a Work Breakdown Structure (WBS) very valuable. Every task that has to be completed should be there, so you should not forget anything. You can estimate task by task, at the lowest level of activity on the WBS, which most people find easier, then apply your findings to a network diagram that shows the sequence and dependencies of all the tasks. Provided that the network is logical and complete, you will be able to forecast the overall duration in working days, weeks or months. You now also have valuable data for critical path analysis, and finally for a schedule, when you will convert the duration represented on the network to actual dates on the calendar.

ESTIMATING – WHAT MIGHT YOU DO OR CHECK?

For high-level estimates, such as when completing a Feasibility Study:

- Do you have access to project histories?
- Can you find anything analogous with that for which you need an estimate?
- Are the size and complexity similar, or might you need to apply a factor to increase or decrease the estimate because of increased or decreased size or complexity?
- If historical information is not available, have you considered some form of Group Analysis guesstimating?

For detailed level estimating (bottom–up):

- Will the PERT approach be useful?
- Do you have access to project histories for an analogous approach?
- Does your organization have standard time information for project tasks?
- Is the work of a nature that you could benchmark tasks and use this information for subsequent tasks?

- If detailed historical information is not available, have you considered some form of Group Analysis guesstimating with other Project Managers and Project Team members?

GREAT ESTIMATING IN HISTORY

'I think there is a world market for maybe five computers.'

Thomas Watson in 1943 – son of the head of IBM, its President from 1952, Chairman from 1961 and CEO from 1972 to 1979, when he became US Ambassador to the USSR

SEE ALSO

Controlling Against the Schedule
Feasibility Study
Lessons Learned
Scheduling
Work Breakdown Structure

Exceptions (and Management By)

An exception is a serious variance between what has been planned or budgeted, what has happened or is forecast to happen, and which has gone, or will go beyond a level deemed by the Project Sponsor or Steering Group in advance as acceptable, or beyond the agreed Tolerance. The exception needs to be reported urgently to management (escalated) for decisions on its resolution. Note that such exception situations can arise from a number of different sources. These may include a Project Risk that has now become a live Project Issue – what was feared has now become reality, though, in this case, corrective actions and contingency provisions of time and money should have been made. Of course, the impact may now be seen to be much worse than feared, and further provisions may need to be made. The second source could be a Project Issue that has not been managed effectively, which is poor project management, or was simply underestimated. The third might have occurred because of an unchecked and unreported build-up of many smaller variations that has now reached critical mass. This third situation might indicate an abdication or omission that is one of the deadliest sins in project management.

Exception management is a 'hands-off' management philosophy which allows Project Managers to get on with the work of delivering the project without the need for frequent authorization, provided that any variances being experienced or forecast are within a clear and pre-defined range established by the Steering Group, Sponsor, Corporate Board or other project authority.

It is the nature of projects that there will be variances between what is planned and budgeted and what actually happens. If a Project Manager has to report every small variance and seek permission to correct it, this would consume much of her or his valuable time, and the time of the project's decision-makers. It is more sensible to accept that variations will happen, for the Steering Group or Project Sponsor to define the limits of acceptability and then let the Project Manager get on with delivering the project. This should continue unless those limits have been, or are forecast to be, exceeded. In a project environment, exception management could be described as allowing Project Managers and teams the freedom to do their work unless and until unacceptable variations arise.

An exception situation arises when whatever control method being used indicates that 'plan' and 'actual' have deviated or varied beyond the pre-defined acceptable level (or, better, are forecast to be about to deviate unless corrective action is taken). Most often, these variations are against the schedule or budget. This should then trigger a report to the project's decision-makers (Exception Report) and the subsequent implementation of whatever corrective actions are then approved. These could range between stopping and reviewing the project, to authorization of changes to one or more of budget, timing, scope and quality.

Clearly different projects will need different ranges for acceptability of variations. This may depend on such aspects as size, risk, urgency and so on. The two elements normally defined are cost and time, with a cost range of plus or minus so many units, or expressed as a percentage range. For time, the range might be expressed as plus or minus so many units of time, such as days, weeks or months, and the quotation of percentage ranges may not be clear or universally understood. Note that variations indicating under-running or under-spending might free resources that are much needed elsewhere, so should also be reported.

WHAT MIGHT YOU NEED TO CHECK?

- Is the philosophy of 'management by exception' part of your organizational project culture? (If not, the following three points might be theoretical.)
- Are limits set for your projects (tolerances) that give Project Managers freedom to handle normal variations?
- Are these limits expressed in time and cost units?
- Do they allow for things taking less time and incurring less cost, as well as exceeding these parameters?
- Does your monitoring and control method enable reasonable tracking of progress against schedule and budget, and thus of forecasting or spotting exceptions?
- Does your monitoring and control method include 'estimates to completion' for unfinished tasks that would enable forecasting of looming exceptions?
- Do you have established formats and methods for reporting exceptions?

SAMPLE EXCEPTION REPORT FORMAT

An exception arises when controls indicate or forecast that 'plan' and 'actual' or 'budget' and 'spend' have deviated or are about to deviate beyond pre-defined acceptable levels. An Exception Report triggers corrective actions by alerting the Project Sponsor or Steering Group, identifying optional solutions and their implications. Possible content includes:

- the quantified problem
- its probable or known cause
- its likely implications, quantified to show the size of the problem
- options available to resolve the situation
- the pros and cons of each option, and the implications for plans, Business Case, risks and issues
- recommendations.

SEE ALSO

Budget Control
Business Case
Controlling Against the Schedule
Issue Management
Reports in Projects and Programmes
Risk Management
Sponsor
Steering Group
Tolerance

Feasibility Study

A feasibility study is an early, high-level assessment of whether it would be practicable, desirable and worthwhile to pursue an opportunity, or a solution to a problem, and if so, how. It should identify and evaluate optional solutions, their justification and viability, and how you might implement each. The study needs to provide sufficient information to justify any recommendations on whether and how to proceed. It should attempt to answer questions such as:

- What do we need to achieve and why?
- What solution options do we have? What are the costs, benefits, risks and other implications likely to be?
- What approach options do we have? What are the costs, benefits, risks and other implications likely to be?
- Which combination of solution and approach, if any, is likely to meet our needs best, and why?
- How long might it take? How much might it cost? What returns can we expect on our investment over what period?
- What do we need to do next?

In some project life cycles, a Feasibility Study is conducted as an early stage, immediately following Project Initiation. The drawback with this approach is that a project has been authorized with little knowledge of what it might produce, when, and at what cost. Experience has tended to show that such a study is often better conducted as a separate mini-project. This will have minimal risk, limited scope, objectives, constraints and funding, enabling it to take a 'helicopter view' of a problem or opportunity. When conducting a Feasibility Study, you should evaluate all identified solution options and methods of implementing each (see Figure 21). However, as soon as you identify a 'showstopper' for any option, you should normally record that it is not feasible, with reason(s), and discontinue analysis.

You should also include an assessment of the status quo (the 'do-nothing' option) if there is one, as this may still turn out to be the best (or least worst!) available option, and will also provide a baseline for comparing other options. The likely costs and benefits of each can be estimated, and the issues and risks identified. Recommendation can then be made

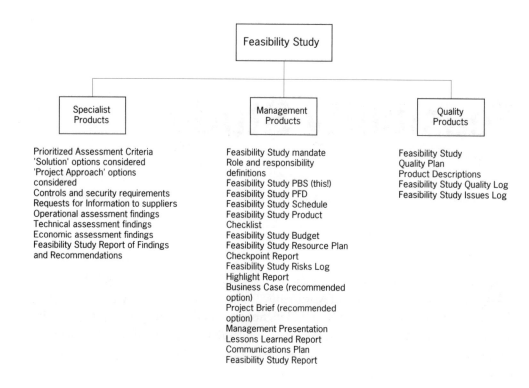

Figure 21 Possible Feasibility Study Product Breakdown Structure

for the option that looks like the 'best buy', what type of project if any should be initiated (for example, procure from third party for own use, 'do-it-yourself', outsource, modify what you have already), what precise objectives and scope and following what project life cycle.

WHAT MIGHT YOU NEED TO CHECK?

● Does the Feasibility Study have its own clear Terms of Reference?

● Do you have a plan for the conduct of the study and delivery/approval of its findings? If so it might beneficially follow three main steps:
1. definition of the problem or opportunity, and of what any resulting project must achieve
2. identification and evaluation of solution options, and recommending the way ahead
3. documenting, communicating and securing approval for the recommendation.

● Are there any constraints that already preclude some possible recommendations? For example, if your organization has a hardware or software purchasing policy, it may automatically mean that some options cannot be considered.

● Are you aware of any circumstances that would make a normally feasible solution unacceptable? This requires awareness of the politics of an organization, and should always be handled with tact and diplomacy. For example, an organization may be seeking a solution that will enable it to reduce headcount. Though this may be unwritten and unspoken, any solution not enabling it would be rejected.

- Does your plan allow time to work with others to identify all potential solutions and approaches (for example, by brainstorming following definition of problem/ opportunity)?

- Does your plan enable you to follow a route to evaluation that addresses operational aspects first, technical second, and economic third, which can have the advantage of making you concentrate initially on the sort of solution your customers need/want.

Operational aspects

- Will the proposed solution 'do the business'? Will your proposed deliverables meet all your customers' needs? If not, why pursue it further?
- Will the organization be able to 'live with' and use what you deliver? Is any training needed?
- Does the organization have, or how can it acquire the skills, knowledge and experience to optimize the use of what you deliver?

Technical aspects

Once you have set aside solutions that your customers do not need, want, or will not risk, evaluate your technical and delivery requirements and capabilities:

- Does your proposal conform to existing or proposed strategies for such things as equipment, hardware, software and telecommunications links?
- Can you use existing equipment, hardware, software, telecommunications links, or will you need something new?
- If it is something new, can your project team create or obtain this, do everything required to set it up, make it work, keep it working?
- Will your 'solution' interface with existing or developing parts/systems?

Economic aspects

- Once you have discarded options you cannot deliver, or dare not risk, you can then complete a cost-benefit analysis on those remaining, to try to establish which might offer best 'value for money'. (Economic – can we afford it? Is it a sound investment?)

- Will the organization be able to afford this, and will it achieve the required level of benefit?

- Do you know the organization's policy on what capital and revenue costs should include? Have you followed this? Note that the 'capital' costs incurred by a project tend to include those items such as equipment, property, systems and other things that are likely to exist for several years and may depreciate during those years. 'Revenue' items tend to include such costs as wages, professional fees, consumables, rentals and other day-to-day costs incurred and paid throughout the project.

- Have you estimated all likely revenue costs? Is this based on the project approach and life cycle you would recommend? Have you validated your estimates?

- Have you estimated all likely capital expenditure? Have you validated your estimates?

- Does/will the organization have funding available to meet the costs at the times you have identified?

- Have you estimated likely cash flows?

- Have you discounted cash flows to today's values (Net Present Value calculations)?

- Have you followed the organization's policies for project costs and benefits?

- Are there stated financial criteria for project acceptance? (For example, some organizations state that if a project's DCF Rate of Return is not equal to or greater than n per cent, the project will not be accepted. Would any project you recommend meet these requirements?)

- Is your justification for rejecting all other solutions clear, auditable and quantified?

Policy and politics

Do not ignore policy or politics. Policy is usually clear and defined. Company politics can sometimes be less clear and, like authority, may only be clarified when you step outside of its limitations! I once worked as a consultant for a large organization that, for systems proposals, insisted that everything came out of a 'blue box' (all systems must use IBM mainframe solutions). When conducting a Feasibility Study, everyone was constrained to examining IBM mainframe solutions only, even if they could identify something more appropriate. This was policy.

In the same organization, the hardware and software was always one or two steps behind the latest available developments. It was understood, though unwritten, that other organizations could risk the latest hardware and software. This organization would follow on later, after all the technology wrinkles had been removed. They would be 'close followers' – but not too close!

Organizational politics becomes altogether more dangerous when key individuals or power groups do not see eye-to-eye. If you face such circumstances, all you can do is remain detached and professional. As always, you will need to show why some options have been discarded, and present proposals and recommendations that will stand up to the most rigorous scrutiny. Avoid any temptations to skew figures, or overstate or understate benefits or risks in an attempt to justify someone's 'favourite' option.

SEE ALSO

Business Case
Investment Appraisal for Projects
Project Life Cycle
Reports in Projects and Programmes

FEASIBILITY
STUDY

Filing and Document Management in Projects

Reliable information about a project has two main uses:

1. to help you manage a current project effectively
2. to help *everyone* manage *future* projects effectively.

In a dynamic project environment, it is all too easy to lose track of important documents. Information must be in the right place at the right time, accessible to managers, project staff, reviewers, auditors and stakeholders. Project documents and files have to provide clear and accurate accounts. Some information may need to be kept secure.

Information about what actually happens on a project, compared with what was planned and expected to happen, provides valuable lessons learned to improve future projects. A good filing and retrieval system must satisfy all these needs. This section explains why and how such records might be organized and maintained.

WHEN MIGHT YOU NEED IT?

You will need good provisions for the safe storage and effective retrieval of information, from the pre-project situation until long after a project has closed. What we learn on projects can be immensely valuable in the future. This is probably why Fred Brooks' *The Mythical Man Month*, (Addison Wesley, 1975), describing the earlier development of IBM's s360 operating system, is still regarded as a classic work on the management of software projects – a lessons-learned gold mine!

HOW DO YOU USE IT?

You will need to:

- maintain information about a project's deliverables, which can be shared in a controlled and effective way throughout and beyond a project's life
- ensure that the status of deliverables is known
- ensure that only the current version of a deliverable is released for use
- safeguard all original deliverables, including signed approvals and authorizations
- provide good-quality information to project evaluations, to enhance the effectiveness of the 'lessons learned' process
- provide information on project status and history so that audits and reviews can be conducted effectively
- ensure that Change and Configuration Management decisions are based on accurate and up-to-date information
- provide reliable information to all involved with, and affected by, a project.

You may prefer to keep a hard copy of all deliverables, or to keep as little paperwork as possible. For some items, it will only be possible to keep paper, particularly signed originals. You will also need to file correspondence, contracts and any paperwork received from outside your organization, although where scanning is available, this may not always be necessary. It is important that your filing system can handle any combination of deliverables and supporting documents, so that a complete audit trail and history of your project is available and accessible.

Your system should provide for documents, electronic copies and for 'baselined' or Configuration Items.

You will probably need three sets of logical files for:

- **Management** – information about running the project
- **Quality** – information to assess 'fitness for purpose' of outputs
- **Business** – information about the outputs the project was established to deliver.

A logical file may be set up as several physical files. The contents will vary according to the project, and security might also determine physical location and access rights. Each type of file is described below.

MANAGEMENT FILE

You will use this to store 'management' deliverables created during the project, including information on the organization, planning and control of the project. You may consider sub-dividing your Management File into:

- a Project File
- Stage Files (one for each stage).

You are likely to use your Management Files to hold correspondence and any other documentation associated with the project as a whole. Make sure you do not allow the file to become unwieldy – store background paperwork and general correspondence in a separate file. You will find suggestions below where you might consider keeping an original hard copy (H) or an electronic version (E). For some items, you may choose to keep both. Where you have created documentation internally, you should try to keep only electronic versions, provided you are confident about the security and backup provisions.

You will probably need to keep such items as:

- your signed Project Initiation Document (H)
- the approved initial Project Plan and any subsequent baselined versions; all the components of each version should be kept, with clear identification of their date, version number and reason for creation (E)
- planning support documentation, such as the Work Breakdown Structure and PERT diagrams, kept with the plan to which they relate (E)
- Steering Group Meeting Agenda and Minutes (H/E)
- Progress Reports (E)
- Exception Reports (if a stage is going off track) (E)
- signed Approval Forms (such as End of Stage) (H)
- signed Authorization Forms (such as to start a new Stage) (H)
- Evaluation and Audit Reports and Health Checks (E)
- Roles and Responsibilities and organization details (E)
- contracts, purchase order copies, invoice copies for services and supplies to the project (H)
- timesheet copies (E).

QUALITY FILE

You should use one Quality File for the whole project, rather than trying to divide it into Stage Files. You might also consider three sub-files:

- **Quality Review File** – containing administration and control documents covering the evaluation of outputs against specification (E)
- **Change Control File** – containing change control administration and control documents (E)
- **Product Descriptions or Specifications** – containing current baselined Product Descriptions; you should have a Product Description or written specification for every major deliverable in the project.

The Quality File should also provide for records of any audit work on quality and adherence to standards.

BUSINESS FILE

You should consider using this to contain all the baselined business outputs delivered by the project, usually referred to as 'Configuration Items'. You will find it impossible to standardize its structure, since deliverables will be unique and vary with the type of project. You will need to decide on an appropriate setup.

Your Business File could contain:

- **Deliverable Log** – a filing index that identifies the physical location of each deliverable
- **Business Deliverables** – deliverables that can be physically filed and which do not need to be filed separately because of their security or sensitivity rating
- **Held-over Requests for Change** – as deliverables, these should be filed in a separate section of the Business File
- **Test Deliverables** – the results of Test Executions, such as Test Logs, Test Results, Incident Logs, Incident Reports or Test Completion Reports
- other key outputs, such as decision documents and documented analysis outputs.

HOW DO YOU KEEP IT ALL UP TO DATE?

You will find that the maintenance procedures you choose to use will depend on your project and whether you have dedicated Project Support staff or a Project Office. You might consider the following basic principles:

- You should set up Project Files early in the Start-up or Initiation Stage. Before you start any stage, you should also set up appropriate filing for that stage, as you will be working on its plans and budget before the current stage ends.

- Keep your final versions ('ready for review' status) separate from working documents or drafts.

- Try to structure your files logically, and organize them physically to ensure completeness, ease of access and to reflect the current status of the project and its deliverables.

- Store information recording the location and status of any deliverable that cannot be filed.

- Use 'revision marking' where possible as your documents evolve. Insist that all changes to baselined documents are 'revision-marked', so that you maintain an audit trail. Keep both the revision-marked version and the new baselined version with revisions accepted.

- Always use electronic filing, unless there is an overriding reason for not doing so, as it normally benefits from good security benefits through backups and offsite storage.

● A lot of project information is shared by e-mail. Much of this is transient, and some of the information may be crucial and worth saving. It is efficient and effective to copy, paste and save e-mails using a suitable word processor text format, such as Rich Text Format (RTF). This should save 80 per cent of the disk storage space you would have consumed if you had saved it as a normal word processor document.

Typical filing conventions follow.

File names

You should find file naming conventions very useful. Persuade everyone to use the same folder structure and file naming conventions, and you will find negotiating your way around documentation and configuration management much easier. If you have completed a Product or Work Breakdown Structure, the number assigned to each item should stay with it permanently as a unique identifier. If you also add a standard abbreviation, acronym or mnemonic, it will simplify access, maintenance and control of products.

Repeating products

You will find that repeating products such as reports, memos, forms, letters and e-mails, can present more of a challenge. You may find it useful to use a reverse-date system, (YYMMDD) as part of the reference: for example, if you use 030303, this would at least identify the document as having been created on 3 March 2003, allowing it to be placed in date order. Unfortunately, this is too simple, because if more than one document originated on the same day, you would risk duplicating the identifier. There are various ways of dealing with this – for example, when you create more than one product of the same type on the same date, you can simply add two further digits (for example 030303.02), which will mean that you can create up to 99 on the same date without a problem, and they will still be listed in order, though this may not be relevant. You will also find that some products, such as letters and memos, lend themselves to sequential numbering. You can simply assign the next number from a log, prefixing a letter with 'L' and a memo with 'M'. Tedious, but not rocket science!

Version numbering

Finally, you will need some method of identifying the latest version of a product and whether it is a draft or a baselined product. It is conventional to start draft versions at 0.1 and to increment the version number by 0.1 for each subsequent draft.

Again, you will probably find that version numbers for completed products are always integers, starting at 1 as soon as you baseline a product. If you ever change it, simply increment the version number by 1. You should find that one digit will be enough.

It is sensible to show document history on all the documents your team produces, similar to that shown in Figure 22.

Version	Date	Changes Incorporated and Change Log reference
0.1	3 March 2003	First draft issue
1.0	1 April 2003	First approved issue

Figure 22   Example document history

HARD COPY PROJECT FILING SUGGESTIONS

Note that Figures 23 and 24 are suggestions only. They are not exhaustive, and you will need to tailor them to your use. (PRINCE® names are largely used in these examples.)

Name	Contents	Comments
Project Initiation	Project Brief	External Product
Project Initiation Document (PID)	Project Initiation Document Updates as required	Your PID should be approved and signed by the Steering Group. You should update the Project Plan and Business Case at the end of each stage. You must not change your PID other than through formal Change Control. If minor aspects change, then appropriate notes, letters, memos, amended sections and so on can be inserted in this sub-section to provide an accurate status of the PID.
Planning Support Documents	Product Breakdown Structure Product Flow Diagrams Product Descriptions Gantt/bar chart Resource Plan Project Organization Chart	Working documents. Sub-divisions of this section may be created for these documents. The file organization will depend on the volume of documentation.

Figure 23   Sample filing scheme for plans

HARD COPY STAGE FILING SUGGESTIONS

As before, you will need to tailor Figures 25–29 to your specific needs.

Name	Contents	Comments
Steering Group Meeting Records	Templates Agendas and Meeting Papers not filed elsewhere Meeting Records and Minutes	
Highlight Reports		File in date order.
Acceptance Letters	User and Business Acceptance Letters	
Approvals to Proceed	One for project, and one for each stage	File in stage order.
Review	Project Evaluation Review	
Miscellaneous	Miscellaneous documents relevant to your project	File in date order.

Figure 24   Filing scheme for controls

Name	Contents	Comments
Stage Organization	Recording changes or additions to the organization shown in the Project Initiation Document	

Figure 25   Sample stage organization filing scheme

Name	Contents	Comments
Stage Plan	Stage Plan Updates as required	As agreed by the Steering Group
Planning Support Documentation	Product Breakdown Structure Product Descriptions Product Flow Diagrams Gantt/bar chart Resource Plan	Stage and Team Plan working documents
Exception Plans	Exception Plan(s)	Only if needed in an Exception Situation
Team Plans	Work Packages (if used) Products Activities Resource Loading Detailed Gantt/bar charts	The Stage Plan may be adequate.

Figure 26   Sample plans filing scheme

Name	Contents	Comments
Stage Controls	Checkpoint Reports Resource Usage	
Stage Progress and Resource data	Resource Usage Reports	File by week.
Stage Costs data	Copies of orders and invoices Staff costs	File in date order.
Project Manager's Log	Brief log of significant events (for example, dates of signing contracts, visits to suppliers, problems, questions/answers, informal discussions with Steering Group, actions for stage, and so on.	File in date order.
Timesheets	Completed timesheets	Files in date order.

Figure 27 Sample controls filing scheme

Name	Contents	Comments
Miscellaneous	Miscellaneous documents that are relevant to the stage Correspondence at stage level	Filed in date order.

Figure 28 Sample miscellaneous filing scheme

Name	Contents	Comments
Quality Log	Log of Quality Reviews showing current status of all Quality Review products	
Quality Review Records	Quality Review Invitations Error Lists from reviewers Follow-up Actions List Quality Review Result Notification Forms	File by product.
'Off Specification' File	Details of current status of all 'Off Specification' Reports	File in Issue Number order.
Requests For Change (RFC) File	Details of current status of all Requests for Change	File in Change Log Number order.

Figure 29 Sample Quality filing scheme

BUSINESS FILE

You will need to make the Business File structure specific to your project. You should be able to use your Product Breakdown Structure for guidance. You might find the list of headings in Figure 30 useful, showing examples of product groups.

Name	Contents	Comments
Product/Product Log	Log identifying location of each product/output that will be used by the business post-project – the reasons for there being a project!	Either its location in the Business File or its physical location if elsewhere
Technical Products	Example grouping are: Specifications Design Products Development Products Support Products Testing Products Installation and Conversion Products Training Products Acceptance Products Documentation Products Procurement Products	
Held-over RFCs	Held-over Requests for Change – Requests for Change not completed within the project, but handed over to a post-project maintenance function	Will become part of hand-over documentation

Figure 30   Sample Business File structure

ELECTRONIC PROJECT FILING

You will find a well-planned filing system very helpful for the effective maintenance and control of electronic documents. If you proceed on an *ad hoc* basis, you will find that control is difficult, and you risk multiple unsynchronized copies, lost items, multiple versions, disorganized version numbering, inappropriate access, poor security and poor confidentiality. You will spend much more time trying to sort out the muddle than you would have spent organizing it properly in the first place. You may be aware of the many possible electronic filing options, but will find the suggested structure, based on practical experience, a reasonable starting point.

You know that it is impossible to file all project documents electronically, particularly external documents, signed internal documents, orders, contracts, invoices, correspondence and documents with high security and confidentiality. You need to ensure that your hard-copy filing system is designed to complement, not duplicate, your computer-based system.

You will need permanent space to create and store your project files on the network. Your next decision will concern security and access controls, including read and write access. You and your staff are likely to have full access to all folders, whereas others may have full access to Work Files, but maybe 'read-only' access to others. 'Read-only' means that full access is limited to nominated individuals, including the Stage and Project Manager and designated staff, such as those in a Project Support Office.

You will probably need to create the following folders:

- **Project** – for the project's products
- **Stage** – one for the products of each stage.

Each Stage File might have the following folders:

Name	Contents
Work in Progress	Working documents and deliverables
Ready For Review	Draft deliverables submitted for Quality Review
Management	Baselined management deliverables
Business	Baselined business deliverables
Quality	Quality deliverables
Archive	Superseded versions of baselined deliverables

A suggested outline of each folder type is shown below.

Work Files

Create a sub-folder for each project team member. When they create new a document they can store it in a personal folder until complete, when the author or some other designated person, such as a Team Leader or Stage Manager, will *move* (not copy) it to the 'Ready for Review' folder.

Ready for Review

This should be a 'read-only' folder that you will use as a temporary store for completed documents, submitted for review. You need to do this to ensure that the original is preserved. If changes are needed following the review, the document should again be *moved*, rather than copied back from whence it came to. If it passes the review, it becomes baselined and should be moved to one of the Management, Business or Quality folders, as appropriate.

Management, Business and Quality

These should be 'read-only' folders. Once your reviewers accept a product, if necessary after any post-review changes, you need to baseline it by *moving* it (again, not copying it) from Working (or Ready for Review if no corrections were necessary) to either the

Management, Business or Quality folder, as appropriate. The Management and Quality folders also contain day-to-day administration and control sub-folders.

Archive

This should be a 'read-only' folder. When a baselined product is changed, the previous version should be moved to the Archive File, to provide an audit trail and a fall-back and recovery option.

Sample electronic Project folder

The Microsoft Windows® screenshot in Figure 31 shows a sample Project folder and its sub-folders.

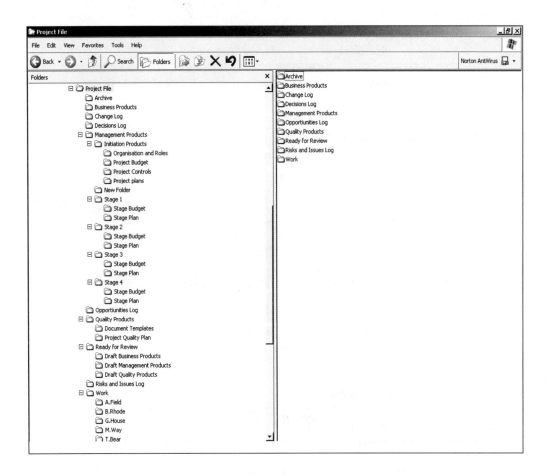

Figure 31   Sample Project folder and sub-folders

You may find the typical folder contents lists shown in Figures 32–38 useful.

Folder	Files	Comments
Name	One folder for each team member	Internal structure at the owner's discretion, but similar conventions to those used in the other folders will enable easier control and ('read-only'?) access by other people when necessary

Figure 32   Sample 'working' folder

Folder	Files	Comments
Management	Management products	Drafts of unique management products that have been submitted for Quality Review
Quality	Product Descriptions (Specifications)	The only relevant quality deliverables are draft Product Descriptions
Business	Business deliverables	Drafts of unique Business Products

Figure 33   Sample Ready for Review folder

Folder	Files	Comments
Project	External products	Any relevant product which was produced externally from the project (for example, Project Brief, Feasibility Study)
Project Planning	Project Initiation Document	Latest version of the PID, and all its components
Project Planning	Project Plan Support Documents (for example, PBS, PFD, Resource Data, Financial Data	Working documents when preparing the Project Plan
Project Planning	Project Plan and Project Budget	
Project Control	Memo Log Individual Memos Letter Log Individual Letters	You may need to use a log to identify individual memos and letters, by file name, brief description, date and author. Number all Memos and Letters from 0001 to 9999. Retain at Project rather than Stage level.
Project Control	Miscellaneous	All miscellaneous documents that are relevant to the project as a whole.

Continued

Folder	Files	Comments
Project Control	Meeting Records Invitations to Meetings	Note that some Meeting Records must be retained on hard copy, since they require authorizing signatures (for example, Approval to Proceed and Acceptance Letters)
Risk Log	Updated details of all identified risks, their status and counter-measures and outcomes	Note: Risks can be closed, but never removed from the Risk Log during a project. If a Risk occurs and becomes an Issue, the new Issue must be cross-referenced to the original Risk Log entry, and vice versa.
Issue Log	Updated details of all Issues, status, ownership and outcome. Central repository of decisions taken during project	Note: Issues can be closed but never removed from the Issue Log during a project
Opportunities Log		Note: Opportunities can be closed but never removed from the Opportunities Log during a project. If an Opportunity arises and becomes an Issue, the new Issue must be cross-referred to the original Opportunity Log entry and vice versa.
Project Control	Highlight Reports Project Evaluation Review Risk Register	

Figure 34 Sample Management folder

Folder	Files	Comments
Planning	Detailed Plans at stage level. Products include: work packages, activity lists, resource loading, detailed Gantt charts	Detailed Plans are produced for a fixed period, and updated with progress at one- to two-week intervals
Planning	Exception Plans	There will be one Exception Plan for every Exception Situation that arises in a stage
Planning	Stage Plan	
Planning	Stage Plan Support Documents (for example, PBS, PFD, Transformations, Resource Data, Financial Data)	Working documentation created when preparing the Stage Plan
Control	Stage Budget: Actuals, Commitments, Forecast Spend	
Control	Miscellaneous	All miscellaneous documents that are relevant to the project as a whole
Control	Project Manager's Log	Brief log, notes and miscellaneous products of significant events, actions and so on
Control	End Stage Report Checkpoint Reports Resource Usage	
Control	Completed Timesheets	

Figure 35   Sample Stage folder

Folder	Files	Comments
Quality	Product Descriptions	Product Descriptions for key and major products may also be contained in the Project and Stage Plans. Ensure that these do not get out of step if they are also retained in the Quality File. Use Configuration Management to ensure everyone uses the current version. All lower-level Product Descriptions are held in the Quality File only.
Quality Review	Quality Review Meeting Invitations Quality Review Error Lists Quality Review Follow-up Action List Quality Review Result Notification	Each unique major product may have a file of quality documentation. The Product Description identity is an ideal way to identify the files. Some Error Lists may be hand-written. The Follow-up Action List and Result Notification are in blank format only, since the signed versions will be filed as hard copies.

Figure 36   Sample Quality folder

Folder	Files	Comments
External	Technical and business products	Products on which the project is dependent, but which are supplied from external sources
Held Over	Held-over Requests for Change Held-over Off-Specifications Concession Off-Specifications	These are part of the project's final documentation, to be handed over to the owners when the business product goes operational.
Products	Product Log Business products	The Product Log lists all product identities plus their names. If a product (because of its nature) is not in the folder, its physical location should be entered (for example, equipment, hardware, furniture).

Figure 37   Sample Business folder

Folder	Files	Comments
Management	Superseded versions of unique management products	Amend file names to identify version numbers
Quality	Superseded versions of Product Descriptions	As above
Business	Superseded versions of unique Business Products	As above
Change Control/ Issues	Project Issue Log Project Issues	
Change Control/Off Specification	Off Specification Log Off Specifications	

Figure 38   Sample Archive folder

SEE ALSO

Please refer to the figures above for all the related topics, and the Glossary if you need to check any terms with which you are not familiar.

Handover Options

When you conduct a handover, you put a project's deliverables into operation, making them available for whatever use they are to have. It makes good sense to select the handover option during start-up, and to plan the project accordingly. The approach may vary considerably between projects but, for a business or IT system for example, there are at least five possible main approaches:

1. **'Big Bang'** – where everything comes to life or into use at one time, as if someone had flicked a switch

2. **'parallel running'** – sometimes used when new business systems are installed and the 'old' system continues alongside, either for benchmarking or 'security blanket' purposes

3. **'pilot' scheme** – you arrange some form of route-finding exercise by installing some or all of your project's outputs, probably in prototype form, to gain stakeholder input to ongoing development before final development and widespread installation; a 'Model Office' can be established to try out office furnishing, equipment, system and layout options as part of a relocation or major business system change, such as the introduction of a call centre

4. **'phased' implementation** – where an agreed sub-set of a project's outputs is installed at time intervals across an organization until all have been installed, or all the project's outputs are installed at once in part of an organization, and then at time intervals in other agreed parts of the organization until complete

5. **'production line'** – where many small outputs will be created, and each can be used on completion.

WHEN MIGHT YOU USE EACH?

Probably the best-known **'Big Bang'** example in the United Kingdom introduced changes to Stock Exchange rules and systems on 27 October 1986, when old systems were switched off and new ones switched on. The systems, which had been rigorously tested, ran into early difficulties, handling unexpectedly high transaction volumes, generated not just by normal business, but by the apparent race to be 'first' on the new system and the curiosity of thousands of 'browsers'. You might need to use a 'Big Bang' approach when there is a similar fixed regulatory or legislative deadline, where you must use existing methods up to the deadline and new methods immediately after, or where other perhaps more 'comfortable' approaches such as parallel running are impractical or too expensive. This approach is perceived as most risky, but may be less costly, highly motivational and will sometimes be the only way. More familiar examples might be such projects as office relocations, where you close down one office on, say, a Friday and open the new one on the following Monday. You will need to plan, test and review thoroughly, and make sure that all communications with stakeholders are clear and comprehensive.

You might be required to conduct **parallel running** when introducing mission-critical business systems. There may be a perception that if old and new run side by side and the 'new' fails, nothing will be lost. What you need to consider first is how long the parallel run will last, because the costs and resourcing difficulties might be considerable. Imagine for a moment parallel-running two network-based business applications, where you may need two personal computers on every desk, every transaction entered twice (once into each system), two sets of controls, two databases, and the need to make enquiries and seek information from two systems. Your organization might be tempted by three common and potentially dangerous assumptions when faced with a strategic implementation decision and selecting the parallel approach. These are: (a) that the staff can handle double the volume of work, (b) there will be space for all the extra equipment and cabling, and (c) if there is a reconciliation problem, the old version must be correct (so why replace it?).

You may consider a **pilot scheme** where the customers and users need a low-risk opportunity to experiment with possible solutions and to develop specifications for eventual project outputs. If you select this option, you may plan a sub-project to establish and install the pilot outputs, tune the outputs according to feedback, and to agree the specifications and installation approach for the ultimate outputs. You might then start the second sub-project to develop these outputs, and then implement them by the chosen method. This approach might help to contain risks, but could also extend the timescale and add to the costs.

Your may work to a **phased implementation** for your project's outputs in circumstances such as the introduction of a new system, office-by-office or region-by-region. If you are building a new stretch of motorway, you may build one carriageway and use a contra-flow while you build the other. When this is ready, you will need a brief closure of both carriageways while signs are uncovered and cones removed before both are finally opened. This is one approach where you need to avoid any bangs, big or otherwise! Your Steering Group will need to be aware of the benefits and risks of phasing. On the plus side, you can start to gain benefits earlier than if you waited for completion, and may reduce risk by limiting exposure to the new, particularly if any flaws are uncovered by phased operational use. On the minus side, you may add complexity to the project, its communications plan, and between users of its outputs at varying phases.

A **'production-line'** approach might be used in circumstances similar to those experienced by the author in a major project to clean up records of trademark information. This tackled problems in over 160 countries, on a country-by-country basis, prioritized according to business risk. As soon as trademark registrations and agreements had been examined by lawyers, information was updated on a new computer database, registration renewals were implemented or planned, and pursuit of uncollected royalties was initiated immediately. There had been an early sub-project to develop the database using rapid applications development techniques, a seven-month sub-project to clean up data for countries where the risks were seen by the business as highest, then a subsequent and final sub-project to tackle all the remaining lower-risk countries. This approach was used to manage business risk most effectively by prioritizing countries and achieving early returns by enabling collection of uncollected royalties. You might use this approach, for example, when developing a housing estate, when you plan from thc start to build each house to its earliest completion date and make it available for immediate sale, rather than completing a group of houses in a phase before offering that phase for sale.

You should also consider that some options might not offer quite what is needed, and may need to consider combinations. For example, in the trademark project described above, the computer database was developed and implemented through a 'pilot' approach, while the two major sub-projects were conducted like a production line.

WHEN AND HOW TO DECIDE

Making a decision on how to install a project's outputs probably needs to take place during a Feasibility Study or during the Start-up Stage, because it will be fundamental to how the project will be split into future stages, planned and managed. The decision is also fundamental to the management of business and project risk, so will need to be made at project Sponsor level, or by corporate management.

Your role as Project Manager might be to describe all the available options, their advantages and disadvantages, and maybe even to make a recommendation on which makes the best project management sense.

SEE ALSO

Starting a Project

HANDOVER
OPTIONS

Impact Analysis

Impact analysis is used to forecast the possible effects of any proposed or imposed changes on the justification, schedule, budget, risks, issues and other requests for changes, so that decision-makers can have the opportunity to consider the full implications before committing to a course of action that was not in the original plans, or alternatively to maintaining the status quo. It is another form of 'What if . . .' analysis, comparing the potential impacts of various events or conditions that we may or may not be able to influence, once we have considered all the implications.

WHY MIGHT IT BE USEFUL?

'Just one or two small changes ...'

Projects exist because of the constant pressure for change and innovation in all areas of human endeavour. Projects are established and live out their life cycles in dynamic conditions, subject to continuing pressures to 'change the changes'. Each time a variation away from the intended course of action is proposed, someone usually has to make a decision – to allow the change or not.

'What will happen if this happens ...?'

All projects co-exist with risk. We are often replacing something that works, however badly, with something that does not yet exist and is thus unproven. If there is no risk here, we misunderstand the word. We may be developing a new product that has been market researched extensively, with confident forecasts of its commercial success, but can we really develop it and make a profit at the researched price – will it really sell? Will it repay its development costs? If changes occur part-way through, what then?

'This is causing real difficulties ...'

Imagine you have two key stakeholders with very different requirements for what is intended to be a single outcome from your project – a critical Project Issue. If a *laissez-faire* attitude is taken but the protagonists grow no closer in their outlooks, the project is heading for deep trouble. If you pursue one of the two courses, what will be the impact for the stakeholder who misses out? You might consider Impact Analysis to look at the effects of not doing something, as well as of doing something else, but this problem should be recorded and acted upon in any pre-project activities, such as a Feasibility Study.

WHEN MIGHT YOU USE IT?

In any of the above scenarios, you should conduct some form of Impact Analysis on the outcomes of the various courses of action open to those who own the decision. Impact may bear positively, negatively or be neutral on:

- scope, objectives, constraints and assumptions
- stage or project durations
- the Business Case and budgets
- people
- existing or new Project Risks or Project Issues
- work already completed and now perhaps invalidated, requiring it to be re-done to meet changed circumstances
- other changes, perhaps under way but not completed.

HOW DO YOU USE IT?

For each option that appears available to a project, including the 'do nothing' option, here are ten suggested points you might wish to check, identify and to aquantify the likely effects on:

1. the planned duration
2. the Business Case
3. stage and project budgets
4. Project Risks (Will this create any new Risks or trigger existing ones?)
5. Project Issues including other proposed changes (Will this create any new Issues?)
6. Project Opportunities (Will this create any new Opportunities?)
7. customer stakeholders
8. the project team
9. suppliers
10. contractual obligations or legal commitments.

WHAT SHOULD YOU CHECK?

- Have you identified all the optional courses of action likely to be available to you and the stakeholders, including the 'do nothing – status quo' option?
- Have you asked and answered each of the ten questions about each option?
- Have you attempted to quantify the answers?
- If quantification is difficult, have you considered applying some form of structured ranking to answers, such as 'Red, Amber, Green' or even 'High, Medium, Low' impact?

- Have you included the positive as well as the negative impacts of any course of action considered?
- Will any 'drop-dead' dates be put at risk by any of the options? If so, your analysis needs to make this clear and unmistakeable.

SEE ALSO

Budgets for Project Work
Change Control
Issue Management
Procurement
Project and Stage Plans
Project Opportunities
Risk Management

Investment Appraisal for Projects

Investment Appraisal gives an estimate of the cost of a project and of the possible future costs and benefits that may flow from operational use of its outputs, which should enable an organization to determine whether the investment will be worthwhile.

Do you know whether your proposed project is a really sound business investment? Can you prove its worth to decision-makers? How will your justification be judged by those who hold the corporate purse strings? Don't forget: money talks!

We have several types of calculations, which we often refer to collectively under the umbrella name of an 'Investment Appraisal'. We should (though may not always) use one or more of these calculations to forecast whether investment in a project makes good financial sense. Will a project pay for itself, or perhaps better, add to the bottom line? We can use such appraisals:

● to compare different projects, if an organization cannot afford to do every project that has been identified (quite a common situation)

● to compare when there is more than one available solution to our problem, and more than one approach to acquiring it: for example, you could provide a river crossing by bridge, tunnel, cable car, ferry, or even helicopter; you could build it yourself, sub-contract or outsource the entire construction effort. Whichever options are considered, someone will need to compare the costs and benefits of various means and ends. This is often done as part of a Feasibility Study.

Although you may think this could be a daunting undertaking, you can do a few relatively simple calculations and produce valuable financial headline information, provided that your estimating and its raw data are cautious, sensible and complete. You should also remember that it is important to use only significant numbers – express your currency in round thousands or possibly in tens or hundreds of thousands, or in millions if, say, you are comparing the costs of building either a three- or four-lane toll road. This is an area where it will be valuable use of your time to examine what has been spent on previous projects in your organization, which might provide some basic data for your global estimates. Even if you cannot find a close match in terms of size and complexity, you might be able pick brains and work up factors that take account of the differences, so that you can adapt your findings, and use these in your estimating.

WHAT SHOULD YOU CHECK?

Do you know which method(s) are standard in the organization for financial evaluations of projects and project options? (There may be one or more of: Payback Period; Calculation of Net Present Value (NPV) of future net benefits using Discounted Cash Flows (DCF); Internal Rate of Return (IRR; also known as DCF Rate of Return, DCFRoR).). Once you know which to use, there are some more questions you will need to answer to conduct such an appraisal. These are likely to include:

- How much will it cost to complete and deliver this project?
- What might be the likely useful life of the output?
- How much might it cost to run and maintain the project outputs, over each forecast year of their useful life?
- What financial (net) benefits might be expected, and over what time period should they be earned?
- What percentage is currently used by the organization for such calculations?
- Is there a period mandated by the organization within which any project must pay back its investment?

PAYBACK PERIOD

The simplest technique is to calculate how long a project might take to recover the money invested in it. This is referred to as its Payback Period. It is calculated by adding together the hoped-for project net benefits (estimate of annual benefits to be gained minus estimated annual costs to be incurred) until they equal the investment made in the project (break-even point is reached, the net benefits equal the investment). The result is expressed in the number of years (and maybe part-years if such a level of accuracy is required) it should take to happen. This gives a rough guide to organizations on how long it should take to recoup their investment. Some may also have rules such as 'We will only invest in projects that pay back in less than five years', though cynics will tell you how they can massage figures so that any project pays back a short time before such a deadline.

Example 1

XYZ is considering investing in a new information system. After all the factors are considered (including initial costs, running and maintenance costs, future cash flows and expected life), XYZ forecasts the following cash flows (net benefits) from the system:

- Year 0 – (£150 000) (Project costs – the investment)
- Year 1 – £50 000
- Year 2 – £50 000
- Year 3 – £40 000

- Year 4 – £40 000 (expected system life)
- Total – £30 000 (an apparent net return of £30 000, and a **Payback Period of 3 years 3 months**, calculated by adding the net benefits until they equal the investment, and expressing the result in years and months).

In this case, these benefits total £140 000 at the end of year 3, and an assumption has been made that the next £10 000 will occur in the following three months. Of course, this may not be the exact case, but is only intended to produce a guideline.

NET PRESENT VALUE AND DISCOUNTED CASH FLOW

Other organizations are more interested in currency. They will require you to estimate how much a project will cost, and predict future costs and benefits from using its deliverables. A simple calculation normally suffices, but it is conventional to recognize the time-value of money. £1 put in your bank today is worth more than £1 received at some time in the future because, if you invested cash in an interest-bearing account today, it would earn interest. When investing, you can use interest tables to calculate the future value of your money. There are also tables available that work in reverse, to 'discount' the value of future amounts and tell you what they are really worth in today's terms. You will hear the terms Discounted Cash Flows (DCF) and Net Present Value (NPV). Tables are widely available that help you do calculations for different rates and different periods. See the table in Figure 39.

Note that project costs incurred before live date (your investment) are regarded as occurring in 'year zero', and are therefore not discounted. An example of the type of calculation follows. However, before you can use the tables (and similar to what you would have done to calculate payback), you need to establish:

- an estimate of the investment you will be making (all the forecast outgoings before project closure)
- the number of years of the likely life of the project deliverables, or such other period as mandated by your organization
- the net value of future cash flows from use of the project deliverables (savings or revenues minus running and maintenance costs).

Check with your accountant/accounts department to determine what percentage interest rate to use in your calculations. Then:

1. From your table select the column under the chosen percentage rate.
2. Identify each of the rows representing the years within the life you have forecast (Year 1 to Year n).
3. The cells where the selected percentage and years intersect contain the factors you need to use to calculate the value of the future amount in today's terms. Note these factors.
4. Multiply each net amount by the appropriate factor to find the 'present' value of that amount.
5. Do this calculation for each year's net cash flow.

Present Value of £1 in the future (Discounting Table)
(Investment durations of between one and ten years, and rates from 3% to 10.5%)

Years	3.00%	3.50%	4.00%	4.50%
1	0.971	0.966	0.962	0.957
2	0.943	0.934	0.925	0.916
3	0.915	0.902	0.889	0.876
4	0.888	0.871	0.855	0.839
5	0.863	0.842	0.822	0.802
6	0.837	0.814	0.790	0.768
7	0.813	0.786	0.760	0.735
8	0.789	0.759	0.731	0.703
9	0.766	0.734	0.703	0.673
10	0.744	0.709	0.676	0.644

Years	5.00%	5.50%	6.00%	6.50%
1	0.952	0.948	0.943	0.939
2	0.907	0.898	0.890	0.882
3	0.864	0.852	0.840	0.828
4	0.823	0.807	0.792	0.777
5	0.784	0.765	0.747	0.730
6	0.746	0.725	0.705	0.685
7	0.711	0.687	0.665	0.644
8	0.677	0.652	0.627	0.604
9	0.645	0.618	0.592	0.567
10	0.614	0.585	0.558	0.533

Years	7.00%	7.50%	8.00%	8.50%
1	0.935	0.930	0.926	0.922
2	0.873	0.865	0.857	0.849
3	0.816	0.805	0.794	0.783
4	0.763	0.749	0.735	0.722
5	0.713	0.697	0.681	0.665
6	0.666	0.648	0.630	0.613
7	0.623	0.603	0.583	0.565
8	0.582	0.561	0.540	0.521
9	0.544	0.522	0.500	0.480
10	0.508	0.485	0.463	0.442

Years	9.00%	9.50%	10.00%	10.50%
1	0.917	0.913	0.909	0.905
2	0.842	0.834	0.826	0.819
3	0.772	0.762	0.751	0.741
4	0.708	0.696	0.683	0.671
5	0.650	0.635	0.621	0.607
6	0.596	0.580	0.564	0.549
7	0.547	0.530	0.513	0.497
8	0.502	0.484	0.467	0.450
9	0.460	0.442	0.424	0.407
10	0.422	0.404	0.386	0.368

Note: These tables are often published to an accuracy of six or seven decimal places, but have been truncated here to only three for our purposes, which may still give unnecessarily detailed results. For example, the Net Present Value of a return of £10 000 in ten years at 4.5 per cent would be £6439.28 using tables accurate to six decimal places, and £6440.00 using this table. It appears unlikely that a shortfall of £0.72 would jeopardize an investment decision.

Figure 39   Investment Appraisal – Table 1 (DCF)

6. Add the discounted amounts over the given number of years before comparison with the sum invested, as in Example 2 below, which has identical investment and cash flows to Example 1.

Example 2

Assume that XYZ's cost of capital is 5.5 per cent. Use of the Net Present Value table (Figure 39) shows more realistically whether the new system would cover its costs:

Year 0	(£150 000)	Discount factor 0.000000	Cost	(£150 000)
Year 1	£50 000	Discount factor 0.948	Benefit	£47 400
Year 2	£50 000	Discount factor 0.898	Benefit	£44 900
Year 3	£40 000	Discount factor 0.852	Benefit	£34 080
Year 4	£40 000	Discount factor 0.807	Benefit	£32 280
Total	**£30 000**		**Total**	**£8 660**

The total is the Net Present Value (NPV) of the now discounted cash flows. Although still positive, it has apparently 'shrunk' by £21 000. Any financial decision to go ahead with this project now appears somewhat harder to justify. However, selecting the rates and estimating the cash flows are always important judgements.

DISCOUNTED CASH FLOW RATE OF RETURN – KEEPING IT SIMPLE

This approach to the investment appraisal of projects (or other investments) is less widely used, but probably more informative. One of its strengths lies in comparing 'like with like', where the contribution each project might make to an organization's prosperity is assessed only on the percentage return on the investment made in it. A small project that returns 10 per cent could be considered a better investment than a larger project that returns only 5 per cent, even though the larger project may produce seemingly better net revenues. However, in the real world there are often many non-financial factors to be considered when selecting which projects to finance. One strength of the DCFRoR approach is that a common denominator is established (percentage return on investment). One weakness is that this method is often taught to Project Managers in the most complex way possible, rather than by application of the 'keep it simple' approach, which you will now read. It is variously referred to as 'DCF Rate of Return' (DCFRoR) or 'Internal Rate of Return' (IRR). From this point forward, the term IRR will be used.

Calculating the Internal Rate of Return for a project investment

Investment Appraisal – Table 2 in Figure 40 can be used to calculate the IRR of a project. A required percentage rate is usually set by an organization's management accountants as a baseline for determining whether investments, including projects, are likely to be financially worthwhile. The rate is normally based on what an organization believes it can theoretically earn from other interest-bearing investments, so will vary from time to time

Rate of Return of £1 in the future (Discounting Table)

(Investment durations of between one and ten years, and rates from 3% to 10.5%)

Years	3.00%	3.50%	4.00%	4.50%
1	0.971	0.966	0.962	0.957
2	1.913	1.900	1.886	1.873
3	2.829	2.802	2.775	2.749
4	3.717	3.673	3.630	3.588
5	4.580	4.515	4.452	4.390
6	5.417	5.329	5.242	5.158
7	6.230	6.115	6.002	5.893
8	7.020	6.874	6.733	6.596
9	7.786	7.608	7.435	7.269
10	8.530	8.317	8.111	7.913

Years	5%	5.50%	6%	6.50%
1	0.952	0.948	0.943	0.939
2	1.859	1.846	1.833	1.821
3	2.723	2.698	2.673	2.648
4	3.546	3.505	3.465	3.426
5	4.329	4.270	4.212	4.156
6	5.076	4.996	4.917	4.841
7	5.786	5.683	5.582	5.485
8	6.463	6.335	6.210	6.089
9	7.108	6.952	6.802	6.656
10	7.722	7.538	7.360	7.189

Years	7%	7.50%	8%	8.50%
1	0.935	0.930	0.926	0.922
2	1.808	1.796	1.783	1.771
3	2.624	2.601	2.577	2.554
4	3.387	3.349	3.312	3.276
5	4.100	4.046	3.993	3.941
6	4.767	4.694	4.623	4.554
7	5.389	5.297	5.206	5.119
8	5.971	5.857	5.747	5.639
9	6.515	6.379	6.247	6.119
10	7.024	6.864	6.710	6.561

Years	9%	9.50%	10%	10.50%
1	0.917	0.913	0.909	0.905
2	1.759	1.747	1.736	1.724
3	2.531	2.509	2.487	2.465
4	3.240	3.204	3.170	3.136
5	3.890	3.840	3.791	3.743
6	4.486	4.420	4.355	4.292
7	5.033	4.950	4.868	4.789
8	5.535	5.433	5.335	5.239
9	5.995	5.875	5.759	5.646
10	6.418	6.279	6.145	6.015

Note: These tables are often published to an accuracy of six or seven decimal places, but have been truncated to only three for our purposes, which should still give adequate results. In the five-year example in the text, scanning for the answer closest to 4.2 would still only tell us that the rate falls between 6 and 6.5 per cent. When organizations have to be very selective about the projects they can afford to undertake, they are unlikely to choose one project over another solely because the calculated IRRs of one is 0.5 per cent better than the other.

Figure 40   Investment Appraisal – Table 2 (IRR)

with the financial markets. Projects with forecast IRRs that exceed the organization's current agreed rate are more likely to be approved. It is a particularly important method, as it can be used on large and small projects to ensure that those with the best returns on investment can be identified. A number of small projects with good IRRs may be a better bet than a large project with a poorer IRR when money is tight.

To use Table 2 (Figure 40) to forecast the IRR of a project, as with earlier methods, you need to:

- forecast the likely costs and benefits of the project and the life expectancy of its outputs. Use these to calculate a number that you can then look up in the table. To do this:
  - divide the total forecast net cash outflows (costs) by the forecast arithmetic mean (average) of the total annual net cash inflows (earnings/savings)
  - search for a result across the rows containing the 'life expectancy' year. The IRR will be at the head of the column where you find the closest match. Interpolate if necessary.

Example 3 which follows shows the simple approach to finding the IRR for a project.

Example 3

XYZ is planning the replacement of a system that will cost £210 000 to install and operate but is forecast to save about £50 000 a year over each of five years. In this case, the cost of the project (net cash outflow) is £210 000 and the average annual net cash inflow is £50 000.

£210,000 ÷ £50,000 = 4.2

Look along each of the '5 year' rows in Table 2 (Figure 40) until you find the number closest to your result (4.2). At the top of the column in which the closest number was found, you will see the IRR, which in this case is between 6 per cent and 6.5 per cent. This has to be compared against any rate required by your organization to determine whether or not it will approve the investment. This decision may be taken by a Steering Group, Programme Board, or indeed the Management Board of your organization.

Note that while there are commercial incentives for many projects, you need to be aware that some projects are not carried out for financial reasons. For example, projects related to health, safety, access to premises for disabled people and so on will have costs, but not benefits, at least in the commercial sense. You will need to be as rigorous as always on cost management, but investment appraisal will not be the deciding factor.

SEE ALSO

Benefits
Business Case
Starting a Project

Issue Management

A Project Issue is an existing situation or set of circumstances that is affecting the ability of a project (or programme) to arrive at its intended outcome.

WHY MIGHT IT BE USEFUL?

Managing a project is concerned to a large degree with managing towards certainty, through uncertainty. While you will always try to have a precise statement of requirements, a comprehensive plan, sound estimates, and clear dependencies, known resource requirements, a skilled team and reliable suppliers, you also know that whenever you are dealing with change or innovation, things may not always turn out as expected. You need some procedures in place to record those factors you have identified that are already affecting the project's progress towards a successful outcome. Once you have identified them, you will need measures to deal with them.

WHEN MIGHT YOU NEED IT?

You should identify initial Project Issues as part of any pre-project process. It is very important that if you need to seek approval for one of a range of optional ways forward, or to pursue one project at the expense of another, those making such decisions have a good understanding of the pitfalls. Before you start any project, you should have a Project Issues Log. Once you have created this log, the management of Project Issues should become a continuous process.

Project Issues are in the present, and you can deal with them now, while Project Risks are in the future, waiting to trip you up, for you to avoid if possible. If avoidance fails and the dreaded thing happens, you will then be in the present, so a 'Project Risk' becomes a 'Project Issue' and needs to be dealt with.

If you do not face a new situation on your project every working day, something is wrong. If you do face a new situation every day, something has changed. If changes have happened, have they been affected by a Project Issue or changed the nature of a Project Issue? Have new Project Issues emerged? You should see now that you need a Project Issues Log nearby. You will find a daily inspection valuable, and will not waste the five minutes it might take.

HOW DO YOU USE IT?

You will need a Project Issues Log for your project. I have set up and successfully used such a log and procedures in several companies using Microsoft Excel®, and you will see sample pages below. You will be able to set up similar logs using any spreadsheet software.

If you use a similar approach, perhaps with your own ratings and calculations, you can keep all the pages and procedures together. In the sample in Figures 41 and 42, you will find Risks, Issues and Procedures on three tabs in the same workbook. I have reprinted the guidelines below, and you can use similar logs in both project and programme environments.

There are a number of sources for identifying Project Issues:

- existing Project Issues Logs
- Project Issues Workshops
- generic Project Issues identified in Project Management publications
- new items identified in progress reports

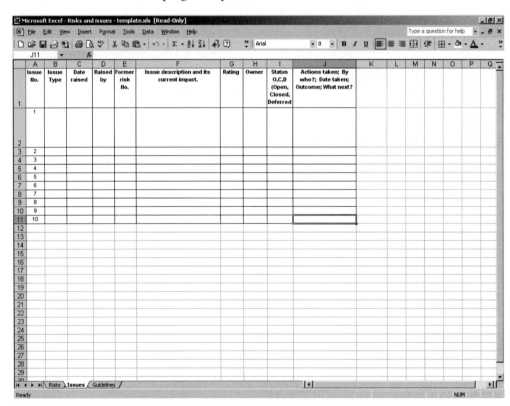

Figure 41 Sample Project Issues Log template

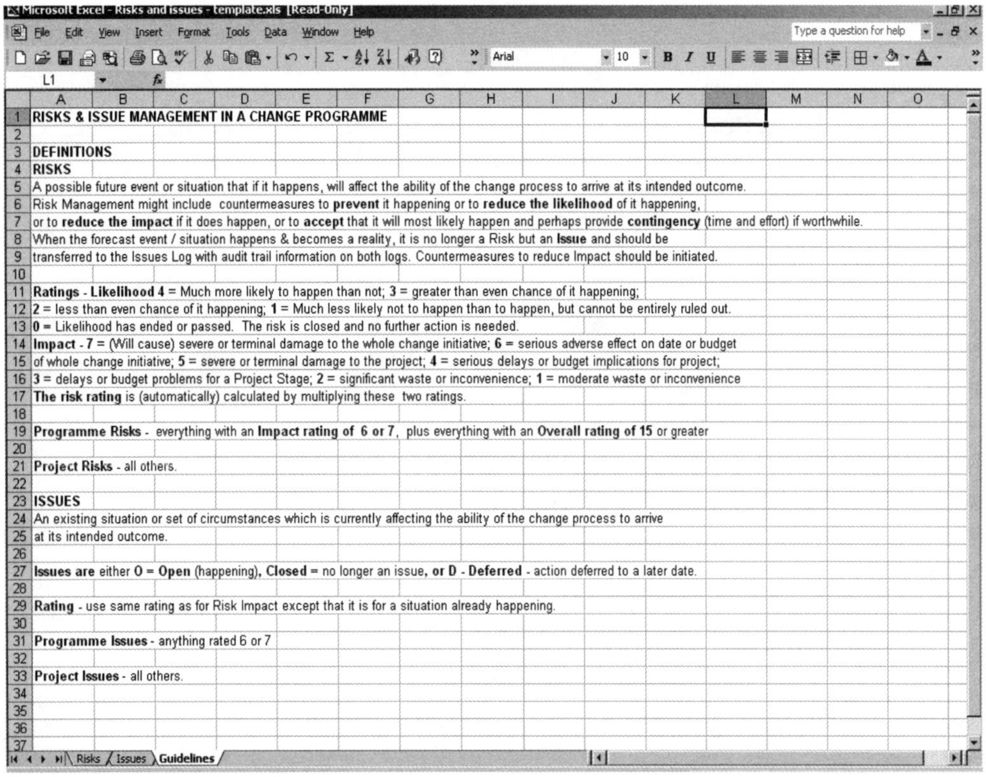

RISKS & ISSUE MANAGEMENT IN A CHANGE PROGRAMME

DEFINITIONS

RISKS

A possible future event or situation that if it happens, will affect the ability of the change process to arrive at its intended outcome.
Risk Management might include countermeasures to **prevent** it happening or to **reduce the likelihood** of it happening,
or to **reduce the impact** if it does happen, or to **accept** that it will most likely happen and perhaps provide **contingency** (time and effort) if worthwhile.
When the forecast event / situation happens & becomes a reality, it is no longer a Risk but an **Issue** and should be
transferred to the Issues Log with audit trail information on both logs. Countermeasures to reduce Impact should be initiated.

Ratings - Likelihood 4 = Much more likely to happen than not; **3** = greater than even chance of it happening;
2 = less than even chance of it happening; **1** = Much less likely not to happen than to happen, but cannot be entirely ruled out.
0 = Likelihood has ended or passed. The risk is closed and no further action is needed.
Impact - 7 = (Will cause) severe or terminal damage to the whole change initiative; **6** = serious adverse effect on date or budget
of whole change initiative; **5** = severe or terminal damage to the project; **4** = serious delays or budget implications for project;
3 = delays or budget problems for a Project Stage; **2** = significant waste or inconvenience; **1** = moderate waste or inconvenience
The risk rating is (automatically) calculated by multiplying these two ratings.

Programme Risks - everything with an **Impact rating of 6 or 7**, plus everything with an **Overall rating of 15** or greater

Project Risks - all others.

ISSUES

An existing situation or set of circumstances which is currently affecting the ability of the change process to arrive
at its intended outcome.

Issues are either **O = Open** (happening)**, Closed** = no longer an issue**, or D - Deferred** - action deferred to a later date.

Rating - use same rating as for Risk Impact except that it is for a situation already happening.

Programme Issues - anything rated 6 or 7

Project Issues - all others.

Figure 42 Risks and Issues – sample procedures for a programme environment

- concerns raised by individuals involved in or affected by a project.
- Project Issues that lead to 'Requests for Change'
- Project Library information on similar projects.

Issue No.	Issue type	Date raised	Raised by	Former Risk No.	Issue description and impact it is having	Rating	Owner	Status O,C,D (Open/ Closed/ Deferred)	Actions taken? By whom? Date taken? Outcome? What next?

Figure 43 Project Issues Log headings

The headings in Figure 43 should all be almost self-explanatory, supported by the following notes and analogies:

- **Column 5, Former Risk No.** – use this when a Project Risk has become reality and is now a Project Issue. This will maintain an audit trail.
- **Column 6, Issue description and impact it is having** – a complete description is essential here. Entries have to stand up to the 'So what?' test. A useful phrase every time you make an entry in this column is 'which means that . . .'. Do not simply write 'X is being delayed', but try to describe the consequences – 'X has been delayed,

which means that we are unable to deliver Y. This has triggered the penalty clause on that contract, now costing the company £Z per month or part month.' This focuses readers' minds better!

- **Column 10, Actions taken** – use this as a diary to record actions that have been completed and to set dates for other actions needed.

Impact Rating

- 7 = Causing severe damage to the whole change initiative
- 6 = Having a serious adverse effect on date or budget of whole change initiative
- 5 = Causing severe damage to the project
- 4 = Causing serious delays with budget implications for project
- 3 = Causing delays and/or budget problems for a Project Stage
- 2 = Causing significant waste or inconvenience
- 1 = Causing moderate waste or inconvenience.

Project Issues are either O = Open (happening), Closed = no longer a Project Issue, or D = Deferred – action deferred to a later (specified) date.

Issue Type – is it affecting the project, a programme, or the business?

Programme Issues – anything rated 6 or 7

Project Issues – all others.

Note that if you use a RAG system (Red, Amber, Green), where Red is a 'showstopper', Amber is a serious warning and Green is OK, you can link number ranges to the colours, such as 6+ is 'Red', 3–5 is 'Amber' and <=2 is 'Green'.

You would be wise to keep your log on a network if possible, though you may wish to apply a 'read-only' restriction, so that if you have a Project Office, the staff here will deal with updates.

WHAT SHOULD YOU CHECK?

Pre-project

- Did you make a candid initial assessment of the Issues facing each possible project option?
- Have you created a Project Issues Log for the selected option?

Project

- Did you conduct an Issue Workshop with project stakeholders during the project start-up, to maximize your understanding of all the issues?
- Have you updated your Issues Log with all this information?

- Is each entry in your log specific and are impacts/consequences clearly described ('which means that …')?
- Are all the actions and counter-measures clear, specific and owned by an individual?
- Do you monitor the issues continuously?
- Do you have a diary system for reminding issue owners ahead of actions needed by them?
- Do all stakeholders have access to the log?
- Is there an agenda item for Steering Group meetings to review Project Issues?

SEE ALSO

Change Control
Project Office
Request for Change
Risk Management
PRINCE® 'Off Specification'

Lessons Learned

The purpose of a 'Lessons Learned' exercise is to recognize and document any experiences that might help improve the running of future projects. The main users of a Lessons Learned Report will include the Steering Group, the Project Team and the Project Office. Such a report might also be circulated to:

- the corporate standards function, or those responsible for Quality Management systems and Project Management standards
- managers of future projects.

You must be careful to concentrate on techniques and practices, avoiding any explicit or implicit personal criticisms. It is also important to record techniques that worked well that are to be encouraged in future, as well as those that did not work well and which ought to be improved for future use. This report will be of little value if all it contains is a list of problems. If it can identify problems, give an indication of why they might have occurred, and recommendations on how they can be avoided or minimized in future, it will serve a useful purpose.

HOW AND WHEN MIGHT YOU RECORD 'LESSONS LEARNED'?

It is an unfortunate consequence of the pressures you may experience on projects that lessons you intend to record are lost along the way, or are diluted or lacking in any useful detail. To minimize this risk, it is good practice to initiate the process of recording and reporting lessons learned at the start of the project, so that as you close each stage, you can record its lessons while they are still fresh in your mind. There is no reason to wait months before you share these lessons with others, as many are stage-specific and might be of value to another project about to start the same stage as, or one similar to, that you have just finished.

SUGGESTED CONTENTS OF A LESSONS LEARNED REPORT

You may use an existing standard format for such a report, and it may be worth checking whether it is intended to be a 'stand-alone' document or whether it makes extensive use of other documents through cross-referencing. In many ways, it makes better sense to write a stand-alone report, so that the aims, outcomes and lessons remain closely related. The difficulty with this approach concerns keeping your report to a modest size while maximizing its usefulness. If you take this approach, the content might include:

- **Project Background and Objectives** – briefly summarizing what the project was set up to achieve and why, and listing the main objectives
- **Project Scope** – briefly describing the original scope of the project (what was defined as 'in scope') and anything explicitly defined as being 'out of scope'
- **Any significant constraints on the project** – such as deadlines and resource shortages
- **Project Deliverables** – listing the main (probably not lower than level 3 on your WBS):
  - deliverables needed by the customer for use by the organization
  - deliverables needed by the Steering Committee to manage the project successfully
  - deliverables needed to assure quality (fitness for purpose).

  These should show for each, where appropriate:
  - OT (on time), AS (ahead of schedule), BS (behind schedule), ND (not delivered)
  - OB (on budget), UB (under budget), EB (exceeds budget), and summarizing reason(s) for any significant variances and any lessons that should be learned, including strengths or weaknesses of the estimating method(s) used, the estimates made, and the actual duration and effort on key deliverables.
- **Project Budget** – showing the original approved budget, summarizing what was actually spent by the end of the project and reasons for any significant variance(s); if the budget was changed during the project, state briefly why and when, and record any budgeting lessons learned
- **Monitoring and Control methods used** – and any lessons learned from these
- **Risks and Issues** – describing the main project risks and issues, their impact, and any lessons learned
- **Quality methods and any relevant outcomes**
- **Conclusions and any recommendations** – to improve project management methods and techniques in your organization.

SEE ALSO

Project Office
Reports in Projects and Programmes
Task Checklist
PRINCE® Product Checklist

Matrix Management

atrix Management is a term normally used to describe an approach that uses 'borrowed' project team members who report to a Project Manager on project matters, and to their normal Line Manager on all operational matters, such as 'pay and rations'. It can be very successful in organizations with a fair degree of project orientation. Such organizations may be less likely to face some of the problems outlined below, which might sidetrack sporadic users of a matrix approach. Figures 44 and 45 show typical structural differences between a hierarchical or functional approach and a matrix approach.

THE HIERARCHICAL/FUNCTIONAL APPROACH

A hierarchical/functional approach is shown in Figure 44. This approach will probably be found more often in enterprises that are organized along strong traditional lines and where projects tend to support those functions. In the example, each participating department sets up its own project and team. This retains all the strengths of functional

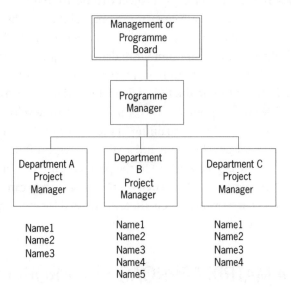

Figure 44   Hierarchical/functional approach

experience, within existing reporting lines, but may not achieve flexible or economic resource utilization, nor be appropriate for any cross-functional needs. No-one will be in any doubt as to who their boss is. Outcomes should be customer-focused and functionally strong, but may not always have seamless joins with other external functions and systems. An additional disadvantage is the 'day-job' syndrome, where pressing operational needs tend to be given priority over project needs, however urgent. As Henry Ford once said: 'It's the product that pays the wages.'

WHY MIGHT A MATRIX APPROACH BE USEFUL?

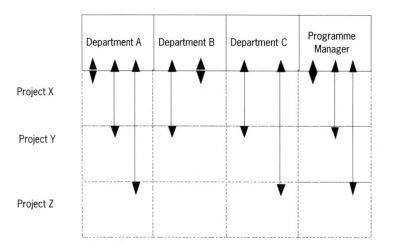

Figure 45   Matrix approach

Under the matrix approach, people work between business and project depending on needs and priorities. A matrix organization, as shown in Figure 45, can provide a temporary multi-disciplinary team for any project that needs to deliver across organizational boundaries and provide cross-functional solutions. When such a team is created, much of the required business knowledge, experience and skills will exist within that project team, facilitating the establishment of detailed requirements, gaining early input to any design work, improving business interfaces, and promoting shared responsibility for, and ownership of, the final deliverables. Matrices can also be highly motivational when they create opportunities for individuals to develop their skills by doing something very different. Staff remaining in the areas from which team members are 'borrowed' can also enjoy development and additional responsibility while they deputize for those who have been seconded to the project team. This approach is very flexible, in that when resources are not needed on the project they can return 'home', and when a matrix team is created or disbanded, there is no need for any major organizational change around the project.

WHY MIGHT A MATRIX APPROACH BE PROBLEMATIC?

The 'day-job' syndrome is similar to the hierarchical approach. It surfaces whenever there is contention between line and project for the services of team members. A team member may be willing to give the project priority, but his or her line manager may insist that line responsibilities come first, and can use influence over performance reviews, pay and privileges to lean on an individual. In addition, those used to having one 'boss' may be uncomfortable and confused by the less clear lines of authority in a project matrix. It is important that individuals be reassured that recognition and rewards can be influenced from within the matrix, as well as from the line.

WHEN MIGHT YOU NEED TO CHOOSE?

You will have realized that there are shades of grey when considering how to organize a project. Much will depend on your corporate structure and traditions. Consider a matrix approach whenever you need to deliver cross-functional solutions, maximize resource utilization and avoid duplication of effort, while retaining some the benefits of a functional organization and experience, and gaining some of the benefits of a natural project approach.

WHAT SHOULD YOU CHECK?

The totals of 'Yes' and 'No' answers in Figure 46 should give you a guide as to whether a matrix approach might be appropriate for your project or not. If you have more 'Yes' than 'No' answers, it should encourage you to explore the potential of a matrix approach for your project.

	Yes	No
1. Does your project operate across functional, organizational or political boundaries?		
2. Will your team benefit from having members seconded part-time from business areas?		
3. Might it be difficult to get people resources if not 'borrowed' from business areas?		
4. Could your project and the business work effectively with a matrix approach?		
5. Would projects be able to influence recognition and reward in a matrix solution?		
6. Do you have established methods for resolving potential matrix resource contention?		
7. Could your organization set up a matrix team and approach in time for your project?		
8. Is it clear that no one joining a matrix team would lose out by working on a project?		
9. Are you short of realistic options other than a matrix approach?		
Totals		

Figure 46 Checklist for a matrix approach

Milestones and Milestone Plans

Project milestones have been variously defined as follows:

'A reckoning point; an important event, stage, etc.'	Chambers
'A significant, measurable event in the project life cycle.'	Young
'Significant event used to monitor progress.'	Buttrick
'State the project should be in at a certain stage.'	Andersen, Grude & Haug

Traditional roadside milestones or mileposts contain three items of information, useful to those on long and often uncertain journeys:

1   exactly where you are
2   how far you still have to go to your final destination, the next resting place, or perhaps change of a horse
3   how far you have come (and, by checking the time, seeing whether you are on schedule).

Projects are oriented towards completed packages of deliverables, but in most cases it is both undesirable and impractical to monitor progress towards this completion without some interim checkpoints. These checkpoints are often referred to as 'milestones', and are important project management tools. There should be no room for doubt as to whether any milestone has been achieved. Milestones are most useful when they are associated with significant deliverables, so that such checkpoints provide progress information together with useful, tangible outputs.

If you manage your projects using 'technical' stages, you are likely, for example, to deliver a 'design' at the end of the 'Design Stage'. This important event coincides with the end of a stage, and will be included in the Stage End reporting. If you use 'Management Stages', as advocated in the PRINCE® project management method, delivery of the 'Design' may be planned to occur mid-way through a Management Stage, and this could be marked as a significant milestone.

If you are working within a programme or portfolio of projects, the Programme Plan might sensibly just show major milestones imported from the detailed plans of each of its component projects.

WHAT SHOULD YOU CHECK?

- Are important milestones documented in the plans?

- Are these milestones identified on the Project Schedule/Gantt chart?

- Are the milestones distributed through the project's planned life cycle so that progress measures can be made throughout, rather than leaving many towards the end when information regarding lack of progress may be 'too little, too late'?

- Does each milestone have 'SMART' characteristics (**S**pecific, **M**easurable, **A**greed, **R**ealistic and **T**ime-based)?

- Is each milestone related to at least one major and tangible output from the project's work?

- Does each milestone have some significance for the project's customers and, if not, can significant customer milestones be identified and included?

- Is there a sensible number of milestones? Are there enough to enable measurement of significant progress (or its lack), but not so many that they risk being regarded as trite?

- Are milestones included in the Communications Plan?

While many people in organizations use Microsoft Office®, or a similar integrated package, not all of them are likely to have access to Microsoft Project® or other scheduling software used to generate Project and Stage Plans. If this is the case, did you know that you can copy and paste 'milestones' from Projec®t into Excel®, or from other scheduling tools into other spreadsheets, complete with end dates, then circulate this valuable information to a much wider readership?

SEE ALSO

Communications Plan
Project and Stage Plans
Project Life Cycle
Scheduling
Stages – Start and End Procedures

Network Analysis and the Critical Path

You will find several acronyms when you start to use networks as part of your planning approach. Some of the most important are listed here.

PERT

Lockheed and Booz-Allen and Hamilton developed the Program Evaluation Review Technique for the US Navy's Special Projects Office, which introduced it in 1958 to help manage and implement the huge and complex Polaris missile system at the height of the Cold War. The Special Projects Office had become concerned with performance on large military projects and needed to make Polaris effectively operational as quickly as possible.

PERT is a planning technique that uses time-based networks to show the relationships and dependencies between project tasks. The US Navy used it to improve project planning, optimize resource allocation, and ultimately to have better control over time and costs.

CPM

In 1957–8, DuPont (E.I. du Pont Nemours & Company) introduced their Critical Path Method (CPM). They had two concerns: one about the time and cost of bringing newly developed products from the laboratory to the marketplace, and another about the time and lost revenues when overhauling production plants. CPM is the diagrammatic network technique they introduced to provide more structured management of complex projects.

Both are 'network' methods, used to analyse diagrams showing the often complex dependencies between tasks within projects. Although PERT and CPM differed in some significant ways, they have been adapted in hybridized form to give us today's valuable project management techniques, which we refer to as Network Analysis. One significant difference is that CPM estimates 'normal' and 'crash' estimates (fast at any price), while PERT uses a formula based on pessimistic, likely and optimistic durations.

CRITICAL PATH

A 'critical path' is any route through a network, from the first to the last, which has the longest duration. You use it to forecast the overall project duration and to determine the path(s) through the network where any delays will extend the project duration. If *any* delay is unacceptable, all the routes with equal longest duration are 'critical' paths. Paths that are not critical have shorter durations and some 'float' or slack time.

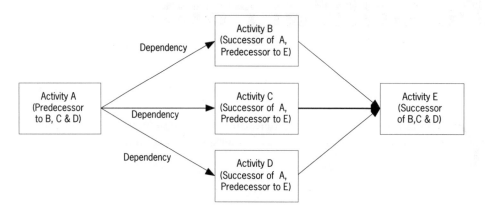

Figure 47   Activity on Node (AON) network diagram (also known as a precedence diagram)

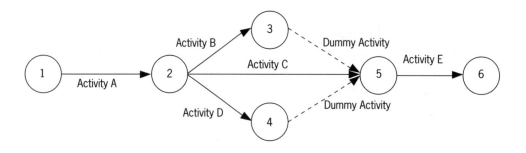

Figure 48   Activity on Arrow (AOA) network diagram (as developed for the PERT/CPM approaches)

Note that the logic of the activities and dependencies in Figures 47 and 48 is identical. AOA 'rules' preclude the use of more than one arrow between any two nodes, so 'dummy' activities are used, in this case to show that Activity E is dependent on B, C and D. The nodes represent nothing other than a status before or after an activity: in the example in Figure 48, (1) is the status before Activity A and (2) is the status when A has been completed. Note that the flow is conventionally from left to right in both types of diagram.

WHEN MIGHT IT BE USEFUL?

When you identify the critical path through a project or stage, you forecast its overall duration in working days, weeks, months or years. Note that you will still need to convert this information into a schedule, to show dates and to allow for non-working days, whether weekends or holidays.

You can use critical path information to:

● help answer the perennial question, 'How long is this all going to take?'
● concentrate your tracking effort on critical path tasks, trying to ensure on-time completion and minimize risks of delays to the project
● see whether resources could be redeployed from non-critical to critical tasks, again to minimize risks of delays to the project. Note, however, that if you take this approach and use up the entire float on a path, it will become critical, too!

HOW DO YOU USE IT?

From this point forward, we will use the Precedence Diagram Method (PDM), with activities on the node.

To start, you will need to create a network diagram showing the sequence of tasks in a project or project stage, as in Figure 49, where each node represents one task.

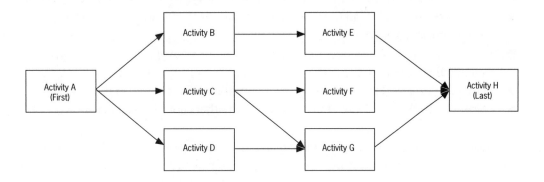

Figure 49   Logical network

Typically, after a stage starts, the tasks fan out – several streams run in parallel, and then all converge at the end of the stage. There are three parallel paths in the example above, and four paths between the first task at the left and the last task at the right. You will need to include all the lowest-level tasks from your Work Breakdown Structure diagram (WBS) on such a diagram. If you use PRINCE®, you would have already created a Product Breakdown Structure (PBS) diagram, and you would transfer all the lowest-level products to a Product Flow Diagram (PFD), similar in style to that above. However, you would still need to identify all the tasks needed to create each product before you constructed an AON diagram.

You need to work out the sequence and dependencies of all the tasks, identifying those tasks you will need to complete before you can start work on others. If you have used

Post-it® notes to develop your Work Breakdown Structure, you will be able to re-use them across a board or wall, to try out sequence and dependencies. You will find that holding a small workshop with team members and customers is an excellent approach, as you will be able to develop understanding and ownership of the plan you will eventually create.

Use a network diagram first to establish the logical flow and sequence between all the tasks. At this early stage, you will not yet have attempted to show any information about the physical aspects of the work, such as who, when, how, how long – hence the term 'logical' network diagram.

When you are satisfied that the logic is as sound and complete as is possible given what you know at this point, you may need to return to your WBS diagram to update it with any new tasks that constructing the network has helped you to identify, or perhaps even to remove any found to be superfluous.

WHAT SHOULD YOU CHECK AFTER DRAWING THE LOGICAL NETWORK?

- Is the flow from left to right?
- Does your logical network diagram contain all the lowest-level tasks from your WBS?
- Does every task, other than the first and last, have at least one arrow entering at the left and one arrow leaving at the right?
- Is there a complete flow along every path through the network that you can trace from the first activity to the last?
- Have you developed the logic of the diagram with others involved in the project?
- Have you checked the logic of the diagram with others not involved in the project?

You will need to maintain the logic and dependencies through the rest of the planning process, unless you find previously unrecognized flaws. You now will be able to add estimates for the duration of all the tasks and analyse the results to establish both the critical path(s) and the overall duration.

DEVELOPING THE NETWORK DIAGRAM

To develop to a level at which you will be able to determine the overall duration and Critical Path(s), you will need to add the information shown in Figure 50 to each task (node on your network). You will already have entered each task name when constructing the logic diagram. Once you have completed your estimating and before you start analysing the whole network, you will have to enter a duration (top centre) for each task (see Figure 51). Now you can start to analyse the network and calculate the remaining data!

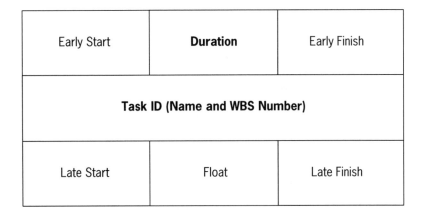

Early Start	**Duration**	Early Finish
Task ID (Name and WBS Number)		
Late Start	Float	Late Finish

Figure 50   Information needs

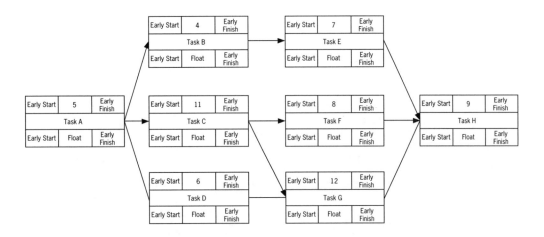

Figure 51   Duration estimates added to PERT diagram

ANALYSING THE NETWORK

The analysis is completed in two passes, which involve first working through the diagram from left to right (start to finish) then working backwards from right to left (finish to start). By convention, the Early Start of the first task is always '0'. The Early Finish in our example is at the end of the fifth hour, day, week or month, depending on the units we are using. From this point forwards, we will assume the time units to be days. The Early Start of Tasks B, C and D are identical with the Early Finish time of task A. To calculate the Early Finish of Tasks B, C and D, we simply add each Duration to the respective Early Start (see Figures 52 and 53).

You already know that the critical path is the longest duration through the network, which in our example is 37 days. This suggests that the Late Finish is 37, too; otherwise, the project will be later. Our second pass through the network is from right to left, and we subtract the duration from the Late Finish to establish the latest time we can start the task

NETWORK
ANALYSIS AND
THE CRITICAL
PATH

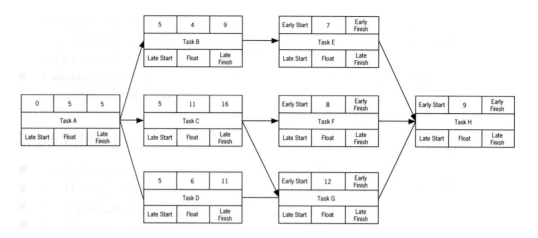

Figure 52 Start of first pass from left to right

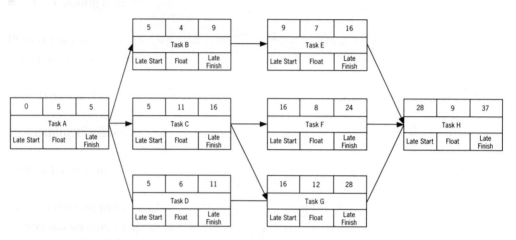

Note: A task can only start when all its predecessors have been completed – so, for example, the Early Start of Task G is 16, not 11, and that of Task H is 28, not 16 or 24. When passing in this direction, we always use the *largest* number where paths converge.

Figure 53 End of first pass from left to right

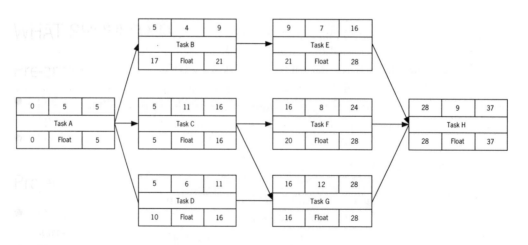

Figure 54 End of second pass from left to right

without causing a delay (see Figure 54). The Late Start of successor tasks will carry back and become the Late Finish of predecessor tasks.

Note that when completing a Late Finish on this pass, where more than one arrow converges backwards into the task box you are working on, always use the *lowest* Late Start figure from the successor task as the Late Finish.

WHAT IS A CRITICAL PATH?

A Critical Path has the longest duration through a network. It is also characterized by there being no difference between Early Start and Late Start, or between Early Finish and Late Finish for every task on the Critical Path. In the example above, the Critical Path is A, C, G and H. Note that for any path to be genuinely critical, there is a requirement for the earliest possible finish and the overall duration to be equal to the time available.

You can now quickly identify and calculate any 'float', by subtracting Early Start from Late Start (or Early Finish from late Finish). Float indicates where there might be freedom for a Project Manager to delay the start of a task and use resources elsewhere (maybe on a Critical Path task).

Figure 55 also shows another characteristic of tasks on the Critical Path: such tasks have zero float.

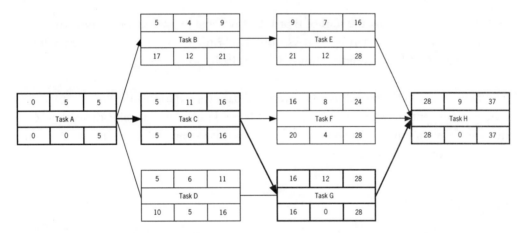

Figure 55   Critical Path and float

One more convention illustrated in Figure 56, is that of showing the Critical Path as a straight line, or as central, parallel paths if more than one is critical. Note that this is not a 'law'.

USING CRITICAL PATH INFORMATION

Note that on the non-Critical Path through B and E above, there is 12 days of float. The float applies to the path, not the task, and you can only use it once. As Project Manager,

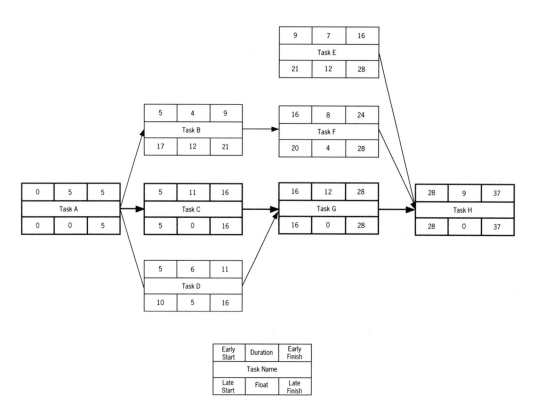

Figure 56 Critical Path drawing convention

you could decide to delay the start of B or E by from one to 12 days. Note however, that if you decided to delay the start by 12 days, until day 17 (that is, by using up the entire float on that path), A, B, E, H would become a Critical Path too.

The next piece of valuable information you will have gained from analysing a network is where to concentrate when tracking progress. If you know the Critical Path and know that any delay on it will delay the overall finish, you also know to concentrate monitoring and control on all tasks on that path.

OTHER FACTORS

So far, we have assumed that a successor task can start immediately a predecessor has been completed, but there are many cases where this may not happen. For example, outside my window as I write, a concrete base has just been laid where a summerhouse is to be erected. The summerhouse will take one day to erect, but this cannot be done until the concrete has hardened and we have had to allow three days for this. This three-day period is known as 'lag' – see Figure 57.

You will have noticed that the first task is (always) on the Critical Path – everything else awaits its completion. As R. D. Clyde once said: 'It's amazing how long it takes you to complete something you are not working on!'

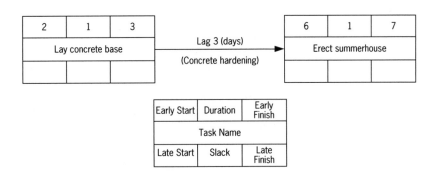

2	1	3		6	1	7
Lay concrete base				Erect summerhouse		

Lag 3 (days)
(Concrete hardening)

Early Start	Duration	Early Finish
Task Name		
Late Start	Slack	Late Finish

Figure 57   Lag time

SEE ALSO

Estimating
Scheduling
Work Breakdown Structures

SUGGES
REPORT

...e an exe...
...chure is intend...
...d content...
...done refer...
...ly with th...
...ts usefulness...

- Project Background
  ...to achieve a...
- ...ject Scope –
  ...what is 'in scope')
- Any significant constraints
  ...straints
- Project Delivera...
  Whic...
  ...liverables nee...
  ...rables needed...
  ...erables needed pr...
  ...se should show (or...
  - OT (on time)
  - OB (on budget)
  - ...son(s) for any...
  - ...cluding strength...
  - ...read, and the...
- Project Bud...
  ...ally spent by...
  ...e budget was...
  ...budgeting...
  ...monitoring ass...
- Risks and Issues –...
  ...s learned
- Quality methods...
- Conclusions and any...
  ...at techniqu...

SEE ALSO

...ject Offic...
...g the Project and Practice...
...rt Concept...

Objective(s)

In May 1961, US President John F. Kennedy set the following famous objective for the USA during an address to a joint session of Congress:

> I believe this nation should commit itself, before this decade is out, to landing a man on the moon and returning him safely to the earth.

You may be familiar with the acronym SMART to help remember the characteristics of 'good' objectives and wonder how Kennedy's objective measures up to:

- **S**pecific? – No ambiguity here.
- **M**easurable? – Yes, straightforward and simple.
- **A**greed? – The President does not appear to have given any indication that agreement had been sought.
- **R**ealistic? – On 5 May 1961, Alan Shepard had just completed a fifteen-minute sub-orbital flight to a height of 115 miles, aboard *Freedom 7*. Now the USA had less than nine years to achieve the almost unthinkable.
- **T**ime-driven? – Clearly.

Seemingly, this single objective fell somewhat short on agreement and realism. However, on Sunday 20 July 1969, Neil Armstrong and Buzz Aldrin flew *Eagle*, the lunar module of Apollo 11, to a landing on the Sea of Tranquillity, while Michael Collins orbited above in the command module, *Columbia*. On Thursday 24 July 1969, the trio landed safely back on Earth and were picked up by the carrier USS *Hornet*. Mission accomplished, with just over 160 days to spare.

Can you manage projects with objectives that are less than SMART? You would be well advised to pursue objectives that are as complete and helpful as possible and to do whatever you can to SMARTen them up. However, in the real world you may have to settle for less on occasions. Work for objectives that are:

- **S**pecific – Ensure clarity and precision about what needs to be done.

- **M**easurable – Implement quantification where possible, so that there will be no argument about whether an objective has been met or not.

- **A**greed – Many projects fail because agreement was never gained in the first place and the expectations of stakeholders differ. One group thinks the objectives have been achieved, while others are puzzled by, and even hostile to, your project's outputs.

- **R**ealistic – Sometimes you might feel you have been given 'mission impossible'. If so, you need to address this directly. However, if all you can say is 'It cannot be done' then you are likely to get nowhere, other than into a different job. It is always more positive to confirm what can be done and to seek a scope reduction, or phased delivery, supported by a risk analysis on the original objective(s).

- **T**ime-driven – You are usually told when something needs to be delivered, and have to put together a plan to achieve it. Time is a project characteristic that can be an objective and a constraint at the same time.

You may already have experienced projects with multiple objectives – a 'let's throw everything into this project' approach. This is rather like choosing to use a cluster-bomb rather than a laser-guided missile – you may hit a lot of things, but not always the right ones. Multiple objectives are quite common, so you owe it to yourself to ask enough questions to determine whatever hierarchy or priorities might exist. Check out which objectives:

- must be achieved and are mandatory
- ought to be achieved if at all possible
- would be nice to achieve, but could be set aside if money and time are running low.

SEE ALSO

Constraints
Project and Stage Plans
Project Strategy
Scope
Terms of Reference

Planning Checklist

Whe tend to think of 'the plan' simply as the bar chart on the office wall showing high-level activities and dates. Whilst everyone might applaud it at the start, it will quickly become forgotten, outdated and irrelevant if hastily conceived and superficial in nature. Such a document ought to represent the culmination of a number of important and thorough processes. We need sound plans so that we can organize, monitor, control and communicate effectively about our project work. If any plan is to guide us effectively and enable us to make informed decisions as circumstances change, we need to plan the time to plan thoroughly. Regard the production of your plans as mini-projects and apply the same disciplines, so that you can create useful and fit-for-purpose deliverables.

In planning, as in many aspects of modern life, style can sometimes seem more important than substance. Some plans may be little better than wishlists masquerading as plans, showing sponsors what they want to see, rather than what they really need to know. This is the 'Yes Plan'. Unfortunately, many projects have been authorized following slick presentations of such plans. Adding substance to plans is important, but can be unpopular because proper planning takes time. The urgency is always to do the 'real project work'. Much will depend whether your organization prefers realism to spin. If you belong to the realistic school of project planning, you may wish to consider trying these ten steps, with occasional iterations:

1. Clarify and agree the Terms of Reference or Project Brief so that it clearly defines your objectives, scope and any constraints, documents any planning assumptions that will need to be resolved, and sets out the responsibilities and reporting lines.

2. A Work Breakdown Structure is probably the single most important planning document. Time invested here, with input from your stakeholders, is worthwhile, so that everyone can contribute to an agreement on what has to be done to satisfy the Brief. Whether you draw a hierarchical diagram, create structured lists, or stick Post-it® notes on the wall is less important than the valuable thinking and discussion that goes into the process. These help guard against errors of omission, and initiate the communications framework you will need.

3. While you have your stakeholders together, try to work out priorities, sequence and dependencies so that you can create a logical flow diagram. This network diagram is also likely to be valuable for communications and can help with decisions on the project's structure into stages or phases.

4. At some point, you will need to estimate the person–days, weeks, months or years of effort you will need to deliver your project. Just how big is it? Use whatever information and experience is at your disposal. It does not even have to be your own experience. You can talk to other project managers and consult project records about similar projects to help give you feel for the work likely to be involved. You might make a high-level estimate for the whole project, then attempt to validate it by estimating and aggregating the effort you are likely to need for each task on the Work Breakdown Structure. This validation can only start after you have developed an initial Work Breakdown Structure.

5. Those paying for the project often have one question, which they ask at the outset and continue to ask throughout the project. The question is: 'How soon can I have it?' Effort estimates tell you something about the size of the project, and thus something about the likely cost. Duration estimates tell you something about how long the tasks and the project may take. If you apply these estimates to the logical flow diagram you created in Step 3, you can give an early indication of the overall likely duration and the path or paths through the diagram that might turn out to be critical. At the end of this step, you might be better equipped to give a theoretical indication of the time it might all take, but the real question relates to when you will deliver – that is, on what dates.

6. You will probably need to iterate during the next steps, during which you add resources by allocating real people to tasks and refine your estimate of how long each might then take, allowing for the skills and availability of the individuals.

7. When you have done this first-pass resource addition, develop a network, apply the updated estimates, and calculate the overall duration and the critical path or paths – the paths through the network on which any delay might delay overall completion.

8. You are finally ready to transfer all the information you have developed onto a schedule, normally in Gantt chart (bar chart) format, showing tasks down one axis and dates across another. Here you have to take account of real-world constraints, such as weekends, public and other holidays, and the prior commitments of team members. Do not forget to take account of the constraints identified in the Terms of Reference or Project Brief. If you are faced with a very tight and fixed delivery deadline, you might consider using a back-scheduling (backward-pass) approach. When you have taken account of all these factors, negotiated any changes, or recognized that you will have to live with any problems, you ought to make a final recalculation of the critical path or paths. Then you can add critical path information as you redraft the schedule, the document that most people will come to know simply as 'the plan'.

9. You may have considered Project Risks and Issues throughout the planning process, but make sure you review this version carefully to identify the impact of known Project Issues, to identify new Project Risks or revise existing ones. In some cases, you may have to add contingency following high-risk activities, or modify estimates or resource usage because of one or more Project Issues.

10. You should make time for and invite participants to reviews of the deliverables you create during the planning process. You might consider a combined review of your Work Breakdown Structure and logical flow diagram to be particularly important. Your estimates of effort and duration should benefit from a peer group review, conducted by those who have estimating experience, even if not on this project. Once you have taken account of review feedback, informally walked through the plan with your Sponsor and either gained tacit approval or been asked to rework parts, you will be approaching the point at which you will seek approval for its use. It may have taken time to get here, but you will have a plan that should repay the investment you have made by giving you a sound basis for control.

SEE ALSO

Back-scheduling
Estimating
Network Analysis and the Critical Path
Terms of Reference
Scheduling
Work Breakdown Structure

Post-project Review

A Post-project Review is an appraisal to determine whether the expected benefits, as documented in the Business Case, have been achieved or are being achieved. The Business Case should also have identified how the benefits should eventually be measured, so this document is a vital input to any review process. Such a review should be planned when you are closing the project, and conducted after reasonable 'settling-in' of a project's outputs, so that they have the opportunity to reach optimum performance and demonstrate achievement of benefits through several business cycles, such as months or accounting periods. However, not all organizations commit the time and effort to such a review, though any brief study to assess whether benefits claimed in a project justification or Business Case have been or are being realized ought to be welcomed. The review should answer the questions: 'How well did the project meet our expectations in delivering the capability to achieve the claimed benefits?' and 'What, if any, significant problems have been experienced when using the project's outputs?'

Note that you may participate in some projects where improved revenues or avoided costs were never sought. However, targets should still have been set, such as for performance improvement or volume handling, and these should have been expressed in such a manner as to make them measurable. For example, if you build a new stretch of motorway to relieve city-centre traffic congestion, the costs will be very high, very public and easy to measure, but proving financial benefits might be much more difficult. However, if the justification was based on a required reduction in volumes of city-centre traffic at peak times and on the volume of traffic using the new motorway, this should be relatively easy and quick to measure and assess. By now, you may have spotted a potential weakness in the post-project review theory. When reviewers collect data, how will they differentiate between the project's delivery of a capability, and the recipient's usage of that capability to realize benefits?

It is important to differentiate between a Lessons Learned Review or Report, which should concentrate on how the project was managed and the project management techniques used (the 'means'), and a Post-project Review, which should aim to concentrate more on the usability and use of the project's outputs in satisfying the original justification (the 'end').

WHO SHOULD CONDUCT SUCH A REVIEW?

As you have already closed the project, it clearly cannot be a project task to complete the review. All you will be able to do is to plan it as part of the closure process. Your organization stands to gain the most by using third-party specialists, perhaps internal auditors, to conduct the review. They will be able to conduct such a review with impartiality and objectivity that may be compromised if such a review was to be conducted by anyone closely linked to the original project or to the current use of its outputs. Bear in mind that it was the project's role to deliver the outputs, and the user's to ensure they were complete, fit for purpose and acceptable before using them to achieve the required benefits. This principle should concentrate the Project Manager's mind on completing all the outputs to universally high standards, and the user's mind on maximizing the potential of what they have received.

WHEN MIGHT SUCH A REVIEW BE MOST USEFUL?

Such a review will be of little value if there is insufficient data to determine whether the forecast benefits are being realized at the expected rate. If, for example, the project has delivered a new business system to improve sales by more selective targeting and prompt follow-up of marketing material, when might the reviewers assess this? This would depend on whether marketing was an ongoing process, or worked in campaigns. In either case, they would need some baseline figures for comparison, but in the former case they might need to let a few (say three) monthly cycles to elapse, then collate sales data and compare with the baseline. In the latter case, you might conduct a review at the end of the first campaign and compare it with baseline campaign results. In both cases, some adjustments might be needed for seasonal or economic variations. The guiding principle ought to be to make this assessment as soon as sufficient reliable data becomes available.

WHY MIGHT IT BE USEFUL?

Whenever an organization is called on to make an investment, it has a right to seek a judgement over whether that investment was worthwhile and seek an answer to the question: 'Did we get what we paid for?' Neither the customers nor the project team would want such a judgement to be intuitive or whimsical, so all should agree on the need for the review to be of firm data about the outputs against the original quantified objectives recorded in the planning documents or Business Case.

A second value of such a review is to identify any problems and difficulties with the outputs, for which users may have invented ingenious work-arounds and suffered in silence, or which they may have identified but not yet actioned.

A third use is in the evaluation of the process and outputs at the start of the project, to see whether there are lessons to be learned that might improve them for the future. It is not uncommon that, at a pre-project stage, expectations are unrealistically high about the outputs and the level of benefits that can be achieved for a perhaps modest investment. If this optimism leaked into the Business Case, the benefits being achieved at the time of the review may be very good, except when assessed against those written into the Business Case, when they may be judged to have failed. Perhaps the project worked well and delivered excellent and effectively used outputs, while the benefits claimed in the Business Case should now be awarded a prize for imaginative fiction!

WHAT MIGHT BE REVIEWED?

Project benefits might be tangible, intangible or indeterminable:

- In order for benefits to be regarded as **tangible**, they would have to have been expressed in quantifiable and thus measurable terms. It should follow that any data you collect about them should be available in some numeric form. In our earlier marketing and sales example, we should have been able to quantify conversion rates (prospect to client) and measure that say, they have increased by 5 per cent each month since we implemented the new system. If we also know the value of typical conversions, we should then be able to express this as in money terms and put a value on the benefit. Either the percentage or the money value expectation should have been documented in our Business Case, so comparison between the two should be straightforward.

- **Intangible benefits** are those that appear to exist, but whose value has to be a matter of judgement, such as, for example, when a business is offered for sale and a value is put on goodwill. In a business environment, while it would be straightforward to find out how many of a workforce had received required training, it is never so easy to express the value or worth of any derived benefits. For example, you could look at training records that will tell you that 100 per cent of a department had received training and passed tests on the use and understanding of a new system. If the system does not deliver the expected increases in revenue, this might be because the system is inappropriate, the training was inadequate, or users do not feel motivated to use or exploit it fully. A highly motivated workforce is always a great asset after a project but, of course, very difficult to measure. It is very reasonable to ask users who were project stakeholders for an opinion about a project outcome, but the responses may be mixed, and overall judgements difficult and variable.

- **Indeterminable benefits** are those that have no definable value, but may be regarded as part of a 'feel-good' factor, such as a view that a campaign must be improving your organization's image.

WHAT SHOULD REVIEWERS CHECK AND CONSIDER?

Note that a question list will need to be created for each project, though some questions will occur during each. This example might be adapted for a business system project:

- Have the benefits been achieved or exceeded?
- Have any 'pleasant surprise' unexpected benefits emerged?
- If not, do trends indicate that they are likely to do so, and if so, when?
- If not, is there any evidence to suggest whether the benefits were realistic and achievable, as stated in the Business Case? Note that it will be of little value to criticize the project or the users of its outputs if it was 'pie in the sky' in the first place.
- Have performance requirements identified in the Statement of Work or Project Brief been achieved? Note that these are not benefits, but are often crucial to the achievement of benefits, and should be capable of measurement.
- Have any shortcomings, transparent when acceptance of the project's outputs was signed, surfaced since? What are the implications for benefits realization?
- Has all training and documentation been delivered? Is it clear, comprehensive and useful?
- How many Requests for Change have been raised since acceptance?
- How many of these have been to address errors or shortcomings in what was delivered, and how many to add newly identified requirements and enhancements?
- How much has it cost to fix both categories?
- Is there a formal method for handling change requests? Does it return timely responses?

WHAT MIGHT BE COVERED IN SUCH A REPORT?

Check your organization's standards for a contents list and format, but if you do not have these, possible contents might include:

- the purpose of the report
- overview of the project's objectives (probably brief extracts from the start-up document)
- abstract of the Business Case benefits and benefits realization timescales
- whether the benefits of the project's outputs have been/are being achieved, along with any supporting data and relevant observations
- description of any problems that are being/have been encountered, along with any supporting data
- observations about any reactions from users of the project's outputs
- conclusions and any recommendations for follow-up actions.

SEE ALSO

Business Case
Closing a Project
Lessons Learned
Starting a Project
Statement of Work

Procurement

Procurement can embrace the purchasing or hiring of goods or services, to satisfy a defined requirement that might include quality, quantity, availability and price, usually with the aim of achieving best value for money. In projects and programmes, you might need some form of procurement to obtain:

- products or services to facilitate execution of the project or programme – for example, contract/agency staff, or perhaps temporary office space to accommodate team members
- products or services that will be an outcome of the project or programme – for example, an installed software package, or perhaps a new building for an expanding or relocating business.

Say you have decided that you would like to replace your car. You should know before you start whether you need a saloon, a hatchback, an off-roader, a people carrier, five, four or three doors, petrol or diesel, and the engine size. Are you one of those who devours test reports, looks in the many available car magazines, visits garages and car supermarkets, compares prices, asks friends and eventually reaches a decision? Will you buy it using your savings, use a loan, buy it on hire purchase or lease purchase, lease it, rent it, or use a personal contract plan? Will it be new or used? What will you do with your existing car? Can you afford it? Can you afford to run it? How much will it cost to insure? Say also the list price was £10 000 – how long would you spend just collecting information and thinking before you made the big commitment? Most people seem to deliberate for months and, even then, some end up with a flashy racer that is completely unsuitable.

If you are a 'deliberator', do you spend a similar amount of time going through all the same hoops before you spend £10 000 of your organization's money on a piece of business equipment or a business service? Whether you buy for yourself or your organization, you need to seek value for money. The time it takes to seek and achieve good value needs to be proportionate to the cost.

You may work in an organization that has very clear guidelines on how to conduct any procurement, or that has existing call-off or framework arrangements. Public sector organizations work within such arrangements as the Public Purchasing Initiative and the

Treasury's Public Purchasing Guidelines, which seek value for money for taxpayers. Commercial organizations should seek value for commercial reasons. Competition should be used, unless there are sound reasons for some alternative approach. Beware the cheap solutions that do not provide what you need. Do not forget that whatever you procure should fully satisfy your requirement(s), and be of appropriate quality, be available in the right quantities, when and where needed. 'Best value' need not mean the same as 'lowest cost'.

Note that civil government procurement projects in the UK are subject to assurance review processes known as a Gateway Reviews, which are briefly covered at the end of this topic.

WHAT SHOULD YOU CHECK?

- Does your organization have a Procurement or Purchasing Unit? Do you know of any rules that state when you must use that unit to conduct or oversee procurement? (You may find that if such rules exist, they may set a price limit on any procurement you can conduct without reference to them.)

- Does your organization have a Procurement or Purchasing Manual? If so, are you familiar with its provisions?

- If you work in the public sector, are you aware of the requirements under European Community (EC) and General Agreement on Tariffs and Trade (GATT) regulations for procurement above specified financial thresholds?

- Does your organization have a code of ethics or rules or guidelines on conflicts of interest and on gifts and hospitality that you should follow when conducting or influencing any procurement?

- Do you know exactly what you need? Is it written, clear, quantified and unambiguous?

- Do you know how much it is likely to cost to acquire, and have you secured budget approval for this level of expenditure?

- Have you estimated 'whole-life' costs and gained approval from whoever will have to meet these costs once your project closes?

- Do you, or someone senior in your team, or someone available to you from purchasing/procurement, have training, knowledge and experience in conducting negotiations?

- Do you have access to legal advice when a procurement contract arrives at the pre-contract stage, including any negotiations?

- Consider using the flowchart in Figure 58 on the following page as a prompt.

PROCUREMENT BY TENDER

Your organization may have rules stating when tendering must be used to procure goods or services. If you work in the public sector, this is almost certainly the case.

Single tender

Note that there are occasions where you might still invite a tender from a single supplier, where:

- compatibility with existing equipment is essential, or patent or intellectual property rights exist which mean that no other supplier can meet your requirements
- you have paid substantial tooling or similar costs for a manufactured item, and would have pay these costs again if you contracted a new supplier
- you have engaged contractors previously, and you have since identified some genuine and proportionate follow-up work.

In such circumstances, you are likely to find it better if you follow processes similar to those you would use in a competitive situation.

Competitive tendering

A competitive tender is one in which you seek more than one tender and your objectives are normally to seek best value, and to minimize risks from cartels or collusion, or any suggestions of favouritism in your purchasing decisions. Your rules might show a series of 'cost-steps' and how many tenders you should seek for each step up to a higher cost range. Your ultimate aim is likely to be awarding a contract to the supplier who appears best able to satisfy your requirements, assessed against whatever criteria you have set.

A sample tendering process

1. Identify potential suppliers. (Who is out there?):
   - Advertise your requirement and main dates.
   - Receive expressions of interest.

2. Pre-qualification. (Weed out the least likely to meet your needs, and ensure you will end up with a sensible number of tenders, each of which might require a substantial amount of work to evaluate):
   - Prepare a preliminary enquiry letter setting out the information an organization will need to submit a tender on time, with the needed information in the required format, plus a pre-qualification questionnaire.
   - Issue this to organizations who have expressed interest.
   - Evaluate responses against your criteria, and shortlist accordingly.

Does your organization have procurement procedures, guidelines, rules or standards for competitive tenders? Are you following them? If you do not have such procedures, you may wish to consider some of the points below. Note that while price is important, you should be looking for best value for money, which may not be the lowest bid. Quality, service and the ability to work in harmony with a supplier are crucial, too.

Have you identified potential procurement needs for:
- resources or tools to be used during the project?
- products or services that you will eventually deliver from the project to its customers?
- both of the above?

↓

Have you checked that these needs can only be satisfied through tendering? For example, does your organization already have:
- existing supplies of the resources, tools, products or services?
- an existing 'call-off' contract?
- a list of 'Approved Suppliers'?

↓

Have you estimated likely timescales for conducting a tender?
Have you estimated the likely costs of buying, leasing, renting or hiring the resources, tools, products or services?
Have you identified both one-off and recurring costs?
Have you gained budgetary and any other approvals to conduct a tender?

↓

Have you created a detailed specification of requirements?
Has this specification been developed by and agreed with key stakeholders?
Has it been approved?

↓

Do you know the likely supplier candidates?
Will you need to advertise? Where?
Have you established criteria for initial shortlisting of suppliers?
Have you designed a package of information that those tendering will need to receive?

↓

Will your Invitation to Tender contain:
- the detailed specification?
- information on how, when and from whom recipients can seek clarification?
- rules they must follow?
- instructions on the format they should use?
- final date and delivery requirements?

↓

Will you decide which supplier has 'won'? Have you developed:
- an evaluation method?
- evaluation criteria derived from the specification?
- scores to record how well each criterion has been met?
- 'weightings' to reflect the relative importance of each criterion?
- a score sheet to record findings?
Have you established an Assessment Panel with the authority, availability and any required training/ briefing to assess responses and reach an objective decision?

↓

If your assessment is inconclusive, consider creating a shortlist of the top-scoring suppliers, then:
- Invite each to a separate negotiating session.
- At the end of the negotiations, invite each of the shortlisted suppliers to submit a revised tender, if they wish. Their other option is to stick with the original tender.
- Re-assess and decide.

Figure 58   Sample process flow for competitive tenders

3. Invitations to tender:
    ●   Finalize the Invitation to Tender (ITT) (also sometimes known as a Request for a Proposal or RFP) and related evaluation criteria.
    ●   Establish and brief a Tender Evaluation Panel on what they will need to do, and when. These are likely to be the customers, and will have helped establish the evaluation criteria.
    ●   Issue the ITT with full instructions on 'How to Tender'.
    ●   Respond to any enquiries from any tendering organization. Circulate responses where appropriate, to maintain a 'level playing field'. Ensure you do not breach any confidentiality arrangements.
    ●   Receive tenders.
    ●   Provide initial tender clarification to tendering organizations, if needed.
    ●   Evaluate the tenders. You will normally need two numbers for each criterion – a score which will be awarded depending on *how well the criterion has been met* – for example, from 0 (does not meet at all) to 5 (meets fully or exceeds) – and a weighting which reflects how important a factor is *to your organization* – for example, from 1 (cosmetic or minor requirement) to 5 (mandatory, will reject any tender that does not meet this need). Calculate the scores for each criterion (often achieved by multiplying the score by a weighting) and record it on a score sheet. Shortlist accordingly.

4. Presentations and any post-tender negotiations with those on final shortlist:
    ●   Presentations are sometimes known disparagingly as 'beauty parades', but it is often very important to see whether the people behind the tender will blend and work well with your organization's people and culture.
    ●   Negotiation and clarification, sometimes straight after the presentation, but beneficially later, enables both sides to research and prepare.
    ●   There should be an opportunity for submission of revised tenders, to take account of the results of the negotiation and clarification session.
    ●   Make a final evaluation and select the preferred supplier(s).
    ●   Agree on any outstanding details regarding the contract(s). Note that if you appoint more than one supplier for the same product or service, it is likely that you will want identical contracts.

5. Contract award.

6. Commencement of service or supply.

See Figure 58 for a sample process flow for competitive tenders.

GATEWAY PROCESS

Although Gateway processes are applied to procurement projects, they appear to have similar aims to a Project Health Check – a similar review process used to help ensure that any type of project is in good order, particularly at crucial stages in its life.
The reviews are conducted by a team that is independent from the procurement and

therefore able to give an objective view. A confidential report is produced for the Project Owner (PO) or Senior Responsible Owner (SRO), who alone is accountable for the implementation of any recommended remedial actions.

There are six Gateways or key points in a procurement project:

0. Strategic Assessment – Review the needs identified and the Project Brief or Terms of Reference.
1. Business Justification – Review the Business Case or justification.
2. Procurement Strategy – Review the procurement approach and requirements.
3. Investment Decision – Review of bid evaluation and bid selection.
4. Ready for Service – Post-contract award, to review readiness for service.
5. Benefits evaluation – Possibly recurring review(s) of value for money and benefits obtained.

Team size and leadership varies according to the size, complexity and risks of the procurement, but team members are always independent of the procurement project. Teams are usually three to five strong. A typical review is intended to last no more than five days, and, conducted in such a way as to avoid or minimize project delays.

SUPPLIER CONTRACT MANAGEMENT

It is one thing to let a contract, and another to maximize its value to your organization. It is very important that you monitor whatever is supplied, whether product or service. A nominated Contract Manager should carry out this responsibility. If you establish a contract for the duration of a project, the Contract Manager and Project Manager may be the same person. If your project establishes a contract for the operational supply of products or services, the Contract Manager should be a senior person from an operational part of the organization who has also participated in the procurement activities in the project. Include the Contract Manager in the procurement and in the setting up of contract terms, as she or he will have to live with the results.

GATEWAY REVIEW

Gateway Reviews are used in UK central government civil procurement projects at pre-identified key points. The process is a 'best practice', supported by the Office of Government Commerce (OGC: <http://www.ogc.gov.uk>).

FURTHER READING

Ministry of Defence (2002), *The Acquisition Handbook* (4th edn), London: MoD.
Your organization's Procurement Handbook, Standards, Guidelines or Manual.

SEE ALSO

Contract Management

Programme or Project?

WHAT IS A PROGRAMME?

The meaning of the term 'programme' varies between one organization and another, but as a general rule, a programme is a group of related though not necessarily concurrent projects, co-ordinated and directed by a single Programme Board or Steering Group, to deliver the resulting benefits of strategic or major change or innovation to an organization.

WHEN MIGHT YOU USE A PROGRAMME?

A Programme Approach is recommended when there is a combination of some of the following characteristics:

- a succession of outcomes is required
- complexity, including interfaces and dependencies
- scarce resources
- activities potentially common to more than one component
- possibility of requirements being fluid as time passes
- uncertainty
- high risk to all or a major part of the organization.

WHAT SHOULD YOU INCLUDE IN A DOCUMENT TO DEFINE A PROGRAMME?

- **Brief background** – how did the circumstances arise to trigger the programme? (This is usually well documented elsewhere, so it is usually better to refer to it, rather than spend time re-writing it.)

- **The Vision Statement** – expectations about the future capability which will be used to agree and communicate about the desired 'end state' to stakeholders.

- **The Blueprint** – defines the approach to delivering the transformation described in the Vision Statement, including, for example, the intended structure and composition of the evolving and final 'to be' organization and such aspects as processes, information systems, people, data, costs and measures

- **Business Case** – potential costs, benefits and risks; use this to justify the investment and monitor its ongoing viability

- **Benefits Management** – how potential benefits will be managed from identification through to realization

- **The Benefits Profile/Plan** – a schedule of expected benefits

- **A Programme Risk and Issue Management Strategy** – how will projects manage the Risks and Issues that affect them directly? What should happen if any Project Risk or Issue puts the programme at risk? How will the programme manage the Risks and Issues that affect it directly? Who will own the different levels of Risks and Issues?

- **Initial Risks Log** – the main possible future threats

- **Initial Issues Log** – the main existing concerns

- **A Quality Strategy** – setting out common standards describing how 'fitness for purpose' will be built in and assessed in all participating projects

- **Financial Plan** – phased over the programme's life. When will investment be needed? How much, and when?

- **Programme Plan** – identifying the portfolio and any proposed tranches; the recommended programme approach, the possible sequence or timing of projects and any major milestones

- **Stakeholder Matrix** – who they are, and their main interests

- **Communications Strategy** – how stakeholders will be kept up to date, and when

- **Programme Organization and Roles** – team roles and responsibilities to enable effective 'steering'

- **Approvals procedure and an approval document** – for signature by the Programme Director and his/her nominees

- **Appendices** – as needed (perhaps including some of the documents referred to earlier)

- **Initial Programme Plan:**
  - likely portfolio, sequence and any tranches
  - possible costs
  - potential benefits
  - likely Risks (possible future events that might affect the programme)
  - known Issues (existing situations that affect the programme)
  - likely resource needs and potential resource constraints
  - outline schedule
  - Financial Plan and Programme Business Case
  - approval and authorization methods.

WHAT ROLES MIGHT YOU NEED?

- **A Programme Director** – accountable for delivering the outputs and benefits of the Programme to the organization, who should be a senior executive with an appropriate level of authority and funding
- **A Programme Manager** – who sets up, runs and co-ordinates activity within the portfolio of projects
- **One or more Business Change Manager(s)** – to ensure business readiness to receive outputs and realize benefits
- **An appropriate number of Project Managers** – to deliver projects to the specifications mandated by the Programme Director.

WHAT IS A PROJECT?

'A unique set of co-ordinated activities, with definite start and finishing points, undertaken by an individual or organisation to meet specific objectives within defined schedule, cost and performance parameters.'   BS6079:1996

Characteristics:

- a defined and finite lifespan (beginning, execution and end are clear)
- defined and measurable deliverables
- a planned set of activities to create deliverables
- a defined amount of resources (people, money, tools, suppliers, and so on)
- clear organization and defined roles and responsibilities for the duration.

WHEN SHOULD YOU CONSIDER A FORMAL PROJECT?

If the answer to one or more of the following is 'Yes':

- Do several tasks have to be integrated?
- Do technical (including any practical, business, industrial, scientific, professional or other) complexities exist?

- Are there dynamic or stringent environmental, regulatory or legal considerations?
- Is there a tight budget, and do schedule constraints have to be met?
- Do functional boundaries have to be crossed?

WHAT SHOULD YOU INCLUDE IN A DOCUMENT TO DEFINE A PROJECT?

You should create a Start-up Document, also known under PRINCE® as a Project Initiation Document (PID), to define a single project, create a basis for its management, and to form the basis for assessing its overall success.

It is likely to contain information under the following headings:

- Background
- Scope, Objectives and Constraints
- Deliverables (also known as products or outcomes)
- Interfaces that will need to be satisfied
- Assumptions made
- Business Case (justification answering the question, 'Why are you doing this?')
- Organization underlying the project (defined roles and responsibilities)
- Project Communications Plan (stakeholders, and how they will be kept in touch)
- Project Quality Plan (how completion and 'fitness for purpose' will be assessed for which types of deliverables)
- Initial Project Plan (scheduled tasks, resources, milestones, dependencies, and so on)
- Controls (how progress will be tracked, updated, corrected and reported)
- Exception handling (including escalation procedures)
- Initial Project Risk and Issue Logs
- Project Filing (how documents will be managed, stored and retrieved).

WHAT ROLES MIGHT YOU NEED?

This will vary significantly with the size of the project. Probably the minimum would be two roles:

- **A Project Sponsor** – who may also be the 'customer in chief', and sets the terms of reference and is accountable for successful delivery of the outputs to the organization

- **A Project Manager** – responsible for planning and managing the delivery of the outputs by the project team, if one is needed; in some small projects, the Project Manager is sometimes the only resource.

If the project crosses functional boundaries, or is otherwise large and complex, the Sponsor may feel the need to have others on a Project Steering Group, each of whom will represent and make decisions for his or her part of the organization. Final decisions on project strategy should remain with the Project Sponsor, who is also likely to chair any group or board.

SEE ALSO

Business Case
Communications Plan
Issue Management
Project
Risk Management
Sponsor
Stakeholders – Identification and Communication
Steering Group
Tranche (of a Programme)

Project

'A unique set of co-ordinated activities, with definite start and finishing points, undertaken by an individual or organisation to meet specific objectives within defined schedule, cost and performance parameters.'   BS6079:1996

'A finite piece of work undertaken within defined cost and time constraints directed at achieving stated benefit.'   Robert Buttrick

'Features that make projects:
- Goal oriented
- Involve the co-ordinated undertaking of interrelated activities
- Of finite duration, with beginnings and ends, all to a degree, unique.'
                                                                    J. Davidson Frame

The pace of business and technical innovation creates endless pressure for change in every sort of organization. Decisions to change can vary from panic-driven reactions through grudging acceptance of the inevitable to considered, soundly justified and prioritized cases. The execution of change can be a bureaucratic nightmare or completely *laissez-faire*, a methodical series of controlled steps or an undisciplined scramble, a voyage into known and monitored risks or into rocky and uncharted waters. A project with a sensible structure and organization, a sound plan and committed people can make the difference between chaos and control, between failure and success.

CHARACTERISTICS COMMON TO PROJECTS

Projects:

- need definition of when and where the project should begin and when, and where and how they should end
- use five resources – time, money, effort, materials and facilities
- (should) follow a structure, plan and budget
- often need a team approach, sometimes multi-disciplinary
- have stakeholders, each with a set of needs, wants and expectations
- are unique, in that they use different combinations of the above characteristics to deliver something that did not exist beforehand.

WHAT SHOULD YOU CHECK?

- Do you have approved Terms of Reference, a Project Brief, a Project Mandate or some similar documented statement with clear Scope, Objectives, Constraints, Assumptions and perceived Risks?

- Is there an established structure (life cycle) for projects in your organization, setting out the phases or stages you will need to go through, and what needs to happen between each stage?

- Is there an established framework for projects in your organization, setting out the reporting structure, typical roles and responsibilities, and limits of authority?

- Do you know what information is needed to gain authorization for the project to start?

- Do all the likely key stakeholders know the answers to the above questions?

- Do you have existing project planning and control methods, and people with the skill and experience to use them effectively?

- Will the organization make the best people available to a project when needed to contribute to its success? Who will do their 'day jobs' when this is happening?

SEE ALSO

Programme or Project?

> 'No great thing is created suddenly, any more than a bunch of grapes or a fig. If you tell me that you desire a fig, I answer you that there must be time. Let it first blossom, then bear fruit, then ripen.'
> Epicetus, first-century Greek philosopher

Project and Stage Plans

How many plans are you likely to need at any particular point in a project? This is not intended as a trick question, but to raise an important point about plans and planning. Many practitioners and organizations are firm believers in the concept of having two levels of plans: the 'soft' and the 'hard' varieties. Project Plans tend to be 'softer', simply because there are often too many unknowns for the plans to be accepted as firm. Conversely, the plan for a stage you are in, or about to start needs to be clear, firm and detailed. These principles are fundamental to the process of breaking a project down into stages, one at a time. Note that many organizations use the terms 'stage' and 'phase' interchangeably. We will soon return to the initial question and suggest answers!

SOFT PLANS

'Soft' plans outline that which you are unable to plan in very much detail, usually because of relative distance. For example, at the start of your project, you may have chosen a handover strategy for making your final outputs operational. You may already know many of the key tasks, but will neither wish nor be able to plan this in detail until you get closer and know much more. You are likely to need to apply this same principle to plans for a whole project, where you know what you want to do and the broad approach you wish to take from the start. However, at this point you may know little about the details. Therefore, your Project Plan will be relatively soft when you start, but will firm up with the delivery of outputs and knowledge gained from each stage.

STAGE PLANS

Stage Plans have to be pitched at a different level. Your team members will need to know precisely what you require them to deliver, and on what days. They will need to know detailed schedule information, specifications, formats, dependencies, arrangements for reviews or tests, and the timing and content of the tracking information you need. Stage Plans need to be 'hard'.

So can we answer the question yet? Well, we now know there will be at least two plans:

one for the project, and one for the stage. Will they give you what you need to steer your project to success? Not quite. If you accept the principles of hard and soft planning, you will also need to accept that if you harden a soft plan, you change it. Are you going to monitor and report progress against the original or the changed version? What will you use for tracking if you need to change your plan again? If you are required to re-plan and set a later delivery date for project completion, is it true that if you complete on the new date, that the project has delivered 'on time'? Well, 'yes' according to the new plan, but 'no' according to the old version!

Elsewhere in this manual, you will read about 'baselining'. When your Steering Group has approved your Project Start-up or Initiation Document, or other similar foundation document that includes the initial project plan and authorized budget and resource commitment, it is recommended that you 'baseline' these documents. Then, whatever changes are made as reality impacts the working version of your plan and the plan changes, as it surely will, you will retain a basis for comparison between 'actual' and 'intention' and for any lessons that can be learned for future projects and planning. It is also good practice to baseline your Stage Plan once it has been approved and the budget authorized. So now you have four plans – the baselined Project and Stage Plans and a working, evolving version of each. These will suffice until you approach the end of a stage, when, unless it is the last stage, you will need to start work on the plan for the next stage and refine and firm up the Project Plan for the remainder of the project.

Returning to answer the original question, you may find that you need to have at least five plans close to hand at any time:

1. Project Plan (baselined)
2. Project Plan (working)
3. current Stage Plan (baselined)
4. current Stage Plan (working)
5. next Stage Plan.

WHAT SHOULD YOUR PLANS INCLUDE?

Whether for project or stage, baselined or working, plans might include all or most of these:

●   Work Breakdown Structure, or Product Breakdown Structure if you use PRINCE®
●   Work or Product Flow diagrams
●   Network diagram with estimates showing duration
●   Schedule (bar or Gantt chart) showing tasks, dates and resources
●   Specifications, or Product Descriptions if using PRINCE®
●   budget
●   Resource Plans.

SEE ALSO

Baselines and Baselining
Budgets for Project Work
Change Control
Project
Project Life Cycle
Stage or Phase
Two-level Planning

Project Health Checks

As with a health check for a person, a Project Health Check is a brief examination to determine how 'healthy' a project is and to prescribe any treatments that might improve, or avoid deterioration, in its condition.

WHEN SHOULD YOU USE IT?

Using a simple checklist and a scoring method you should be able to conduct a DIY health check on your own project at any time – for example, as you approach the end of a stage or a major milestone. However, as a health check is most useful when the review of the main documents and logs, and interviews of the stakeholders, is conducted impartially, it is probably best carried out by a Project Manager who has not previously been involved in the project in question.

You might wish to adapt the following questionnaire, scoring method and suggested recommendations to your organization, but bear in mind that once they have been adapted, it is best to keep to your adapted format throughout the project life cycle.

HOW DO YOU GO ABOUT IT?

You can use the ten sample questions in Figure 59 to review the most important documents and as a basis for interviewing stakeholders, both in the project team and among the project's customers. When you have completed the document reviews and interviews, you will need to make judgements before awarding scores from 1–10 against each question, as suggested below. Justify your scores by using the 'Comments' column to record key aspects of your findings in each area. Finally, total the scores (a perfect project would score 100 points), and award the project an overall percentage. This can then be used as a basis for making recommendations about what needs to be done next – particularly if you have found serious health problems.

Question	Comment	Score
1. Are the Terms of Reference for the project clear? (Are the Objectives SMART – Specific, Measurable, Agreed, Realistic, Time-based?) Is the scope well defined? Are the constraints clear? Are there any unresolved major assumptions? Are the reporting lines, formats and frequencies clear? Are they followed?		
2. Do all the stakeholders understand the Terms of Reference?		
3. Is there a Sponsor or Steering Group at the level and with the authority to 'champion' the project, overcome obstacles and secure budgets and other resources?		
4. Is there a Business Case to justify the project? Does it show how the project supports the organization's business plan?		
5. Are there comprehensive plans for the project and for the stage currently in progress? Do these plans support the Terms of Reference?		
6. Do the plans make the status of the project clear? Can you tell which tasks have been a) completed, b) reviewed and approved (baselined)? Is the project on time and within budget? Do the stakeholders know the project's status?		
7. Are the standards and procedures for planning and controlling against the plan clear and being used?		
8. Are all the participants working to the plan? Do they have the required skills, knowledge and experience? is each task clearly specified?		
9. Are roles and responsibilities clear? Can you see from the documents who is responsible for doing each task, who is accountable for each task being done, who needs to be consulted about each task and who should be informed about each task?		
10. Is there a Risks Log and an Issues Log? Do they appear to be up to date and reflect the size and potential impact of the issues and risks faced? Is the owner of each identified? Are actions to resolve each issue, to prevent or reduce the likelihood of occurrence of each risk, or to reduce impact if it occurs clear? Are the required actions up to date? Are they working?		
Total score		%

Figure 59   Sample Health Check questionnaire

Sample scoring method

You might like to use the following scoring ranges and accompanying findings as a guide:

Score	Findings
10	Documentation and/or interview findings indicate that this area of the project's health is as close to perfect as possible. Every aspect is first-class.
6–9	Documentation and/or interview findings indicate that, whilst this aspect of the project's health is reasonable or good, some improvements may be possible.
1–5	Documentation and/or interview findings indicate that this aspect of the project's health is in need of significant improvement.
0	The lack of documented evidence and/or negative interview findings show that this aspect of the project's health is at critical risk and needs urgent improvement.

MAKING RECOMMENDATIONS

Use the total percentage score from the health check questionnaire as a basis for recommending actions, using the following guidelines.

Score 0–30 per cent

Summary
The project is at serious risk of imminent terminal decline.

Options for action

- Suspend the project.
- Conduct 'damage limitation briefings with major stakeholders.
- Conduct a major review including the project justification (Business Case).
- Replace, or provide experienced support to, the Project Manager.
- Authorize a restart – but only if and when major improvements are in place.
- Monitor all project activities from now on.
- Review the project management and reporting methods that allowed this state of affairs to happen.
- Document the 'Lessons Learned'.

Score 31–70 per cent

Summary
Some major health improvements may be needed – some urgently.

Options for action

- Prioritize corrective actions – highest risk first.
- Manage stakeholder expectations.
- Provide strong support to the Project Manager.
- Review and update the project justification (Business Case).
- Consider stepping up the frequency of management reporting.
- Document the 'Lessons Learned'.

Score 70–90 per cent

Summary

The project is in good health, but some improvements might help.

Options for action

- Support the Project Manager in improving any low-health areas and maintain good health elsewhere.
- Document the 'Lessons Learned'.

Score 90–100 per cent

Summary

Can the project be in this good health? Almost too good to be true!

Options for action

- Recheck the scores before getting too excited.
- Keep up the good work.
- Use the project as a future case study.
- Document the 'Lessons Learned'.

SEE ALSO

Baselines and Baselining
Business Case
Business Case Review
Closing a Project
Controlling Against the Schedule
Filing and Document Management in Projects
Issue Management
Lessons Learned
Milestones and Milestone Plans
Project and Stage plans
Responsibility Matrix

Risk Management
Sponsor
Stages – Start and End Procedures
Stakeholders – Identification and Communication
Steering Group
Terms of Reference

Project Life Cycle

A Project life cycle is the sequences of stages, phases or steps that a project might progress through, from the time that someone has an idea that, if progressed, would need a project to turn it into a reality, until that reality has been delivered, the project that delivered it has been closed down and final reports, disposals and evaluations have been completed. The term 'stage' will be used from here on in this section, but feel free to substitute your own terminology.

Life cycles will vary between one industry and another and even within similar industries. For example, in software development, one organization may use a single comprehensive Analysis and Design Stage, while others may run these as two separate stages, giving approval to a detailed 'Requirements Definition' at the end of the Analysis Stage. Those who separate analysis and design may run just one Design Stage, or a distinct Logical Design Stage, followed by a Physical Design Stage. The most compact systems development life cycle I have used had four stages; the one with the most had nine.

The main characteristics of stages are that they are preceded and followed by short, formal procedures to approve completion and closure of any previous stage, to approve and authorize the plan and budget for the following stage, and to approve the outline (soft) plan and budget for the remainder of the project. There is also an opportunity here to bring any project to a premature end in cases such as when the justification has evaporated, the risks are seen to be too great, or the forecast costs too high. These major decision points are fundamental to good project management practice, and are known by such interchangeable terms as 'Stage Ends', 'Major Milestones', 'Gateways' or 'Decision Points'.

Terminology also varies, with some organizations using the term 'stages' and others using 'phases'. Note that these names often apply to technical sub-divisions of a project, such as an 'Analysis Stage', which may be terminated once a Statement of Requirements' (SOR) has been agreed and approved. Usually the terms are interchangeable, though users of PRINCE 2® will find that the term 'stage' has a somewhat different meaning, in that it is used to describe the sub-division of a project into Management Stages, which may or may not coincide with Technical Stages. (See *Managing Successful Projects with PRINCE2* (The Stationery Office, 2002) for a comprehensive description of this approach.)

WHY MIGHT IT BE USEFUL?

Sub-dividing projects into stages enables your Steering Group to manage the risks associated with change and innovation. It creates the opportunity for a decision on whether or not to release funds, one stage at a time. At each of these decision points, the Steering Group should be satisfied that work to date is complete and adequate, future effort and expenditure are based on sound and realistic plans and budgets, risks are manageable and the venture is still worthwhile.

WHEN MIGHT YOU NEED IT?

You need to know how your projects are sub-divided before you start, so that you can prepare appropriate plans, budgets and reports as and when needed. You should also be familiar enough with your organization's project life cycle to explain and justify its use to stakeholders, who may think that the time and effort consumed by Stage End Reporting is time that could be better spent doing 'real work'. I have worked in organizations where project methods were seen to have been 'imposed', even by the managers who were needed to make them work, but who did not feel motivated to do so.

HOW DO YOU USE IT?

If you have a life cycle based on technical stages, you may find that much of the planning work you need to do has already been done in template form, with Work Breakdown Structures and a task list for typical stages. Do not treat these as the definitive approach; rather treat them as a start point that you should fine-tune to the particular characteristics of this stage in this project. To achieve this, you should be able to justify deleting any tasks whose appearance on a template suggests that they are a standard part of the stage.

You might also consider sub-dividing a very large, complex or risky stage at a natural break point that coincides quite closely with a point at which plans and funding could be examined, such as roughly half-way through on duration, effort or cost, depending on which serves your needs best. At the other end of the scale, you might choose to recommend combining two stages where the work, costs and risks are seen to be modest enough to be manageable as one unit.

GENERIC LIFE CYCLE

Figure 60 shows how British Standard 6079-1:2000 identifies generic project life cycle Phases. This is followed by the author's interpretation of possible main tasks in each phase and the main approvals and authorizations between phases.

British Standard 6079-1:2000 Phase name	Milestone	What might happen here?
Conception		Someone has an idea such as how to solve a problem, grasp an opportunity or develop a new product or service. The idea is developed far enough to justify effort and expenditure on an assessment of its feasibility. No project exists yet.
	Concept feasibility transfer	The Sponsor seeks authorization to apply time and money to an assessment of the technical, operational and economic feasibility of ways of solving the problem or grasping the opportunity.
Feasibility		An early, high-level assessment of whether it would be practicable, desirable and worthwhile to grasp an opportunity or solve a problem and if so, how. It should identify and evaluate optional solutions, their technical, operational and economic feasibility, and how each might be implemented. The study needs to provide sufficient information to justify recommendations on whether to proceed via a project, and if so, following what life cycle.
	Project authorization	The feasibility study findings are approved and a project to deliver them is initiated. The project is planned, a budget developed, risks and issues identified, and the whole package presented for approval and for authorization to work to the plan and incur the forecast costs.
Implementation		This is seldom managed as one phase/stage, and is usually sub-divided into technical phases/stages (or Management Stages, if using PRINCE®). Technical stages might include: ● Requirements Definition ● Design ● Development or Procurement ● Integration and Testing ● Documentation and Training ● User Acceptance ● Commissioning Note that handover can range from 'Big Bang' to a protracted roll-out.
	Handover	This marks the formal handover from development to operational status, at which the Project Manager should be able to demonstrate fitness for purpose and completion of the project's outputs, and the new owner should sign an acceptance document. Some agreement should also be documented about how maintenance will be initiated.
Operation		Live use of the project's outputs, with performance monitoring. Managed change of outputs that do not perform as needed. Support and maintenance.
Termination		Project closure. Completion of any 'Lessons Learned' document. Disbandment of the Project Team and disposal of unused facilities, if appropriate.

Figure 60 Generic life cycle definition

SEE ALSO

Approval
Authorization
Budgets for Project Work
Stage or Phase
Steering Group
Work Breakdown Structure
PRINCE® Project Board

Project Office

A Project Office can be established as a permanent function to supply support to projects in a project-based business, or to an organization that often runs several projects side by side. It can also be a temporary arrangement made to support a single project through its life cycle.

WHY MIGHT IT BE USEFUL?

The more projects an organization runs, the more it stands to gain from running a Project Office. The benefits are likely to include:

- consistency and growing experience in the use of project management tools and techniques
- improving project management and project team skills, attitudes, enthusiasm and professionalism
- nurturing a 'management by projects' culture
- contributions to the bottom line through effectiveness and efficiency in many project tasks and in overall project delivery
- a project 'centre of excellence' and a learning organization
- access to a 'one-stop shop' for lessons learned from projects, project histories, 'plan' and 'actual' information, techniques that have worked well and those that have not done so, sample plans, project documentation and filing methods and systems
- skilled and experienced staff to provide project support and administration services, giving the Project Manager more time to manage successful delivery
- consistent standards and templates.

WHAT SERVICES MIGHT A PROJECT OFFICE PROVIDE?

This will vary between basic administrative support and a full project management support service, depending on what each organization seeks and the stage in the development reached. Many organizations will start by piloting then establishing one function, often on a part-time basis. Additional functions may follow gradually. The following list shows a range of possible Project Office functions, but does not imply any sequence or priority for establishing any one.

Much of the routine work on a project may be carried out by Project Office staff on instructions from a Project Manager, such as:

- developing and maintaining the schedule, probably using a software tool

- time recording and keeping track of timesheets for those deployed on the project

- storage and retrieval of project documentation in secure and well-organized filing systems, for both electronic versions and paperwork; in some organizations, provision will need to be made for non-paper items, such as models and prototypes

- configuration administration, based on the established filing system, so that only the most recent version of any document or product is used either operationally or as prerequisite for a dependent product or document; it is also possible that the Project Office would maintain a Change Log and store signed change authorization documents

- maintenance of other logs, including those recording Project Risks, Issues, Quality and Opportunities

- writing regular reports and distributing them after they have been approved by the Project Manager

- organizing and supporting project meetings by distributing agendas, plus pre-reading paperwork, and then recording and distributing minutes, actions and decisions

- some projects establish places that have become widely known as 'War Rooms', where stakeholders can browse charts, diagrams, schedules, notices and a wide variety of project information; such a room is only as useful if the information is current, so maintenance work is needed; Project Office staff are well placed to run such an operation, as they have first-hand knowledge of all the latest material;

- integration of project plans and logs with those for programmes and portfolios.

You will see from this list that administrative support for a project can be very time-consuming if done to a professional standard. If you, as Project Manager, have to keep taking 'time out' from your main responsibilities to do or chase such work, your project may be put at unnecessary risk, and the cost of your doing such work may not represent best value for your organization.

Other important administrative work may be carried out under the direction of the Project Office Manager and may include:

- setting up and maintaining a library of project histories and conducting any required searches and research
- custodianship and maintenance of standards and templates.

STAFFING A PROJECT OFFICE

The requirement for knowledge, experience and skills in project matters might best be filled by the appointment of a person with all of these as Project Office Manager. Many of the support skills and qualities needed, such as use of word processor and spreadsheet software, literacy, numeracy, time-management, adaptability and willingness to learn, might well be found right across your organization. Other skills, for example in the use of a planning tool such as Microsoft Project®, can be developed by training and coaching.

OTHER PROJECT OFFICE SERVICES

The well-established Project Office might have additional capabilities in such areas as project management resources, with a pool of Project Managers. In such circumstances, the majority should be running one or more projects most of the time, but between projects such valuable people can provide:

- independent project assurance to projects
- feasibility studies and project start-ups
- inducting and mentoring newcomers to project management
- coaching other Project Managers and developing project skills
- education and training for relatively new Project Managers, business departments about to embark on major projects and newly established Project Boards or Steering Committees.

CONSIDERING AND JUSTIFYING A PROJECT OFFICE

Your organization may want to conduct some form of feasibility study before making any decision on whether and how to set up a Project Office. It would need to consider options for the scope of any services to be provided, ranging from simple administrative part-time support to an all-embracing, full-service proposal, using full-time in-house staff, or even a contracted-out supply. Options for the approach to setting up a Project Office might range from a small pilot scheme in support of one project, through starting with one service (say planning) and phasing the introduction of additional services, to a big-bang 'let's do it all for all projects' approach. It will always be easier to forecast the costs of a Project Office, rather than the benefits and, for these, your organization may prefer a notional approach, asking a range of people with project knowledge and experience to put a value on the services the Project Office would provide. To do this, potential users would need to answer questions such as: 'What would you have considered paying for a skilled planner to create and update your plans?' or 'What value would you put on services that freed you from project administration work and enabled you to spend your time managing the project?'

PROJECT
OFFICE

SEE ALSO

Filing and Document Management in Projects

Project Opportunities

A Project Opportunity is a situation where a project might benefit from favourable consequences of future events, affecting one or more of costs, timescales, benefits and quality if the opportunity is recognized and acted upon.

Circumstances in which a project is initiated often change. Such changes often evolve rather than erupt, and are not always negative as is sometimes thought. While Risk Management is a Project Management fundamental, Opportunity Management also deserves consideration. To maximize the chances of success, it will pay you to be ready to counter as many risks and exploit as many opportunities as occur. If you do not actively seek opportunities, you may not recognize them at all and miss them completely, or identify them too late to capitalize on them.

PROJECT OPPORTUNITY LOG

You might obtain useful information on opportunities from:

- existing Project Opportunity Logs
- workshops that address Risks, Issues *and* Opportunities
- generic opportunities identified in publications on Project Management
- new opportunities identified during regular monitoring and tracking
- input from stakeholders
- Project Issues resulting in 'Requests for Change' that create additional benefits
- Project Office records and Lessons Learned Reports that document similar projects where opportunities were grasped, or perhaps missed.

If you have a Project Opportunity Log, use it to hold information describing and perhaps quantifying potential opportunities that might enhance the success of your project and improve its benefits. You might also try to identify signs to watch out for ('trigger' events or circumstances) indicating that a Project Opportunity might be about to arise and suggest actions if this occurs. You might consider setting up an Opportunity Log when starting your project and maintaining it throughout.

Suggested procedure

● When someone identifies a potential opportunity, seek any clarification and information from the originator.

● As long as it appears to be an opportunity for the project, add it to the Log, showing any existing references (for example, a progress report or change request).

● In 'Type of Project Opportunity', identify the main potential benefit(s). (Who could gain what from this?)

● Make the description specific by using a phrase like 'which could mean that . . .', in which the benefits of grasping the opportunity are described and quantified as far as is possible.

● Under 'Source', clarify whether the opportunity is internal (such as 'If Project X could set up their database by dd/mm/yy, we wouldn't need to do tasks 7.1.1 through 7.1.9, which could save us 3 months and £10 000') or external, that is outside the control or influence of your organization (such as 'Suppliers X,Y and Z each sell a database very close to our needs'. If we were able to buy a licence for one of these databases for less than £nn nnn, we could save two person-years of development work which costs us £NN NNN, knock six months off the project duration, and start to earn project benefits six months earlier).

● Identify the originator.

● Agree who will 'own' the opportunity (the individual responsible for monitoring the opportunity and triggering any actions needed to grasp it, or closing the opportunity when the time within which it might have arisen has passed).

OPPORTUNITY ASSESSMENT

The selection of ratings has to be a matter of judgment, best done by more than one person, based on the varied experience and expectations of each. Agree a rating for 'likelihood' and another for 'benefit' for each opportunity identified.

Likelihood/probability

Use a grid such as that shown in Figure 61 to estimate what the chances are of this opportunity actually arising.

Benefit

Use a grid like the one shown in Figure 62 to estimate where the benefits would help you.

Your assessment	Rating
More likely to happen than not to happen	5
Even (50:50) chance of it happening	3
Less than even chance of it happening	1
Opportunity no longer exists and is closed	0

Figure 61   Probability assessment grid

Effect on Benefit Rating	Schedule	Budget	Objectives	Quality
5 for each (max 20)	Excellent	Excellent	Excellent	Excellent
3 for each (max 12)	Good	Good	Good	Good
1 for each (max 4)	Marginal	Marginal	Marginal	Marginal
0	None	None	None	None

Figure 62   Benefit assessment grid

Consider the potential benefits for your schedule, budget, objectives and quality if an opportunity was to become a reality. For example, if you assessed the opportunity 'Project X will set up their database by dd/mm/yy' as 'Excellent' on Schedule score 5, 'Excellent' on Budget score 5, 'Marginal' on Objectives score 1 and 'None' on Quality score 0, the Benefit Rating would be 11.

Overall Opportunity Rating

To calculate an overall rating, simply multiply the Likelihood and Benefit ratings. You might regard any opportunity scoring 25 (or more) overall as not to be missed.

WHAT NEXT?

You may choose actions such as:

- **Enabling/facilitating** – planning, liaison and work to help the opportunity to come about
- **Exploitation** – planning and work to be ready to maximize the opportunity when it does happen
- **Tracking** – monitoring possible opportunities for 'trigger' events/circumstances to enable a prompt reaction when needed
- **Seeking provisional approval** – for the possible costs and estimated effort you might incur to maximize any important opportunity that becomes available.

For opportunities scoring, say, 25 or more (at least one benefit rated as 'Excellent'), use an appropriate combination of the following:

- Maximize the chances of it happening.
- Maximize your ability to grasp the benefits if it does happen.
- Have some contingency plans available to exploit it, proportionate to the potential benefits.
- Ensure there is one 'owner', senior enough to approve a rapid reaction if needed.
- Identify 'triggers' – those signs you would expect to see if the opportunity starts to become realistically available.
- Monitor frequently for 'triggers' and any change to the ratings.

For Project Opportunities scoring, say, 15 or more, use an appropriate combination of the following:

- Consider any simple enabling or facilitating measures.
- Prepare in proportion.
- If you have a management reserve in your budget, seek approval to dip into this in proportion to the benefits available.
- Monitor regularly for 'triggers' and any change to the ratings.

For Project Opportunities scoring, say, 9 or more:

- Monitor periodically.

PROJECT ISSUES

You may recall that a Project Issue is 'an existing situation or set of circumstances which is affecting the ability of a project to arrive at its intended outcome'. If an opportunity arises that meets this definition, it makes good sense to transfer it to the Issues Log and manage its exploitation from there. Overall procedure might look something like that in Figure 63.

POSSIBLE HEADINGS FOR AN OPPORTUNITIES LOG

- **Reference number**
- **Description** – potential opportunity, benefits if it happens and when it might happen
- **Raised** – by whom, and when
- **Likelihood** – suggested rating 5, 3 or 1
- **Benefit** – suggested ratings 5, 3 or 1, one each for Schedule, Budget, Objectives and Quality
- **Trigger Signs** – 'It might be happening if . . .'
- **Owner** – who is responsible for action if trigger event or circumstances happen
- **Actions** – 'What should we do when triggered?'

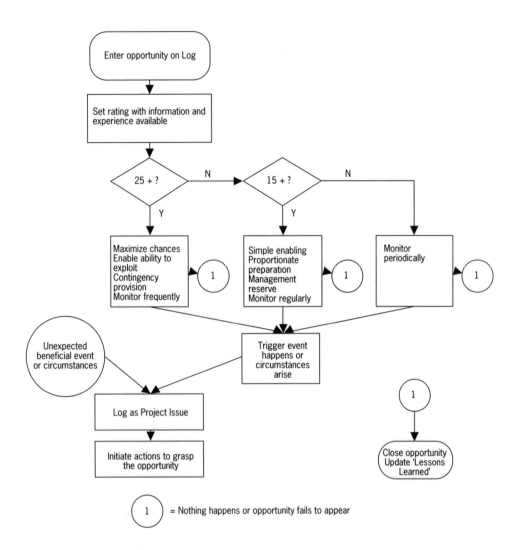

Figure 63 Opportunity management

- **Resourcing** – 'How will any costs or resource requirements be satisfied?'
- **Resolution** – how closed, when, and any Issue Log Number.

SEE ALSO

Change Control
Issue Management
Lessons Learned
Project Office
Request for Change
Risk Management

Project Strategy

A Project Strategy should define a high-level approach to achieve satisfaction of a project's aims, given the prevailing conditions and knowledge of the resources likely to be available (money, people, time). It should provide an answer to the question, 'What do we believe is the best way of going about this?' Such a strategy may be established by a Management Board, a Programme Board, executive-level potential customers who need change or innovation, or those who conduct feasibility studies or other pre-project investigations, all advised as far as possible by those potential Project Managers who would need to apply the strategy and realize a successful outcome. Anyone forming such a strategy will need to consider trade-offs between such approaches as:

(A)   one large, all-embracing, widest scope project
(B)   a series of sub-projects, each with limited objectives and scope, run in series
(C)   a series of sub-projects, each with limited objectives and scope, run in parallel.

For example, as illustrated in Figure 64, a project of the type in (A) above might be dauntingly large, complex, resource-intensive, of long duration, and likely to face all the risks and issues that go along with these characteristics. On the other side of the equation, it will avoid the interface risks and multi-project complexities that types (B) and (C) may face.

The type (B) approach will give you sub-projects that are smaller, simpler, shorter, with lower 'internal' risks, and easier to manage. The achievement of benefits may be strung out; those with a stake in later sub-projects may become disenchanted. Evolving requirements may mean that before you have finished the last sub-project, outputs from the first one have become out of date. Risks with such an approach will usually include those related to dynamic, multiple interfaces.

The type (C) approach will give you sub-projects that are smaller, simpler, shorter, lower-risk, and easier to manage internally. The approach may be even more resource-intensive than the single large project approach. Again, the benefits may be strung out and affected by newly identified requirements and resulting change requests. Other risks may include complex co-ordination and resource problems, particularly when skilled individuals are needed at the same time by different sub-projects.

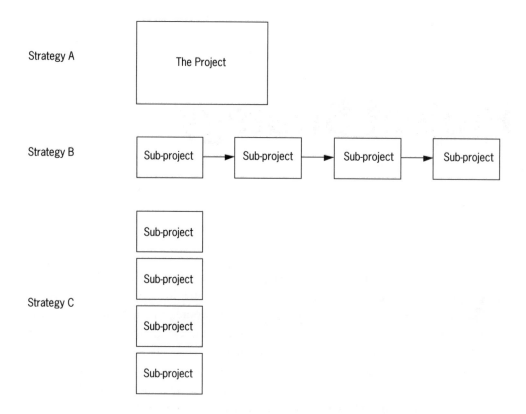

Figure 64   Three possible Project Strategies to deliver the same outputs

You will also appreciate that are several variations on this theme, such as running series of sub-projects in parallel – (B) and (C) combined. Other strategies might involve running sub-projects that require expert subject knowledge using internal resources, while contracting out development, or procuring 'off-the-shelf' solutions for the other sub-projects.

Another strategic decision that could optimize co-ordination and communications might be the number of stages in each sub-project and a high-level definition of the outputs required from them. Using these sub-project approaches, you may well end up with several projects, all of which might be what your organization regards as 'small' projects, each of which you might manage using only two stages (Planning Stage and Execution Stage) or three stages (Planning, Development and Implementation Stages).

WHY MIGHT IT BE USEFUL?

Top–down approaches are valuable across much of the work that Project Managers need to perform. Every project you plan needs to support the bigger corporate picture. Much as a programme or portfolio of change or innovation needs a vision and blueprint to focus thinking and planning, those who establish projects also need strategies within which the practitioners can plan and execute the delivery of the required outputs.

WHEN MIGHT YOU NEED IT?

Clearly, decisions on the approach should be made before any project work is started, so that planning and budgeting will support a strategy formed and approved after consultations with all the main stakeholders on the pros and cons of the approach options.

While the Project Strategy will help provide focus that is sometimes in short supply when projects are launched, it should not be regarded as having been carved in stone. It will be legitimate and proper to keep the strategy under periodic review, to ensure that the approach is still the best available in the prevailing conditions. For example, you may start with a series of smaller projects, and then decide to run those remaining as one project.

HOW DO YOU USE IT?

As a potential Project Manager, you will need to check that the strategy is complete and comprehensive, and that the terms of reference (or Project Mandate if you are using PRINCE®) are clear. If the strategy is for a monolithic project, its objectives, scope, constraints, any assumptions and the reporting lines and method are specified. If the approach is based on serial sub-projects, you need the same information for each, and you will need to know that sequence and the supporting rationale. If the approach is based on parallel sub-projects, each Project Manager will need the same information for each 'module' they will manage and what priorities exist, so that no time need be lost if ever there is resource contention.

If your organization has decided that a single, large project is the best way forward, start-up, though large and complex, should be procedurally routine. You will need to create a normal Start-up Document or Project Initiation Document. You may also have project management standards and templates for a sub-project approach, if selected. What you do with these will depend on the serial/parallel decision and how many Project Managers there will be. Your choice, if you have one, lies between a single document setting out requirements for each sub-project, and one smaller document per sub-project. My preference is to seek approval for and use an umbrella document that sets out all the common information, along with a high-level plan and forecast of likely costs. As the start of each sub-project falls due, appendices containing detailed plans and budget should be added by whoever will manage that piece of work. Approval can then be sought for that sub-project to start. This approach is useful in risk management, as it helps avoid financial over-commitment

WHAT SHOULD YOU CHECK?

- Is there a Project Strategy?
- Is it clear, comprehensive, agreed by all the main stakeholders, and approved by the appropriate decision-makers?
- As a Project Manager for one or all of its parts, are your Terms of Reference (or Statement of Work) clear?

- Did you participate in its formulation?
  - If not, does it appear workable at this point?
  - If not, have you proposed changes that you believe would make it more workable?
- Do the risks appear to be manageable at this point?
  - If not, have you proposed changes that you believe would make them more manageable?
- Have your proposals been accepted?
  - If not, are you in a 'Hobson's choice' situation, having to make the best of it? (Hobson rented horses in Cambridge. You had to ride whichever horse became available next.)

SEE ALSO

Feasibility Study
Issue Management
Programme or Project
Project
Risk Management
Stakeholders – Identification and Communication
Starting a Project
Statement of Work
Terms of Reference

Quality in Project Work

Totality of characteristics of an entity which bear on its ability to satisfy stated and implied needs. (ISO 8402)

You will often hear people discuss quality in terms of 'eminence' or 'superiority'. Such a discussion might include phrases such as: 'Do you know, the sound insulation in my car is so superb that I can hear the clock ticking when I am driving at 70 mph!' You might feel tempted to respond with a question such as: 'Wouldn't it have been much cheaper and just as effective to have ordered sound insulation around the clock, if the ticking bothers you so much?'

The phrase 'fitness for purpose' perhaps comes as close as we normally need to explaining what we mean by 'quality' in much of our project work. We are more usually concerned with the attributes, properties, features or characteristics of our deliverables. If a deliverable contains all the attributes, properties, features or characteristics we have specified, it is complete and we can get on with other tasks.

You will need to know when an output has been completed, in order to update your plan and assign a resource to a new task. To do this, you need to be satisfied that a deliverable fulfils its specification. It is normal to use a Quality Review or similar independent procedure to confirm this status. So while ISO 8402 includes the satisfaction of 'implied needs', you will find it much safer to concentrate on needs expressed in a Specification or Product Description. The alternative is to risk becoming involved in trying to satisfy 'hindsight' requirements, which were not planned, have no budget, and may not deliver what is really needed.

Experience suggests that two related 'quality' issues often contribute to project delays:

1. Work may not have been done properly in the first place, very often as a result of inadequate specification, leading to work having to be redone, with consequent increased costs. If you provide a good, unambiguous specification, your team members will be better able to build in 'fitness for purpose' from the outset.

2. The pursuit of unnecessary polishing and fine-tuning of project outputs wastes time and effort that team members ought to be applying to remaining tasks.

As a Project Manager, you need to have a complete understanding of your customer's quality expectations, but may also need to educate your customer to understand the cost implications of seeking perfect rather than adequate outputs. Your experience here may reinforce the 80/20 rule, when 20 per cent of the effort and cost might regularly deliver 80 per cent of required functionality or content.

When you create a schedule that shows a completion date for a deliverable, it will also focus the developer's mind if you show the date on which he or she should present it for review. Only when your reviewers have completed their task, and the developer has made any required corrections, should you formally approve and 'baseline' a deliverable. This means that once you have done this, you will not permit anyone to do more work on it, unless you authorize it using your Change Control procedures. When you have baselined something in this way, you should be confident in marking it as 100 per cent complete on your plan.

SOME QUALITY MANAGEMENT TERMS AND COMPONENTS

- A quality system should have defined procedures and responsibilities to help ensure that customer 'quality' expectations will always be met in everything your organization does. Note that ISO 9001 provides the international standard for quality systems.

- Quality Assurance – if this function exists, it might establish, maintain and audit the use of your corporate 'Quality System', including that to be used by all projects and programmes. If you do not have this function, your Project Board should try to establish some form of project-level assurance, which needs to be independent of the Project Manager.

- A Project Quality Plan should set out how you intend to use your Quality System to meet customers' quality requirements from your project.

- A Stage Quality Plan is a detailed plan, setting out whether, how, when and by whom the outputs during a stage will be assessed.

- Quality Criteria are the decisive factors against which an output has to be assessed to determine whether it is 'fit for purpose'. Try, wherever possible and worthwhile, to write such criteria to enable objective assessment.

QUESTIONS TO ASK

- Does your organization have a quality management system? If so, are you familiar with all the provisions that relate to project work?
- What form of Quality Assurance do you have for your project?
- Do you have an approved Project Quality Plan? Are you working to it?
- Do you have an approved Stage Quality Plan? Are you working to it?

SEE ALSO

Baselines and Baselining
Change Control
Quality Reviews and Product Descriptions
PRINCE® Product Description

'Who is the designer genius who put frosted glass in the toilet windows of airplanes?'

Harry Scott

Quality Reviews and Product Descriptions

A Quality Review is 'an inspection with a specific structure, defined roles and procedure, designed to ensure a document's completeness and adherence to standards' (Office of Government Commerce, 2002, *Managing Successful Projects with PRINCE2*). While the structure, roles and procedures are important components of the PRINCE® approach, the underlying principles are crucial to managing the quality of project outputs whatever project management standards you follow, and a similar approach is highly recommended.

If you conduct or organize a PRINCE® Quality Review, you will assess the product to be reviewed against criteria in a document known as a Product Description (See Figure 65 for suggested format). In a non-PRINCE® environment, you will normally review deliverables against some form of written specifications.

WHY ARE REVIEWS VALUABLE?

Finding defects in products should not be left to chance, or to your customers after they have put project deliverables to their intended use. Any organization that sanctions this approach will almost certainly find itself with higher costs, operational risks and problems, and disillusioned customers. The costs of fixing errors increase exponentially as time spent on a project elapses, and particularly when other outputs have been based on one that is subsequently found to be flawed. In these circumstances, it may not just be the original flaw that has to be unpicked, but the same output may then have to be recreated, along with possibility that all dependent outputs have to be scrapped and re-done too. Early error detection, conducted promptly within projects leads to earlier, and therefore cheaper, error detection and correction. You will also gain from writing Product Descriptions, or some form of Specification if you are not in a PRINCE® environment, because the person developing each output will have all the criteria that you will use to review that product, enabling a 'right first time' approach. Figure 65 shows a sample format for Product Descriptions.

Product name

Try to give a descriptive, meaningful name to a product. You might also consider showing the unique Work Breakdown Structure or Product Breakdown Structure reference number, to avoid confusion where there are similar but not identical products.

Version

Use this to identify the most recent version of the product. Use version numbering in line with your organization's standards. You can easily identify a draft version using a decimal point (Version 0.1 is a first draft) and a baselined version using an integer (Version 1 is the first baselined version).

Purpose

Explain what purpose the product will serve. What will it be used for?

Components

Specify all the components of the product that must be present when it is complete.

Derivation

Specify what prerequisites will need to be completed, so that all the required information can be found and used to create this product.

Format

Specify the medium that the product must be created in – for example, what software has to be used, if any, what format or template should be used, and so on.

Quality Criteria

Specify quality evidence that will indicate completeness and fitness for purpose. For example, if reviewing your Product Descriptions, does each:

- provide a complete, clear and unambiguous description of the product?
- specify the product, so that a developer should be clear about the characteristics the completed product must possess?
- identify any prerequisites, products or information that must be in place to enable its creation, or which, if absent or incomplete, will prevent its creation?
- help ensure all stakeholders can have a shared understanding of the product?
- define required quality criteria?
- set out how quality will be assessed and any Quality Review conducted?
- identify who will be responsible for developing it?

Criteria Hints

Try to:

- Use 'Yes'/'No'-type questions where possible.
- Set out criteria to seek objective rather than subjective responses.
- Ensure your criteria will assess the product, not its developers.
- Seek 'fitness for purpose' rather than perfection, unless perfection is essential, such as when the product is a banknote design.
- Avoid delays caused by 'cosmetic' errors, particularly for Critical Path products.

Quality Method

Specify how the quality of a product should be assessed, at what point, and by whom.

Assigned to (optional)

Specify who will be responsible for creating the product.

Figure 65   Format for Product Descriptions

WHAT SHOULD YOU LEARN FROM SUCH A REVIEW?

As a Project Manager, you probably need to know four main pieces of information when a deliverable is reviewed:

1. Does it appear to be fit for its intended purpose? If not, what errors or shortcomings have been identified?
2. If corrections need to be made, will another review be needed (usually for major shortcomings) or might it be re-assessed and passed in some other defined way?
3. Does it comply with prevailing standards?
4. Is it complete? Is it ready to be put to its intended use? Can the plan be updated to show completion?

WHEN SHOULD YOU USE REVIEWS?

You should have a Project Quality Plan that sets out how you intend to meet your customers' quality requirements. Quality reviews consume considerable effort and incur significant costs, both in the development of Product Descriptions and in the conduct and follow-up of reviews. They postpone the approval of otherwise completed deliverables. If you are experiencing tight deadlines and quality review resource shortages, you will not be alone, but will need to ensure that you use reviews wisely and cost-effectively. To this end you may need to do some prioritization.

Many organizations use their Project Quality Plans to set criteria for 'major' or 'key' products – that is, those that must be subjected to formal quality reviews, leaving others to be reviewed or checked less formally. For example, if you are managing a project which includes procurement of a product or service through a competitive tender, you should make sure that crucial documents, such as an Invitation to Tender package, are rigorously and independently examined before being sent to the outside world. Errors can cause difficulties ranging from public embarrassment to subsequent contractual wrangles.

WHO WILL NEED TO DO WHAT?

The recommended roles include the following.

The developer or producer

- **Before** – Complete the product, distribute it to the reviewers and prepare for the review.
- **During** – Attend the review, answer questions about the product being reviewed.
- **After** – Action any error list, complete follow-up actions and obtain any sign-offs.

Reviewers

- **Before** – Prepare for the review.

- **During** – Assess the product against the quality criteria in the Product Description.
- **After** – Sign the follow-up action list, if nominated to check it.

Review Chairperson

- **Before** – Check that the product is ready, approve the arrangements, and set the agenda.
- **During** – Chair and control the review, preferably without participating in the review. Gain agreement to the actions and outcome.
- **After** – Update the Project Manager, and give the final sign-off.

Secretary

- **Before** – Prepare for the role.
- **During** - Record the actions identified by the review meeting and the person responsible. Read the notes back to participants.
- **After** – Distribute Action List.

Project Assurance

- **Before** – Check that reviews are set up properly. Suggest suitable reviewers, and check they are briefed and trained as necessary.
- **During** – Check that review procedures being used effectively. Act as reviewer where appropriate, but avoid usurping the Chairperson's role.
- **After** – Check that follow-up actions are monitored effectively.

Project Manager

- **Before** – Plan for all reviews, and identify all the deliverables that will need formal quality reviews.
- **During** – Act as reviewer, if appropriate.
- **After** – Update the plan as appropriate.

TEN-STEP QUALITY REVIEW

1. Plan for required reviews.
2. Plan this review.
3. Complete and distribute the product.
4. Reviewers prepare by reviewing the product against Product Description and returning their findings to Producer.
5. Conduct the review.
6. Record follow-up actions required, and how these will be checked.
7. Check to ensure follow-up actions are successfully completed.
8. Raise a Project Issue if product errors are insoluble

or:

9. Sign off and baseline the product as completed.
10. Update the plan with completion or exception.

FURTHER READING

Office of Government Commerce (2002), *Managing Successful Projects with PRINCE2*, London: The Stationery Office.

SEE ALSO

Baselines and Baselining
Quality in Project Work

For opportunities... appropriate...

- Maximize...
- Maximize you...
- Have some contingency... benefits...
- Ensure there is...
- Identify 'triggers'... become realistically...
- Monitor frequently...

For Project Opportunities... following:

- Consider any...
- Prepare in case...
- If you have a many... proportion to...
- Monitor regularly...

For Project Opportunities...

- Monitor periodically...

PROJECT ISS...

You may recall that... affecting the ability... that meets this d... its exploitation from...

POSSIBLE HEA...

- **Reference number**...
- **Description** – provide... happen...
- **Raised** – by whom...
- **Likelihood** – suggested...
- **Benefit** – suggested... Outlay...
- **Trigger Signs** –...
- **Owner** – who is resp...
- **Actions** – What sh...

Reports in Projects and Programmes

Many Project Managers love their work and the challenges of delivering successful change and innovation in their organizations. However, many of them also strongly dislike report writing, seeing it as a time-consuming chore that takes them away from the dynamic aspects of the role they enjoy. While they sometimes delegate report writing, they may then take the resulting draft home, pull it apart and re-write it in their own style. The final report consumes double the effort, frustrates the Project Manager, his or her family – and the nominated report writer! H. G. Wells once said, 'No passion in the world is equal to the passion to alter someone else's draft' – so beware! Other dangers arise when report writing is unplanned, or when you postpone writing until a deadline is imminent. In both cases, the output may be rushed, incomplete, unchecked, inaccurate, or otherwise flawed.

WHAT TYPES OF DOCUMENTS AND REPORTS MIGHT YOU NEED?

There are a number of typical reports and major documents in and around projects, in two main categories, with examples:

1. **Action** – to identify the need for and to facilitate decisions:
   - Feasibility Study Report
   - Project Start-up Document, or Project Initiation Document if PRINCE®, including Plans, Business Case and budgets
   - Exception Report or other report of serious variance from plan or budget
   - Stage End Report.

2. **Information** – to keep stakeholders up to date, reporting progress and status.
   - Progress or Status Report, or Highlight Report if using PRINCE®
   - Lessons Learned Report, which may need some actions outside the scope of a project
   - End of Project or Project Closure Report.

DO YOU NEED TO GO INTO PRINT?

Why write a report? Is it the best or only way to trigger a decision, or pass on important information? Will it be worth the effort and time? Will it lack immediacy, or be obsolete immediately? Will it answer readers' questions?

What do reports have that other media lack? Reports:

- provide a permanent rather than transient record
- establish or extend an audit trail
- give a substantial and hard-to-ignore prompt when action is needed
- can be thoroughly checked before issue
- do not require an audience in one place at one time
- can build hard, quantified evidence into a compelling case
- are often required by corporate or project standards
- are expected at certain junctures, and thus familiar in purpose and format.

However, reports might:

- be written in such a manner that the message is lost or diluted
- not be read
- be unclear
- not be fully understood
- be dropped in a 'pending' tray
- be too large and cumbersome
- neither anticipate nor answer possible questions
- harm the author's reputation if flawed in any way.

Sometimes you will not need to make a decision on the media for your communications. Feasibility Study Reports, Project Initiation or Start-up Documents, End of Stage and End of Project Reports and other periodic status reports may be familiar and standardized. However, you will still need to write them, and write them well. If you are unfamiliar with report writing in general or project reports in particular, look up some recent examples and see how they are done in your organization. You might also find some 'boilerplate' text to cut and paste and save a little time, though be sparing with this approach.

Sometimes you may choose more than one medium, such as when you deliver a presentation backed up by a report. You may do this, for example, at the end of a Feasibility Study, when you need to generate impetus and enthusiasm for a recommendation, but provide a portfolio of compelling evidence, too detailed for a presentation. Using the dual approach, you can present highlights, and allow your audience to absorb written detail afterwards.

HOW MIGHT YOU START?

Have you ever heard or used the phrase, 'Think before you ink'? It still makes sense in the electronic age. Make sure you form your ideas and know exactly what you have to achieve before you try to write much other than notes. Johann Goethe described the risk of doing otherwise: 'When an idea is wanting, words can always be found to take its place.'

As a Project Manager, you are unlikely to need much research before you write reports. You will normally report on how you have planned a project, how a Project Stage is progressing, or on recommendations following a Feasibility Study. All the information you need should exist. All you need is to present it clearly, simply and logically. You may have heard of 'chaff', strewn out of warplanes to interfere with detection devices – similarly, we sometimes litter our documents with material that hides our intentions.

Suggestions – what you might typically include

Note that you should always use your organization's standards and formats for reports, though nothing should deter you from suggesting improvements.

Feasibility Study Report

A Feasibility Study is an early, high-level assessment of whether it would be practicable, desirable and worthwhile to grasp an opportunity or solve a problem and, if so, how. It should identify and evaluate optional solutions, their viability, and how each might be implemented. The report needs to provide sufficient information to justify recommendations on whether to proceed and, if so, how. So to aid any decision, include:

- brief background to the study
- the study's terms of reference
- the report's objectives
- a management summary (probably no larger than 5 per cent of text, or half a page for every ten pages of the report)
- solutions identified, normally including maintenance of the status quo
- solution approaches identified (such as buy or build, outsource, DIY or hire in a project team); note that you may have a range of solutions, or only one, with optional approaches, such as when the euro (€) replaced European currencies
- operational evaluation (can it satisfy the needs, and will we be able to use it effectively?) plus the rationale for any rejections
- technical evaluation (can we establish and maintain this?) plus the rationale for any rejections
- economic evaluation (will it provide acceptable returns on our investment? Can we afford to establish, operate and maintain this?) plus the rationale for any rejections
- recommendations for the solution and how to approach it, including next steps if the recommendation is accepted; note that this may form a Project Brief, or Project Terms of Reference
- appendices containing detailed evaluations and calculations.

Project Start-up Document (or Project Initiation Document if using PRINCE®)
Possible Contents:

- Introduction and Background
- Project Terms of Reference
- Project Organization
- Responsibilities Matrix
- Business Case
- Main Risks and Countermeasures
- Main Issues and Actions Recommended to Be Taken
- Controls
- Quality Method
- Project Plan and Plan for Stage One
- Project Budget and Budget for Stage One
- Stakeholder Matrix
- Communications Plan
- Exception Handling
- Configuration and Change Control.

Exception Report or other report of serious variance from plan or budget
An exception arises when controls indicate or forecast that 'plan' and 'actual' or 'budget' and 'spend' have deviated, or are about to deviate, beyond predefined acceptable levels. An Exception Report triggers corrective actions, by alerting the Steering Group, identifying optional solutions and their implications. Possible Contents:

- the Quantified Problem
- its Cause
- its likely implications (quantified to show the size of the problem)
- Options Available
- the pros and cons of each option – and the implications for Plans, Business Case, Risks and Issues
- Recommendations.

Stage End Report
The first objective is to show that work from a previous stage has been satisfactorily completed. The second is to verify that the justification for the project is still valid and that the plans and budgets for the next stage and for the remainder of the project are complete, clear and realistic. Possible Contents:

- plan for the stage just ending (updated with actuals) – note that if you use a Product Checklist, you may want to use this simpler format, which should contain all the key data.
- updated project plan and Business Case
- updated Risk and issue logs
- next stage plan and budget
- updated communications plan.

Progress or Status Report, or Highlight Report if using PRINCE®

This is a periodic, often two-weekly, status report in summarized form, hence the term 'highlight'. Possible Contents:

- period being reported (start and end dates)
- Schedule Status
- budget status
- outputs completed during period
- outputs planned for completion during next period
- problems encountered during period (with reference to existing or new Risk, Issue or Change Log entries)
- problems that may be encountered during next period (with reference to existing or new Risk, Issue or Change Log entries).

Lessons Learned Report

The purpose of such a report is to document any lessons that might help improve the running of future projects. It is best created by updates at the end of each stage, so that, where urgent and important, the lessons can be disseminated quickly. Possible Contents:

- project background and objectives
- project Scope
- Significant Project Constraints
- project deliverables (summarizing reason(s) for any significant time or budget variances and any lessons that should be learned, including strengths and weaknesses of the estimating method used)
- project Budget (showing the original budget, what was actually spent, and lessons learned)
- monitoring and control methods used and Lessons Learned
- The Main Project Risks and Issues, Their Impact and Lessons Learned
- quality methods and relevant outcomes
- Conclusions and Recommendations (to improve project management methods and techniques in your organization).

End of Project or Project Closure Report

Its two main purposes are: (1) to summarize the outcome of the project when compared to what was intended, and (2) to make observations and recommendations about the effectiveness, or ineffectiveness, of the project management techniques and tools used. It might usefully summarize such items as:

- what outcomes were planned and delivered, with explanations of any significant variations
- how the project performed against plan and budget
- high-level summary of lessons learned (see **Lessons Learned Report**)
- the impact of authorized changes
- the impact, where significant, of any risks and issues
- any benefits that have already been realized
- any actions recommended for follow-up after project closure.

ADVICE FROM FAMOUS WRITERS

Is it worth writing?

'He can compress the most words into the smallest ideas of any man I have ever met.'

Abraham Lincoln (of another lawyer)

Choosing the right word:

'I never write "metropolis" for seven cents because I can get the same price for "city". I never write "policeman" because I can get the same money for "cop".'   Mark Twain

'Small words work best and old small words work best of all.'   Winston Churchill

Note that the current English language has around half a million words, definitions, references, abbreviations and acronyms, yet we struggle to find one that expresses our meaning in a way that will be best understood by our readers.

Put yourself in the reader's shoes:

'Anything written to please the author is worthless.'   Blaise Pascal

'No-one can write decently who is distrustful of the reader's intelligence, or whose attitude is patronising.'   Elwyn B. White

'The two most engaging powers of an author are to make new things familiar and familiar things new.'   Samuel Johnson

Keep it simple – edit vigorously:

'Run your pen through every other word you have written; you have no idea what vigour it will give to your style.'   Sydney Smith

'Read your composition and when you meet a passage which you think is exceptionally fine, strike it out.'   Samuel Johnson

WHAT SHOULD YOU CHECK?

- Are you clear about the exact purpose?
- Do you know who will read it, and what their expectations are?
- Have you used any words in the report that you would not normally use when conversing on this topic?
- Have you used terms and words familiar to your readers? If unable to do this, have you added a brief 'Glossary of Terms'?
- Have you used any words to describe size or volume, such as 'big', 'many', 'a significant number', 'huge', 'expensive', 'costly', 'cheap', that might usefully be replaced by numbers?

- Have you used simple, clear language?
- Have you used several words where one would do?
- Have you told the readers everything they need to know?
- Have you told the readers anything they do not need to know?
- Have you anticipated possible questions and built in the answers?
- Is the structure and flow logical and helpful?
- Have you drawn any conclusions unsupported by content?
- Have you used appendices to avoid burying your key points under details?
- Have you sought and used feedback from third-party reviews of your report?
- Have you stated your purpose clearly, so that readers know what is expected of them, if anything?
- Did you avoid 'having a little whine' with your report? Have you always tried to express things positively, suggesting solutions for any problems you have identified?
- Have you avoided writing down to readers, insulting their intelligence?
- Have you avoided all flattery and sycophancy?

WHAT SHOULD YOU DO ABOUT JARGON?

What is jargon? It is either professional shorthand, or unintelligible gibberish, depending on the reader's viewpoint. Consider the risks that using jargon might create when you communicate about a project across functional or technical boundaries. Say, for example, you are running a project to set up some procurement functions on a new intranet. Your stakeholders will, as a minimum, include professionals from Procurement, Finance, Legal and Information Technology. You may also have stakeholders in every part of the organization that will use the latest procurement system, from many different professional backgrounds. On top of all this, you, as the Project Manager and at the heart of the communications network, will probably use terms unique to the business of managing projects – your own professional shorthand. There is always potential for a communications nightmare in these conditions. If you have ever heard a senior stakeholder say, 'I would sign this off, if only I knew what it means', you will recognize the problem.

You are likely to be the author of many project documents, so are well placed to minimize the frustration that jargon can create. One of your best options is to create a glossary, so that those unfamiliar with professional or technical terms can look up a definition, without the embarrassment of having to ask. While some professional terms are unique to specific projects, project management terms are not. Once you have created such a glossary, you can file it, perhaps with a Project Office and re-use it. It should be appropriate content for your intranet or online project filing. There is an extensive project glossary at the beginning of this manual.

CLICHÉS

Clichés are stereotyped phrases that, if you litter your document with them, can bore your readers and make your text lifeless and uninspiring. The term 'cliché' apparently comes from the early days of printing, when type had to be laboriously set using individual metal pieces, each containing an individual letter, number or punctuation mark. To save time, regularly used phrases were cast on single metal plates, or *clichés*. The only piece of advice on clichés is to avoid them like the plague!

Here is a cliché decoder:

Avoid like the plague	Don't do, don't use
At this point/moment in time	Now, today
Few and far between	Infrequent, uncommon
Tried and tested	Dependable, reliable
The bottom line	Profit, loss, or the main factor
In the not too distant future	Soon, on (date)
The reason being	Because

Check your documents to make sure that you have not over-used such phrases!

SEE ALSO

Glossary of Common Project Management Terms
Closing a Project
Lessons Learned
Post-project Review
Stages – Start and End Procedures

Request for Change

A Request for Change (RFC) is used in PRINCE® and non-PRINCE® environments when a stakeholder asks for a change to a product, or to one or more of its Acceptance Criteria. It is regarded as good practice for you to enable any such person to raise such a request directly, in which case it should also be recorded as a Project Issue. You may also find that someone will raise a Project Issue which, after examination, may then be recorded as a Request for Change.

WHY MIGHT IT BE USEFUL?

Projects stimulate their stakeholders to think about change and innovation, yet many Project Managers express pained surprise when someone requests even more change, even when it is relatively minor. You need to anticipate change requests and build in a simple process to handle them as a normal part of your project business.

WHEN MIGHT YOU NEED IT?

During the life of a project, it is unreasonable and irrational for you to require the rest of the world to stand still until you have finished. Changes will take place in the wider environment, your business organization, and its needs. Problems will arise, and opportunities will come and go. You need to provide ways of handling or deferring all these possible change pressures throughout.

HOW DO YOU USE IT?

1. Someone identifies a potential change. Check to see whether it has already been raised and examined, either as a Request for Change or a Project Issue.

2. Help the individual raise a Request for Change and explain the process.

3. Use normal methods for examining any Project Issue and, if appropriate, treat this as a 'Request for Change'.

4. If a customer wants to change something that had originally been agreed and planned, or to add to the requirements in any way, he or she needs to understand that the customer is likely to need to pay for the change if the request is accepted.

5. You will need to follow your Change Control Procedures and advise the customer of your forecast of any impact on project and stage objectives, scope, time, cost, other products, interfaces and risks.

WHAT SHOULD YOU CHECK?

- Is the description of the change clear and complete?
- Is the rationale for the change clear?
- Are the implications of not making the change clear?
- Is the importance of the change clear? Is it a 'must do', 'ought to do' or 'nice to do' type of change?
- Is the timing and urgency of the change clear?
- Are the objectives, scope and constraints of the change clear and quantified?
- Do you have enough information to conduct an Impact Analysis?

SEE ALSO

Change Control (includes sample forms and log)
Impact Analysis
Issue Management
PRINCE® 'Off Specification'

Responsibility Matrix

A Responsibility Matrix is a simple table that identifies accountability and responsibilities for project tasks, and records how you and your Steering Group have allocated them. While several individuals may be responsible for completing a task, only one named individual should be accountable for its completion. If accountability is shared, you risk hearing: 'I thought x was dealing with that.'

Have you ever been in a situation where something important has not been done because everyone thought someone else was doing it? Yes? You will probably be in a minority if you answered 'No.' Figure 66 shows a RACI Matrix, a table which lists some typical project tasks and identifies who is responsible, who is accountable, who should be consulted, and who should be kept informed. You may find it, or something similar, very useful at the start of a project or stage. You can 'lift' the tasks and the name of the person responsible for doing them directly from the Stage Plan, and fill in the blanks at the Steering Group meeting that approves the plan and authorizes work. You should be able to use your RACI Matrix at the heart of communications efforts for the stage.

WHAT SHOULD YOU CHECK?

- An important question: is it clear to you who is responsible for doing what in your project?
- A more important question: is it clear to each of them?
- Where does the buck stop if any project task is not done (on time, within budget, to specification, and so on)?
- Are there any overlaps in accountability? If so, can they be reduced or eliminated?
- Is it clear that if an accountable individual is not available, his or her accountability passes *upwards* to the next individual?
- Do you know who ought to be consulted on tasks in the project?
- Do you know who will need to be informed about tasks in the project?
- Have you forgotten any tasks or individuals?

Task	Who is Responsible for completing this task? (whole or part)	Who is Accountable for ensuring this task is done? (With what *individual* does the buck stop?)	Who should be Consulted about it?	Who should be Informed that it is being/has been done?
Agree Terms of Reference for Transition Stage	Transition Manager	Programme Manager	Programme Delivery Manager	Business Change Manager
Establish Transition Strategy	Transition Manager Transition Consultant	Transition Manager	Programme Delivery Manager Business Change Manager Project Managers	All potential Transition Stakeholders
Define Release Criteria	Transition Manager	Programme Manager	Programme Delivery Manager Business Change Manager Project Managers	All potential Transition Stakeholders
Design releases	Transition Manager Business Change Manager Project Managers Design Authority	Transition Manager	Programme Delivery Manager Business Unit Managers IT Support	All potential Transition Stakeholders
Plan a release	Release Manager Business Change Manager Release Project Managers	Transition Manager	Business Unit Managers IT Support	All Release Stakeholders
Authorize a release	Programme Manager	Programme Director	Business Unit Managers	All Release Stakeholders
Prepare user environment	Business Change Manager	Business Unit Manager	Release Manager Business Change Manager Release Project Managers	All other Release Stakeholders
Plan user resourcing	Business Change Manager	Business Unit Manager	Release Manager Business Change Manager Release Project Managers	Human Resources Manager
Design End to End Processes	Design Authority Business Unit Managers	Design Authority	Project Managers	All potential Transition Stakeholders
Create user procedures	Business Change Manager Project Managers	Business Unit Manager	User Procedures Standards	Trainers
Manage Release Stakeholders	Transition Manager Release Manager Project Managers	Programme Manager	Release Stakeholders	Programme Director
Commission hardware and IT infrastructure	IT Support Manager Suppliers Project Managers	IT Support Manager	IT Technical Strategist	All potential Transition Stakeholders
Create and manage Release Business Case	Release Manager Business Change Manager	Release Manager	Programme Delivery Manager Project Managers Business Unit Managers	Programme Director Programme Manager
Set up Rapid Response Team for transition support	Programme Manager	Programme Director	Transition Manager Business Change Manager	
Manage communications with participating Business Units	Business Change Manager Transition Manager Release Manager Project Managers	Business Change Manager		

Note: This is an example only, not intended to represent a complete Transition Stage, and not for use without amendment to satisfy particular project characteristics. It is also recommended that you attach a page showing the named individual holding each role at the start of the stage, and issue amendments if job-holders change.

Figure 66 Sample matrix for programme transition (development to operations)

SEE ALSO

Communications Plan

RESPONSIBILITY
MATRIX

Risk Management

A Project Risk is a possible future event or situation that, if it happens, will affect the ability of a project to arrive at its intended outcome.

WHY DO YOU NEED TO MANAGE PROJECT RISKS?

Managing a project is concerned to a large degree with managing through uncertainty towards certainty. While you should always try to have a precise statement of requirements, a comprehensive plan, sound estimates, and clear dependencies, known resource requirements, a skilled team and reliable suppliers, you also know that whenever you are dealing with change or innovation, things may not always turn out as expected. You need some procedures in place to record those things you can identify that might throw you off course, and some measures ready to deal with them.

WHEN DO YOU NEED TO MANAGE PROJECT RISKS?

You should identify initial risks as part of any pre-project process. It is very important that if you need to seek approval for one of a range of optional ways forward, or to pursue one project at the expense of another, those making such decisions have a good understanding of the pitfalls. Before you start any project, you should have a Risk Log. Once you have created it, the management of risks should become a continuous process.

Risks are in the future, waiting to trip you up, and for you to avoid if possible. If avoidance fails and the dreaded thing happens, you will then be in the present, so a 'Risk' will become an 'Issue' and will need to be dealt with.

If you do not face a new situation on your project every working day, something is wrong! If you do face a new situation every day, something has changed. Have changes triggered a Risk that has now become a reality? Has a new Risk emerged? You should see now that you need your Risk Log nearby. You will find a daily inspection valuable, and will not have wasted the five minutes you might use.

HOW MIGHT YOU GO ABOUT IT?

You can set up Project Risk Logs and procedures using Microsoft Excel® or any spreadsheet software, and you will find sample pages below. You may be wise to keep your log on a network if possible, making it readily accessible to stakeholders, though you may wish to apply a 'read only' restriction, so that updates are dealt with by the Project Office if you have one, or under your control if you don't.

If you use a similar approach for your projects, you may wish to apply or adapt your own ratings and calculations. You can also keep all the log pages and procedures together by using several worksheets in the same workbook. You will see in the sample in Figures 67 and 68 that Risks, Issues and procedures appear on three tabs in the same workbook. You will find guidelines below, and can use very similar logs in both project and programme environments. This is very useful to enable you to escalate Risks or Issues from project to programme level for management, or to receive those delegated from programme to project.

Risk No.	Risk type	Date raised	Raised by	Risk descriptions and likely consequences	Likelihood (1–4)	Impact (1–7)	Overall Risk Rating	Owner	Action type (Prevent/ Reduce/ Accept/ Transfer	Countermeasures

Figure 67   Possible Risk Log headings

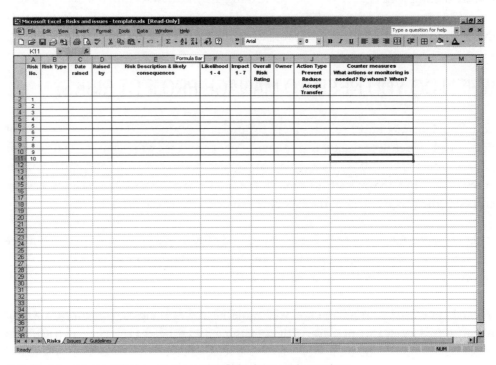

Note: The tabs at bottom left give access to project Risks, Issues and procedures

Figure 68   Sample Risk Log spreadsheet template

There are a number of sources for identifying risks:

- existing Risk Logs
- Project Risk Workshops
- generic Project Risks identified in project management publications
- new items identified in progress reports
- concerns raised by individuals involved in or affected by a project
- Project Library information on similar projects.

The headings in Figure 66 are almost all self-explanatory. See the following notes where this is not the case and where I have used some analogies.

Column 2, Risk type

This typically refers to the project, programme or business.

Column 5, Risk description and likely consequences

A complete description is essential here. Entries have to stand up to the 'So what?' test. A useful phrase every time you make an entry in this column is '... which would mean that ...'. Do not simply write 'X might be delayed', but try to describe the consequences – 'X might be delayed, which would mean that we do not deliver Y by dd/mm/yy. This would trigger the penalty clause on that contract which would cost the company £nnnn per month or part month.' This should help focus the attention of those reading the log!

Column 10, Action type

Risk prevention is similar in its aims and implications to fire, crime and accident prevention. It may incur costs, take time and may or may not work all the time, but if you compare the costs of the prevention with the losses you might incur if the Risk becomes reality, it is a sensible investment. Your main aim is to prevent a particular Risk striking your project, and if 100 per cent security is not possible, to reduce the likelihood.

Risk reduction (mitigation) is usually a second line of defence aimed at minimizing the impact of any risk that becomes a reality. In the 'fire' example, you can do many things in the home and office to help prevent it, but if it happens, the investment you have made in smoke detectors, alarms, sprinklers and extinguishers can save life and property.

Risk acceptance might appear where the likelihood is high, the impact is moderate or low and you do not believe that the costs of prevention or impact reduction are justified. In these circumstances, you might consider adding some contingency time to your plan, so that when 'it' happens, you can resolve the damage and move on, still within your plan. If 'it' does not happen, you might even be ahead of the game.

Discussions on **Risk transfer** seem to generate heat in discussions between Project Managers. Transfer approaches might include insuring yourself against the consequences of some misfortune, using penalty clauses in contracts, or suing whoever you believe to be responsible or negligent. If you are running a project, this might provide some (very) long-term compensation, but your project may have been wrecked and irrecoverable years earlier.

Risk Management should include countermeasures to prevent something happening, or to reduce the likelihood of it happening, or to reduce the impact if it does happen, or to accept it and perhaps provide some contingency (time and effort). When the forecast event/situation happens and becomes a reality, it is no longer a Risk but an Issue, and should be transferred to the Issues Log, with audit trail information on both Logs. You should initiate countermeasures to reduce its impact. Note that the opposite situation can exist, where you need to *ensure* that something will happen (failure to happen will be the problem).

Impact

This can be ranked using the following scale:

7   severe or terminal damage to the whole change initiative
6   serious adverse effect on date or budget of whole change initiative
5   severe or terminal damage to the project
4   serious delays or budget implications for the project
3   delays or budget problems for a Project Stage
2   significant waste or inconvenience
1   moderate waste or inconvenience.

Likelihood

You can use the following scale to assess this:

4   much more likely to happen than not
3   greater than even chance of it happening
2   less than even chance of it happening
1   much less likely to happen than to happen, but cannot be entirely ruled out.

You can use a simple spreadsheet to formula to calculate the overall risk rating automatically when you enter the numeric Likelihood and Impact ratings.

You may need to consider the role of a programme here:

● **Programme Risks** – If there is a programme, it may need to own and manage everything with an Impact rating of 6 or 7, plus everything with an Overall rating of 15 or greater.
● **Project Risks** - All others, or *all* if there is no programme.

RED/AMBER/GREEN RATINGS

A number of organizations use a RAG system (Red, Amber, Green) where Red is a potential 'showstopper', Amber is a serious warning, and Green indicates that you know a risk is there but will not lose sleep over it unless it worsens. With a numeric system, you might link number ranges to the colours – for example, an overall risk rating 15+ is Red, 9–14 is Amber and ≤ 8 is Green.

OPTIONAL RATING METHODS

You may prefer to use a simple, judgemental, non-numeric matrix based on the following judgements.

For Likelihood/Probability, you can use the following rating system:

- **High** – more likely to happen than not to happen
- **Medium** – even (50:50) chance that it might happen
- **Low** – more likely not to happen than to happen.

For Impact, you could use the schema set out in Figure 69. A 'High' or 'Red' rating should be given if any one of schedule, budget or objectives is likely to be seriously affected.

Effect on ⟶	Schedule	Budget	Objectives
Impact rating			
High/Red	Serious	Serious	Serious
Medium/Amber	Significant	Significant	Significant
Low/Green	Minor	Minor	Minor

Figure 69   Rating system for risk impact

RISK TRIGGERS

A Risk Trigger is any signal, such as an event or non-event by a defined date, that what you feared has started to happen, a Risk has become a reality or its likelihood or potential impact has grown and you need to implement agreed actions to prevent or minimize damage to your project. An example might be when you have logged a Risk that a third-party supplier might fail to deliver a vital component on time. If this delivery is delayed, it would mean that you will have insufficient time to test it before you need to assemble it with components you produce, test the full assembly, and install and commission it on your client's site. Risk Triggers that your stakeholders should be able to identify might include late design, late prototype and lack of information on progress at checkpoint meetings or at 'show me' reviews. Early triggers should ensure you tighten up monitoring; later triggers might enlist the aid of your Sponsor, Champion, or even Chief Executive to 'influence' his or her opposite number in the supplier organization. An even later trigger might be for your team to set up a shiftwork approach, to speed up the testing, assembly and re-testing.

RISK RESPONSES

For any Project Risk, your actions may include one (or possibly more) of the following:

- **Acceptance** – Project Managers accept many Risks as part of their role in handling uncertainty, change and innovation. In this context, it implies formal acceptance that you will do nothing specific to manage a Risk you have identified, and if it then happens, you will put up with the consequences.

- **Avoidance** – Some Risks may arise as features of an approach or solution you consider. There may be other approaches or solutions that do not incur this Risk, and selecting one of those is a risk avoidance decision.

- **Reduce probability** – This is a 'prevention is better than cure' approach, where the actions you take attempt to prevent or minimize the likelihood of it happening. This response may be more relevant when you have some ability to control or influence the circumstances in which the Risk might become a reality, such as when the source is within your own organization.

- **Reduce impact** – You may establish contingency or fall-back measures, including plans and budgets that you will use to minimize the adverse effects of a Risk if or when it happens.

- **Transfer** – Your organization may be able to share Risks with customers and/or suppliers, using incentives, warranties or penalties. Insurance may also be an option. Though none of these approaches is likely to keep a project on track, they might later help to defray additional costs.

When considering insurance, remember the late Tommy Cooper once said that his insurance policy covered him against falling off a roof, but not against hitting the ground! You will need to specify very carefully the cover you need, and check the small print carefully first. Better still, ask an insurance specialist or commercial lawyer to do this.

WHAT SHOULD YOU CHECK?

Pre-project

- Did you make a candid initial assessment of the Risks for each possible project option?
- Have you created a Risk Log for the selected option?
- Have you established criteria for Risks that you will simply accept? Note that the terms 'Accept' and 'Acceptable' mean that you know the Risk is there, but have decided to live with it without taking any action, unless monitoring indicates that the threat is about to grow or has grown.

Project

- Did you conduct a Risk Workshop with project stakeholders during the project start-up to maximize your understanding of all the Risks?
- Have you updated the log with all this information?
- Is each entry in each log specific, and are impacts/consequences clearly described ('... which means (would mean) that ...')?
- Are all the actions and countermeasures clear, specific and each owned by an individual?
- Do you monitor the Risks continuously?
- Do you have a diary system for reminding risk owners ahead of actions needed by them?
- Do all stakeholders have access to the log?
- Is there an agenda item for Project Board meetings to review risks?

See Figure 70 below for a sample spreadsheet, where you can include guidelines, procedures and rating 'rules' on a worksheet, accessible via a tab. See Figure 71 for a diagram showing a simple risk procedure. Note also that the procedure does not continue beyond escalation to a Steering Group, because of the many variables that might come into play at this point. Options might range from abandoning the project, through abandoning the current plan and implementing an Exception Plan, updating the current plan and funding some contingency measures, or even taking the same approach as the RMS *Titanic* – steaming on at full speed aboard the unsinkable project.

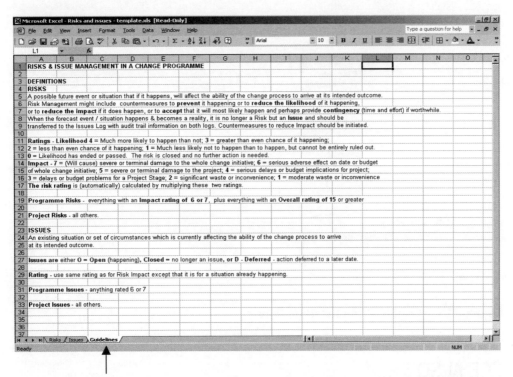

Figure 70   Risks and Issues – programme procedures sample (numeric rating method)

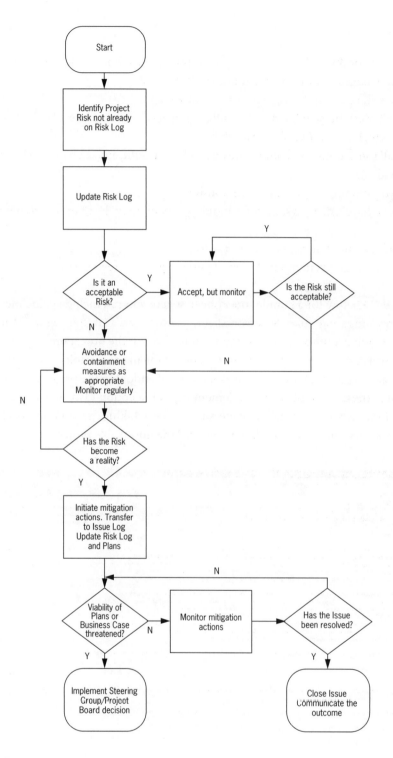

Figure 71   Possible Risk procedure flow

SEE ALSO

Impact Analysis
Issue Management

Scheduling

A Project schedule is normally presented as a Gantt or bar chart, listing each task down the left side, illustrated by a horizontal bar to show the start, duration and finish, which readers can interpret by reference to dates across the top of the chart.

Henry Gantt (1861–1919) was a pioneering management consultant in the USA who developed a system for predicting and tracking production figures over time. Gantt charts and their derivatives have evolved from his production work to become one of the main tools of project management.

When people talk about a Project Plan, it is very likely that they are referring to a schedule, which is usually the culmination of a series of planning tasks that may well have started with the creation of a Work Breakdown Structure. You may then have translated this into a precedence (network) diagram to establish sequence and priorities, then estimated the effort needed to complete each task, and calculated the overall duration after considering resourcing options and plotting the critical path(s). Finally, you would have been ready to produce a schedule by transferring all this information to a calendar-based format, taking account of working and non-working days, holiday periods, and known milestones and date constraints. Figure 72 shows a simple schedule.

ID	Start	Task Name	End	Duration	Mar 2 2003							Mar 9 2003							Mar 16 2003					
					3	4	5	6	7	8	9	10	11	12	13	14	15	16	17	18	19	20	21
1	03/03/2003	Task 1	06/03/2003	3d 4h																			
2	07/03/2003	Task 2	11/03/2003	2d 4h																			
3	07/03/2003	Task 3	07/03/2003	1d																			
4	11/03/2003	Task 4	14/03/2003	3d 4h																			
5	17/03/2003	Task 5	24/03/2003	6d																			

Figure 72   Example of a project schedule

WHY MIGHT IT BE USEFUL?

As a Project Manager, a stakeholder question you are likely to need to answer frequently is: 'When can I have . . . ?' Whether the question is about the final delivery date for a project, such as 'When can my staff move into the new office accommodation?', or something lower down the priority range, such as 'When can I see the first draft of the Issue Log format?', you need to be able to respond. Your Project Plan or your Stage Plan, presented in schedule format, will help you answer these questions.

WHEN MIGHT YOU NEED IT?

There is a more fundamental need for your scheduling skills when you present both Project and Stage Plans for approvals at different times, to gain authorizations to proceed. Those giving the approvals will be most interested in plans that show what they can expect, when, from whom, what resources will they need to commit and pay for when, and how tasks will be sequenced to deliver the required outputs. You will present this information in a schedule, most often as a Gantt or bar chart and, of course, you will need to use a schedule so that you can develop the budget for the project and its stages.

HOW MIGHT YOU APPROACH SCHEDULING?

A suggested six-step scheduling approach follows, with examples and illustrations.

Step 1: Create a Work Breakdown Structure

It has been indicated elsewhere that a Work Breakdown Structure (WBS) is one of the keys to successful planning, and you should consider developing a WBS as the first step in developing each plan you create, both for a project and for each of its stages. A WBS is a planning structure, usually a list or chart, that you create to show how the work to deliver a given project or stage is to be broken down into the tasks and sub-tasks that you and your team will need to complete. For example, if you needed to plan the Requirements Definition Stage for a systems upgrade, you may start the creation of a structured list WBS as in Figure 73.

Your WBS might then continue by showing tasks for analysis of findings and writing a report of the findings and recommendations. Note that some find it useful to work with a group of project stakeholders to develop a Work Breakdown Structure and often use Post-it® notes to workshop the first-pass diagram. Note that the example in Figure 73 is only an illustration of the planning technique, and is not intended for practical use in requirements definition work.

Step 2: Create a precedence diagram

A precedence diagram shows the logical flows and dependencies between tasks. You need to work out the sequence of all the tasks, identifying those you will need to start or

```
1    Existing system fact-finding
     1.1    Conduct user interviews
            1.1.1    Interview Department A Users.
            1.1.2    Interview Department B Users.
            1.1.3    Interview Department C Users.

     1.2    Identify interfaces
            1.2.1    Identify inter-departmental interfaces.
            1.2.2    Identify external interfaces.

     1.3    Review documents and files
            1.3.1    Review procedures.
            1.3.2    Review internally created documents.
            1.3.3    Review externally created documents.
            1.3.4    Review files and contents.

     1.4    Document existing system
            1.4.1    Create physical data flow diagram.
            1.4.2    Create data model.

     1.5    Review findings with users, and update as needed
            1.5.1    Review with Department A Users.
            1.5.2    Review with Department B Users.
            1.5.3    Review with Department C Users.
            1.5.4    Update findings following reviews.
            1.5.5    Review all findings with combined users.
```

Figure 73   Sample structured list WBS for a Requirements Definition Stage

complete before you can start work on others. If you have used Post-it® notes to develop your Work Breakdown Structure, you will be able to re-use them across a board or wall, to work out sequences and dependencies. You will find that a Stakeholder Workshop is an excellent approach, as you will be able to develop understanding and some ownership of the eventual schedule.

So, use a precedence diagram to establish the logical flow and sequence. At this early stage, you will not attempt to show any information about the physical aspects of the work, such as who, when, how and how long; hence the alternative term, 'logical' network diagram. An example is shown in Figure 74.

When you are satisfied with the first-pass precedence diagram, you may need to return to

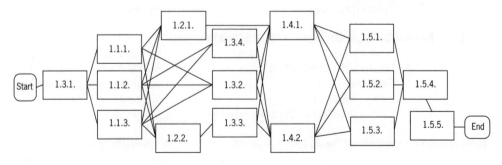

Figure 74   Sample precedence diagram (logical flow)

your WBS diagram to update it with any new tasks that constructing the network has helped you to identify, or perhaps even to remove any found to be superfluous. At the end of this second step, you have a working idea of the required tasks and their logical dependencies.

Step 3: Estimate the effort required

Effort is the amount of work needed to complete a task – an assessment of 'how big' the task is. In project work, this is typically measured in person-hours, person-days, person-weeks, or even person-months or years. For this purpose, it is best to regard a person as a 'standard' individual with the ideal mix of knowledge, skill and experience to do each specific task. You can adjust the estimates later, when you allocate real people to each task and assess each individual's actual knowledge, skill and experience. Once you have estimated standard times for each task, you can then move on to Step 4, where you can use the Critical Path Method to estimate the duration – that is, how long the whole process might take in elapsed days, weeks or months, whichever is appropriate to the work you need to undertake. Let us assume that we will estimate in person-days, which is probably appropriate for this kind of work. Figure 75 shows sample estimates against the tasks needed for this sub-section of a Requirements Definition Stage.

1	**Existing system fact-finding**	
1.1	**User interviews:** Assumption made that each interview will take one person-day each to plan, conduct and document, except for Department A, which has added complexity and may take one more day, both for interviews and for reviews.	
	1.1.1 Interview Department A Users.	4 person-days
	1.1.2 Interview Department B Users.	3 person-days
	1.1.3 Interview Department C Users.	3 person-days
1.2	**Identify interfaces**	
	1.2.1 Identify inter-departmental interfaces.	2 person-days
	1.2.2 Identify external interfaces.	1 person-day
1.3	**Review documents and files**	
	1.3.1 Review procedures.	5 person-days
	1.3.2 Review internally created documents.	3 person-days
	1.3.3 Review externally created documents.	2 person-days
	1.3.4 Review files and contents.	6 person-days
1.4	**Document existing system**	
	1.4.1 Create physical data flow diagram.	1 person-day
	1.4.2 Create data model.	2 person-days
1.5	**Review findings with users, and update as needed**	
	1.5.1 Review with Department A Users.	2 person-days (excluding user)
	1.5.2 Review with Department B Users.	1 person-day (excluding user)
	1.5.3 Review with Department C Users.	1 person-day (excluding user)
	1.5.4 Update findings following reviews.	3 person-days
	1.5.5 Review all findings with combined users.	1 person-day
Total resource requirement for Systems Analyst		**40 person-days**

Figure 75   Sample estimates added to the Work Breakdown Structure

You now have enough information to estimate the overall duration and any potential critical path(s). To do this, you need to move on to Step 4.

Step 4: Estimate first-pass overall duration

To do this, you can use a PERT/CPM approach by adding estimates to the network, as shown in Figure 76.

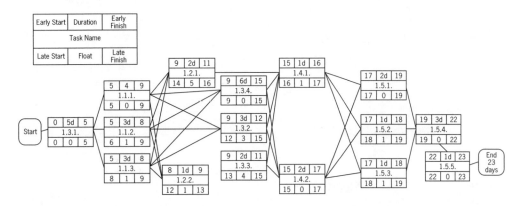

Figure 76   PERT/CPM diagram to calculate first-pass overall duration

For a refresher on this technique, see the entry on **Network Analysis and the Critical Path**. In Figure 75, you will see that the overall duration has been calculated as 23 days, and the longest duration from Start to End flows through 1.3.1, 1.1.1, 1.3.4, 1.4.2, 1.5.1, 1.5.4 and 1.5.5. If you only have 23 working days to complete the work, this would be the critical path. However, we have made some assumptions that need to be checked out now, the most significant being that we will have three business analysts to conduct the work where it looks realistic to conduct tasks in parallel, such as the interviews (1.1.1 to 1.1.3 inclusive). If we only have one business analyst, requiring all the tasks to be done in a straight-line sequence, you will have an overall duration of 40 days, minus any loss factors yet to be considered.

Step 5: Create the schedule

The final step requires us to transfer all the information we have developed thus far on to a schedule – a Gantt chart with our tasks on the vertical axis and real dates on the horizontal axis. Let us also assume that our assumption that we would have three business analysts at our disposal is also correct. At last, we can start to develop a schedule. The first pass through this using 'standard' Business Analysts should look something like Figure 77.

You will notice that only the Level 3 tasks (for example, 1.1.1) use resources; the Level 2 (summary) tasks (for example, 1.1) are group related tasks. At Level 1 on this diagram, you just have the 'project' name. The duration in workdays is still 23. We now need to assign 'real' resources, rather than those notional 'standard' business analysts. For simplicity, we will call them Analysts X, Y and Z. Analyst X is also a supervisor and has to run a small team. For this reason, we can only assign 60 per cent of her time to project work, though

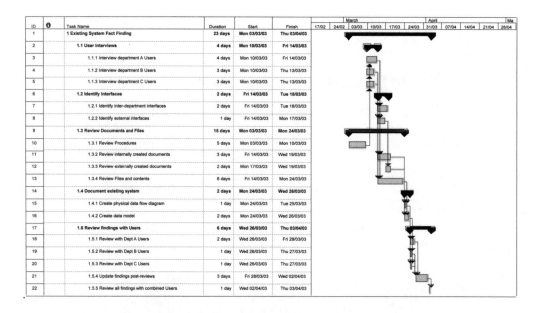

ID	ⓘ	Task Name	Duration	Start	Finish
1		1 Existing System Fact Finding	23 days	Mon 03/03/03	Thu 03/04/03
2		1.1 User Interviews	4 days	Mon 10/03/03	Fri 14/03/03
3		1.1.1 Interview department A Users	4 days	Mon 10/03/03	Fri 14/03/03
4		1.1.2 Interview department B Users	3 days	Mon 10/03/03	Thu 13/03/03
5		1.1.3 Interview department C Users	3 days	Mon 10/03/03	Thu 13/03/03
6		1.2 Identify Interfaces	2 days	Fri 14/03/03	Tue 18/03/03
7		1.2.1 Identify inter-department interfaces	2 days	Fri 14/03/03	Tue 18/03/03
8		1.2.2 Identify external interfaces	1 day	Fri 14/03/03	Mon 17/03/03
9		1.3 Review Documents and Files	15 days	Mon 03/03/03	Mon 24/03/03
10		1.3.1 Review Procedures	5 days	Mon 03/03/03	Mon 10/03/03
11		1.3.2 Review internally created documents	3 days	Fri 14/03/03	Wed 19/03/03
12		1.3.3 Review externally created documents	2 days	Mon 17/03/03	Wed 19/03/03
13		1.3.4 Review Files and contents	6 days	Fri 14/03/03	Mon 24/03/03
14		1.4 Document existing system	2 days	Mon 24/03/03	Wed 26/03/03
15		1.4.1 Create physical data flow diagram	1 day	Mon 24/03/03	Tue 25/03/03
16		1.4.2 Create data model	2 days	Mon 24/03/03	Wed 26/03/03
17		1.5 Review findings with Users	6 days	Wed 26/03/03	Thu 03/04/03
18		1.5.1 Review with Dept A Users	2 days	Wed 26/03/03	Fri 28/03/03
19		1.5.2 Review with Dept B Users	1 day	Wed 26/03/03	Thu 27/03/03
20		1.5.3 Review with Dept C Users	1 day	Wed 26/03/03	Thu 27/03/03
21		1.5.4 Update findings post-reviews	3 days	Fri 28/03/03	Wed 02/04/03
22		1.5.5 Review all findings with combined Users	1 day	Wed 02/04/03	Thu 03/04/03

Figure 77   First-pass schedule

we will also assign her to Department A work, the main user, and 40 per cent to those tasks the team needs to work on together. Analyst Y is as close as we get to a 'standard' resource – capable and experienced. He has some small residual maintenance duties from earlier projects, so we will assign him for 80 per cent availability on Department B, and 60 per cent on joint tasks. Finally, Analyst Z has just completed training, so is less experienced, though has no other competing tasks. We will assign her at 60 per cent availability as a relative newcomer on Department C tasks, and at 50 per cent on joint tasks. You will see in Figure 78 that things have now changed significantly, and the overall duration is down to 17 days over a 23-day period, with 5 working days every week.

ID	ⓘ	Task Name	Duration	Start	Finish	Resource Names
1		1 Existing System Fact Finding	16.78 days	Mon 03/03/03	Tue 25/03/03	
2		1.1 User Interviews	4 days	Wed 05/03/03	Tue 11/03/03	
3		1.1.1 Interview department A Users	4 days	Wed 05/03/03	Tue 11/03/03	X[60%]
4		1.1.2 Interview department B Users	3 days	Wed 05/03/03	Mon 10/03/03	Y[80%]
5		1.1.3 Interview department C Users	3 days	Wed 05/03/03	Mon 10/03/03	Z[60%]
6		1.2 Identify Interfaces	4.2 days	Tue 11/03/03	Mon 17/03/03	
7		1.2.1 Identify inter-department interfaces	2.1 days	Tue 11/03/03	Mon 17/03/03	X[40%],Y[60%],Z[50%]
8		1.2.2 Identify external interfaces	0.5 days	Tue 11/03/03	Tue 11/03/03	X[40%],Y[60%],Z[50%]
9		1.3 Review Documents and Files	10.83 days	Mon 03/03/03	Mon 17/03/03	
10		1.3.1 Review Procedures	2 days	Mon 03/03/03	Wed 05/03/03	X[40%],Y[60%],Z[50%]
11		1.3.2 Review internally created documents	1.7 days	Tue 11/03/03	Wed 12/03/03	X[40%],Y[60%],Z[50%]
12		1.3.3 Review externally created documents	2.63 days	Tue 11/03/03	Mon 17/03/03	X[40%],Y[60%],Z[50%]
13		1.3.4 Review files and contents	3.2 days	Tue 11/03/03	Fri 14/03/03	X[40%],Y[60%],Z[50%]
14		1.4 Document existing system	1.95 days	Mon 17/03/03	Wed 19/03/03	
15		1.4.1 Create physical data flow diagram	1 day	Mon 17/03/03	Tue 18/03/03	Y[60%],Z[50%]
16		1.4.2 Create data model	1.95 days	Mon 17/03/03	Wed 19/03/03	Y[60%],Z[50%]
17		1.5 Review findings with Users	4 days	Wed 19/03/03	Tue 25/03/03	
18		1.5.1 Review with Dept A Users	2 days	Wed 19/03/03	Fri 21/03/03	X[60%]
19		1.5.2 Review with Dept B Users	1 day	Wed 19/03/03	Thu 20/03/03	Y[80%]
20		1.5.3 Review with Dept C Users	1 day	Wed 19/03/03	Thu 20/03/03	Z[50%]
21		1.5.4 Update findings post-reviews	1 day	Fri 21/03/03	Mon 24/03/03	X[40%],Y[60%],Z[50%]
22		1.5.5 Review all findings with combined Users	1 day	Mon 24/03/03	Tue 25/03/03	X[33%],Y[33%],Z[33%]

Figure 78   Resourced schedule

We have now reduced the duration by assigning more than one resource to some tasks, so that, for example, a task which requires six days of effort (1.3.4 – Review Files and Contents) should be completed in 3.2 days using all three business analysts. Note that some tasks, such as this one, might lend themselves to this approach – more resources means less time – but some do not. For example, if three interviewers attend one interview, not only is it unlikely to be completed in one-third of the time, but it may actually take longer.

Now you have a schedule. Before you take it any further, you need to check to ensure that any milestones set for your project will be achieved, and any time constraints satisfied. You may need to go around the loop another time to achieve this, though it is possible that, with the resources at your disposal, you cannot achieve what is required in the available time. It is better that you recognize this now and alert your Sponsor or Steering Group to the risk immediately, rather than when the problem surfaces in due course.

Even when notionally complete, your schedule is not fully 'fit for purpose' yet, as you should arrange for a third-party review, preferably by a project management peer group, to make sure that the schedule is complete, free from errors as far as possible, and forms a sound basis for decision-making. Once reviewed, you will be able to use it as a basis for budgeting, then submit it for approval by your Project Steering Group or Sponsor, and gain authorization to use it.

You may also wish to revisit the critical path. You should be able to switch the view in your planning software to see a PERT Chart view with the critical path highlighted. If this path is critical, there are a number of things you can still do in an attempt to achieve on-time delivery of the outputs. These could include:

1. **Move people away from work on non-critical tasks onto the critical tasks** – Be aware that this can be risky if there is insufficient 'float' on the non-critical tasks, which could mean that if they are deferred, they could soon become 'critical', too. Check your float!

2. **Extend the working day and use overtime** – This usually needs both goodwill and rewards, either in the form of overtime pay if available, or time off in lieu at a later date if not.

3. **Institute weekend working** – This requires even more goodwill and incentives.

4. **Engage highly skilled contract staff short-term** – This can be a pragmatic solution, provided that you do a simple cost-benefit analysis on the implications of lateness versus the extra costs of contract staff. The other potential problems here are that getting the right skills at short notice may be impossible, and the work to induct people into the team and train them to use your standards and tools may consume other vital resources.

You will note that solutions 2–4 may have budget implications, so make sure you consider these, too.

Step 6: Calculate schedule costs for input to your budget

You will need to follow your organization's standards on project budgeting, so ensure you are familiar with the approach and the rules. Your budget is likely to consist of direct and indirect costs, and capital and non-capital items. Your project team will be 'direct' costs to the project, and you should be able to use your planning software to produce cost information for inclusion in the budget. If, for example, Resource X costs £40, Y £35 and Z £20 per hour, the planning software should tell you that for the work in our example, the total direct cost would be £5648.36. Clearly, there will be other costs, such as office space, equipment, supplies, computer network usage, telephones and so on, that you will need to include in the budget.

WHAT SHOULD YOU CHECK?

Step 1: Create a Work Breakdown Structure

- Have you created a WBS? If not, do you have a reliable method for identifying all the work to be done?
- Have you engaged your stakeholders in the development of a WBS, where this is appropriate?
- Did you arrange a third-party review of the WBS, to help ensure its completeness and logic?
- Do all the tasks on the WBS have unique identities, probably numeric, that will stay with them throughout? If not, how do you plan to link tasks to higher-level groups of tasks or differentiate between similar tasks?

Step 2: Create a precedence diagram

- Have you created a precedence diagram or logical network diagram, to help establish sequence and dependencies between tasks?
- Have you engaged your stakeholders in the development of a logical network, where this is appropriate?
- Did you arrange a third-party review of the logical network, to help ensure its completeness and logic?
- Have you carried forward the unique identifiers from the WBS?
- Have you checked to make sure that all the lowest-level tasks on the WBS appear on the logical network?

Step 3: Estimate the effort required

- Have you estimated how big each task on the WBS is in person-time units?
- Have you used 'standard' skill levels (a person with the ideal mixture of knowledge, skill and experience)?
- Have you used project histories or a formula to create the estimates. Have you checked your estimates with fellow professionals?
- Do you now have an estimate for the total effort required by the project or stage? If so, move on to Step 4.

Step 4: Estimate first-pass overall duration

● Have you brought together the information from the 'effort estimating' and the logical network?
● Have you completed a left-to-right pass, to establish the possible overall duration?
● Have you completed a right-to-left (reverse) pass, to identify the possible critical path(s) and the float on non-critical paths?
● Does the overall duration meet your organization's requirements, or is it too long?

Step 5: Create the schedule

● Did you use a planning software tool with which you are fully familiar?
● Have you retained the structure developed during development of the Work Breakdown Structure? Are all the lowest-level tasks grouped under the higher-level tasks, as they were on the WBS?
● Have you retained any unique identifier for each task, so that it is easy to relate a task on the schedule to the same task on the WBS?
● Have you assigned resources and adjusted their availability to allow for non-project work and the level of knowledge, experience and skill they have in relation to the tasks they need to perform?
● Did you seek a third-party review from other experienced planners, and respond to their input?
● Is there any need to adjust assignments in order to meet any deadlines? If so, have you assessed the cost implications, if any?
● Will the schedule meet milestones and work within known constraints?
● If there are one or more tight 'drop-dead' dates, have you considered back-scheduling to establish the latest dates on which the project, stage or specific tasks must start in order to give some chance of success? Have you discussed the risks with your Sponsor or Steering Group?
● Will the schedule provide you with a sound basis on which to track and control progress? Does it show who should be doing what and when all tasks should be completed?

Step 6: Calculate schedule costs for input to your budget

● Have you assigned costs for the resources to be used in the plan?
● Have you allowed for any overtime rates, if likely to be used?
● Have you transferred this direct cost information to your budget?

SEE ALSO

Back-scheduling
Budgets for Project Work
Change Control
Constraints
Milestones and Milestone Plans

Network Analysis and the Critical Path
Planning Checklist

Scope

When you conduct a project, you should have a precise set of aims, and a plan and a budget to enable you to achieve them. You should be aiming to deliver specific outputs to identified stakeholders for a pre-defined purpose within a pre-defined period. Many projects encounter difficulties directly related to scope. If the project scope is inadequately defined from the outset, you will be left unsure whether to include or exclude certain tasks. If you ask, you risk being told to include them, but with no extra budget. If you do not ask and stick to what you think, one or more stakeholders may say: 'I did not get what I expected from the project.' On other occasions, the scope is well defined and agreed at the outset, but then grows to include tasks never originally planned.

When projects fail, they often do so not because of one catastrophic problem, but as the result of the unnoticed accumulation of many small ones. This often comes about because of a well-known, sometimes fatal disease known as 'Scope Creep' that can attack previously healthy projects. You project can catch it when you agree to a small 'favour' to help one stakeholder with a minor extension to the scope. Unfortunately, Scope Creep is a progressive condition that spreads insidiously. The best cure, as always, is prevention – firstly by rigorous work to define the scope before the project starts, and secondly by applying the same change control procedures and authorization to proposed changes to project scope as to any other aspect.

WHEN MIGHT YOU NEED TO CONSIDER SCOPE?

Your Terms of Reference

When you are given an assignment, such as a project management role, you should seek written Terms of Reference to define that role, so that every interested party is clear about what you have been instructed to do. Scope is a key item in your Terms of Reference, to help you go right up to, but not beyond, any required limits. In the absence of written Terms of Reference, it usually makes good sense for you to draft your own and to seek approval for them, so that you start out with clear scope and objectives.

Feasibility Study

When you conduct a Feasibility Study, you will need careful scope-definition for that study. For example, if the study is into ways of improving use of information technology to solve a business problem or grasp a business opportunity, you will need the study to concentrate its investigation on acceptable options only. There may be some options that, while they might work, would be unacceptable to the organization for one or more reasons. For example, if your organization uses established hardware, software and telecommunications technology, you will be stuck with that, despite your belief that there is a 'better' platform out there. Before you start the study, identify every possible scope option, and then seek management guidance as to what is worth looking at and what is not. Your solutions will need to be politically acceptable, as well as technically, operationally and economically feasible.

Project

Clear scope is crucial to project success. You will need to deliver all the required outputs to all the customer stakeholders, within any time limits that have been agreed or mandated, within the agreed budget. You should develop the schedule and budget from a Work Breakdown Structure that reflects the agreed scope.

HOW DO YOU USE IT?

At the beginning of most projects, few stakeholders know precisely what they need for their part of the business. Often, their ideas are at the start of an evolutionary process. Unfortunately, if we set plans, schedules and budgets on this basis, then respond to evolutionary growth in the scope, we will invariably finish late and over budget – a classic 'failed project' scenario. But is this really failure if our stakeholders are satisfied with what they get out of the project? If we recognize that our scope may expand, we can live with this, provided everyone understands that for every expansion in scope, there will be a price to pay in time and money. If you have to change scope, make sure that you do so under proper control, and that you assess the likely impacts on time, cost and risks. The alternative is to stick rigidly to the agreed scope, but to record all the identified 'extras' that will need to be added post-implementation, in a planned and budgeted maintenance mini-project. The choice here must be made by the project's Sponsor as a matter of policy, binding on all the stakeholders, including you as Project Manager.

WHAT SHOULD YOU CHECK?

Do you know:

- that the written and agreed scope definition accurately reflects the Work Breakdown Structure?
- the boundaries within which you need to work?
- what you must include?

- what you must exclude?
- standards that must be used?
- specifications that must be satisfied?
- any scope assumptions that still need to be resolved?
- what you will need to do if you, or any other stakeholder, comes to believe that the scope is no longer correct or appropriate?

SEE ALSO

Change Control
Constraints
Impact Analysis
Objective(s)
Risk Management
Terms of Reference

Sensitivity Analysis

A Sensitivity Analysis is a 'What if …?' examination in which you analyse the consequences of variations in costs and benefits on the financial viability of a project.

WHY MIGHT IT BE USEFUL?

You may use some form of Sensitivity Analysis to help determine the conditions under which a project might remain financially viable if forecast costs increase, benefits reduce, or both. It will be useful preparation for any presentation of an Investment Appraisal, a Feasibility Study or a Business Case, as you are likely to be asked "What if …?" questions by members of your Steering Group. You may find that such an analysis is a requirement, and that you will be told what parameters to use.

WHEN MIGHT YOU NEED IT?

1. It would be normal to conduct Sensitivity Analyses during any pre-project work such as a Feasibility Study, when your management needs to consider various optional solutions and approaches.

2. This form of analysis may also be useful part-way through a project, when changing financial circumstances look as if they may threaten the ongoing viability of the Business Case. For example, if you make a forecast that 'Cost at Completion' is likely to increase by, say, 20 per cent, but that benefits could remain static, you would naturally want to check the implications on the Business Case, to see whether the project is still worthwhile. If it is, you would be well advised to continue the analysis, to establish at what level of increase it would become non-viable, and monitor cost trends carefully from that point forward.

3. You should also consider Sensitivity Analysis as a normal technique at the end of a stage, when you will firm up and detail the plan and budget for the next stage, and refine the plan and budget for the rest of the project, based on everything you have

learned to date. At the end of every stage, you should have reduced the range and number of uncertainties your project faces, so the gap between 'best', likely' and 'worst' scenarios should reduce too and be reflected in each succeeding stage end analysis.

HOW DO YOU USE IT?

A Sensitivity Analysis uses a range of cost and benefit estimates to help determine whether the project will still be regarded as viable, particularly if costs are likely to increase and/or benefits to diminish. To enable this, the original Business Case should include the expected value of benefits including one or more of:

- improved/increased revenues/income
- reduced costs
- improvements to services.

Improved revenues and reduced costs are usually easier to quantify, but improved service or better infrastructure are less tangible ('hard' v. 'soft' benefits). The timing of the arrival of benefits may also have to be taken into account.

Sensitivity Analysis should therefore examine changes through a 'What if …?' approach, by asking and answering questions such as:

- 'What if the expected benefits are 10, 20 or 30 per cent lower (or such a range as required by your Project Board/Steering Committee, or in your Project Management Standards)?'

- 'What if the project costs are 10, 20 or 30 per cent higher?'

- 'What if the project takes 3, 6 or 9 months longer to complete, with consequent cost increases and benefit delays?'

- 'What if capital costs are 10, 20 or 30 per cent higher?'

- 'Which costs and benefits are most "fragile" (most likely to deviate from expectations)? What are the contributory factors, and do these costs and benefits need to be reviewed more frequently than just at the end of each stage (say, monthly)?'

- For each of the above questions, which is the most likely answer?

Rather than using simple percentage ranges for costs and benefits, you could also choose to use 'best', 'most likely' and 'worst', also known as 'optimistic', 'most likely' and 'pessimistic'.

You should base the 'most likely' figure on the latest versions of your Project Plan and budget. In this way, you should also have information on the forecast project duration, timing of the flow of benefits and forecast project costs (Cost at Completion).

Use project management standards for this if they exist; otherwise seek the advice of your Accounts or Finance Department on the required approach and method, such as Net Present Value (NPV), Internal Rate of Return (IRR) or Payback Period (PP). You may find it helpful to do calculations for all combinations, but with rounded results. For net benefits, you may choose to use Net Present Values, and you may also wish or need to show the Internal Rate of Return and Payback Period for each outcome, presented in tables similar to the one in Figure 79.

Benefits						
Costs	Best		Most Likely		Worst	
Best						
Most Likely						
Worst						

Figure 79   Sensitivity Analysis template

Use results where the 'most likely' columns and rows intersect as a basis for any recommendations on the ongoing viability of the project. As each stage passes, you must update the Business Case, making it a more accurate forecast of the financial outcome for your project. As you make progress, the cost range between 'best', 'most likely' and 'worst' should narrow, as you will have spent and learned more, with less to be uncertain about. If this is not happening, something is not working as it should. However, as project expenditure tends to accelerate markedly once development activities start, your Business Case and forecasts need to be reliable at this crucial point, to enable a sensible and informed investment decision.

WHAT SHOULD YOU CHECK?

- Do you have project management standards for Sensitivity Analysis? If not:
  - check with the Chair of your Project Board/Steering Committee that they would find this approach useful, and whether you should use 'best', 'most likely' and 'worst' scenarios or simple percentage increases and decreases for costs and benefits.
- When you have completed the basic Sensitivity Analysis, will you apply additional methods to show future benefits at Net Present Value?

SEE ALSO

Business Case
Business Case Review
Change Control
Investment Appraisal for Projects
Two-level Planning

Small Project

HOW SMALL MIGHT A 'SMALL' PROJECT BE?

A small project is likely to be an assignment which, because of the relative modesty of its duration, objective(s) and scope, resource needs (the project's likely size in person-days), risk to your business, number of stakeholders, budget or dependencies on its outcome is below any threshold at which your business might have chosen to use formal project procedures, approaches and organization.

Many of today's businesses are owned, managed and staffed by small numbers of people. To such a business, a project costing £10 000 and occupying one or two people for three months, full-time, could be a huge and risky undertaking. In a FTSE 100 or Fortune 500 company, such project expenditure could well be regarded as trivial. Your organization might already have criteria that determine the characteristics of a small project. If not, you might now be able to use this section to understand 'small' projects in the context of your business organization.

A small project is one that you may undertake in a less formal manner than those that are more complex, risky, large in scale, or of extended duration. The latter normally require some formal organization for decision-making, a significant number of people in the project team, possibly several stages, each with 'go'–'no go' decisions and, of course, a larger budget. Just beware of throwing away the good sense that has grown up around formally structured projects for good reasons – what you are likely to need for a small project is likely to be just a simpler, slimmer version.

Small projects have a special 'hidden' value, in that they are excellent training grounds for the Project Managers of the future. Because of this, you should use simple elements of 'best practice' and develop the good habits that will stand you in good stead. These should include following the principle of planning first, then doing. You should always start by gaining an understanding of the objective(s), scope, constraints, any assumptions that have been made and 'who needs to know what' as you progress. Once you have this basic but essential information, you might create a dated 'to-do' list, containing simple prompts. What do you need to do, and by when? Will this enable you to complete the tasks and to minimize or avoid threats that might affect a successful outcome? You should also have a simple method for recording information on what happens. A diary or notebook might suffice, but be aware that others might need to refer to it if you are absent for any reason. Such records are valuable during a project and afterwards, when you can compare what actually happened against what you intended to happen. You might learn useful lessons from any variations.

QUESTIONS TO ASK

- Do you have the Terms of Reference (objectives, scope, constraints, assumptions and reporting needs)? Have you agreed them with the person who has given you the assignment (the Sponsor)?
- Do you know how the Sponsor will assess whether or not the assignment has been completed successfully?
- Have you worked out how you are going to conduct the assignment?
- Have you identified and written down all the tasks, and when they need to be completed?
- Have you estimated how much it might cost, and have you gained approval for such expenditure?
- Do you have (or have access to) the skills and resources needed?
- Have you set up a simple method for monitoring and controlling progress?
- Do you need input from others? Do they know what and when?
- Do you need to let others know anything about what you are doing? Have you identified what needs to be done, and when, on this?
- Have you set up a simple method for recording what happens?
- What might go wrong, and what might you need to do if this happens?
- Will anyone else check the quality (fitness for purpose) of the outputs?
- Will you know when you have finished?

SEE ALSO

Project Life Cycle
Starting a Project
Terms of Reference

Sponsor

In everyday commercial use, the word 'sponsor' refers to an individual or organization providing financial support in return for publicity. In fund-raising, it is used to describe someone who promises to pay a specified amount of money to a charity or club when the person or team being sponsored reaches a certain level of achievement, such as £1 per mile for a sponsored walk. In the project environment, 'Sponsor' describes a senior individual in an organization, normally a person who will seek investment in a project, contribute to and endorse the Business Case justifying the project, in order for her or his part of the organization to benefit from the project's outputs. This individual is usually the customer-in chief, without whose sponsorship there might not be a project, and the ultimate authority with whom the decision-making buck stops.

You should expect this individual to provide political, moral and personal support, to use her or his power and influence to overcome barriers and impediments to project success, and to 'sell' the project at peer group and management levels. You may be aware that many people have an inbuilt resistance to change, and you may need your Sponsor to help you overcome this as the project progresses, particularly later, when you begin to implement the change. John Steinbeck summed this up when he commented: 'It is the nature of man . . . to protest against change, particularly change for the better.'

In government projects, you may find that such an individual is named as the Project Owner (PO) or the Senior Responsible Owner (SRO).

IN PRACTICE

I was once the new Project Manager hired to help the recovery of a faltering project. In addition to the dire problems faced by the project, the entire project team of 40 were suspended part-way through a relocation, held up because the telecommunications supplier was unable to install voice and data lines at the new location when needed. After attempting unsuccessfully to expedite the installation, I spoke briefly to my Sponsor and asked for his help, having explained the problem and its consequences. My Sponsor (the Company Secretary of a blue-chip organization) said: 'Leave it to me. I will phone my opposite number at [the telecommunications supplier].' Engineers were on site the following day, and the installation went ahead immediately and without a hitch.

Do not trouble your Sponsor with every irritation and inconvenience you face, but when important matters are beyond your authority and influence, give her or him the opportunity to exercise the authority and influence you need on behalf of their project.

THE ROLE

It makes very good sense for your Sponsor to take the role of Chairperson on your Steering Group, but he or she may appoint a nominee because of insufficient time and constant diary constraints. Appointing a nominee is not always the most desirable outcome, experience suggesting that whenever you need an urgent, crucial decision and you seek it from the Steering Group through its 'nominee' Chairperson, the decision will be deferred while they seek the Sponsor's guidance and approval.

SEE ALSO

Champion
Steering Group

Stage or Phase

The terms 'stage' and 'phase' are normally interchangeable, and usually have the same meaning. The word 'stage' is preferred throughout this manual. Where it is related specifically to PRINCE®, this is mentioned. Be aware that a PRINCE®-based environment, stages are generally timed for management rather than technical purposes, and a Stage End may occur part way through a piece of technical work. In other approaches, stages often follow the technical work more closely. For example, you may divide your projects into stages called 'Requirements Definition', 'Design', 'Build and Test' and 'Implement'. You may have a management review point between each, following the same principle as PRINCE®. Whenever you run a project that you have divided into stages with interim reviews, you create an environment favourable to effective management and control.

WHY USE STAGES?

We usually sub-divide projects into stages. Our aim in doing this is to create manageable pieces of work, to enable us to:

- assess the project's continuing viability, check that we can still afford it, and be confident that it will still deliver what we need

- ensure we are satisfied with what has been achieved before authorizing more expenditure and committing further resources

- make decisions that enable us to steer the project towards a successful outcome

- plan at two levels by having detailed plans for the next tasks (those in the next stage) and by having outline plans for more distant tasks (those in later stages); for example, in certain methods you might plan a stage called 'Requirements Definition' in detail before you start it, but just create outline plans for a following 'Design' stage, the logic behind this being simply that you will be unable to plan any design work in detail until the Requirements Definition has enabled you to complete the design specification.

You could structure small or simple projects in two main steps:

1. Plan the work.
2. Do the work (and close the project).

Between the two, you create an opportunity to approve the plan and authorize use of resources such as time, money, people and equipment.

WHAT SHOULD YOU CHECK?

- Do you use two-level planning?
- Does your organization use a structured approach to projects, with stages, and with management reviews between each?
- Do those who use the approach (including you) and those who participate in any reviews and decisions understand it fully? Has everyone been trained in its use?
- Does your Steering Group, or similar formal group, approve previous-stage outputs and authorize the next-stage and project plans and budgets between stages? If not, when do they do this?
- Do you review Project Risks and Issues at Stage End review points? If not, when do you do this?

Between stages, there is a valid case for you to deliver the following items, in addition to the 'real' outputs from your team's work:

- Updated Plan for Previous Stage
- Updated Budget for Previous Stage
- Detailed Plan for Next Stage
- Detailed Budget for Next Stage
- Updated Project Plan, in outline to project end
- Updated Project Budget, in outline to project end
- Stage End Report and any recommendations
- Updated Business Case
- Updated Project Risks Log
- Updated Project Issues Log
- Updated Assumptions Log and Opportunities Log, if used.

SEE ALSO

Project and Stage Plans
Project Life Cycle
Stages – Start and End Procedures
Two-level Planning

Stages – Start and End Procedures

We divide projects into stages so that we can conduct the work in manageable pieces. By working in stages, we create a series of opportunities where those accountable for steering the project, such as the Project Sponsor or Steering Group, must check two important matters. The first is to ensure that work from a previous stage has been satisfactorily completed. The second is to verify that the justification for the project is still valid and that the plans and budgets for the next stage and for the remainder of the project are complete, clear and realistic.

You will need to understand and follow your organization's Stage Start and End standards and procedures, or perhaps those set out in the PRINCE® method if you are using it.

WHAT SHOULD YOU DO AND CHECK BEFORE YOU START A STAGE?

If you do not have detailed standards, the following hints and checklists may help. Your main aim here should be to create a detailed plan and budget for the work to be done in the next stage. In the entries on **Work Breakdown Structure**, **Network Analysis** and on **Two-level Planning**, you will see that it is normal to have two current plans: one that shows the main pieces of work in the whole project, and another more detailed one that shows all the lowest-level tasks and resources in the current stage, providing a basis for close control. So at the start of each stage, you may need to do the following:

● Review the previous Stage Plan if this is not the first stage.

● Review any Work Breakdown Structure for the project, and make sure it is up to date.

● Update your project logical flow diagram or precedence diagram.

● Review and update the Project Plan.

● Check the Issues Log for any that may influence the next stage.

- Develop a detailed Work Breakdown Structure for the next stage.

- Complete detailed estimates and critical path analysis for the stage.

- Create a schedule for the stage, showing who will be doing what, and when.

- Check to make sure that the resources you need will be available when needed.

- Use your schedule to develop a budget for the stage. Use this as input to a review of the Business Case, to make sure that the justification for the project is still valid.

- Draft a checklist showing all the deliverables for the stage and the dates on which they are due.

- Draft a responsibilities matrix covering the stage tasks, showing those responsible, and accountable for each task, and who should be consulted or informed about each task.

- Review and update the Risk Log.

- Update the Communications Plan.

- Draft an 'approval' document to facilitate sign-off for the plans and budgets.

- Arrange a meeting if this is how your organization requires plans to be presented for approval. Agree an agenda with the Sponsor or the Chair of the Steering Group. Publish all the documents that you will seek approval for in good time for them to be absorbed and understood by the decision-makers.

- Seek and gain approval for plans and budgets, taking any directions and implementing any changes mandated by the Steering Group or Sponsor.

- Publish the Stage Plan, Stage Budget and updated Communications Plan.

- Brief team members, where appropriate.

WHAT SHOULD BE DONE AND CHECKED TO END A STAGE?

You should have been tracking progress and chasing it when appropriate, throughout the stage. As the Stage End approaches, you will need to make sure that all the tasks will be completed on time, or to take advice from the Project Sponsor or Chair of the Steering Group if some tasks look unlikely to be completed in time for the planned Stage End. The options here are to sign off the stage subject to satisfactory completion of the missing tasks within a time limit, or to defer the Stage End pending completion of the tasks. There can be no hard and fast rules here, and such matters might best be dealt with on a case-by-case basis and depending on the criticality of the tasks. Note that if this Stage End is also the Project End, you will need to do and check some additional items to close the project. At all other stage, ends you may need to:

- ensure that you are up to date on the status of stage tasks, and that the current Stage Plan is fully updated

- review the checklist of stage deliverables, and make sure it is up to date

- check that the Quality Plan is up to date, and that all completed tasks that need any quality checks will receive them in time for the Stage End

- review the Project Plan to make sure that it is still appropriate, and update it if appropriate

- ensure that the Issues Log is up to date, and that all actions required during the stage have been carried out

- close down any Risk Log items that relate only to this stage and which run out at the Stage End

- ensure that the Stage Budget is updated as far as is possible, including any costs that are committed but not yet billed. Use this as input to a review of the Business Case

- update your Lessons Learned Report to record any findings from this stage

- write a key management document, the End of Stage Report, to outline progress and summarize project status, so that the Steering Group can fulfil its role and steer the project using the latest information. Typically, you will need to summarize status and prospects, with relevant extracts from the Project Plan, the plan for the stage that is closing and from the plan for the next stage, the Risks and Issues Logs, and from any important lessons learned during this stage.

SEE ALSO

Approval
Authorization
Business Case Review
Issue Management
Lesson Learned
Project and Stage Plans
Project Life Cycle
Reports in Projects and Programmes
Responsibility Matrix
Risk Management
Small Projects
Stage or Phase
Task Checklist
Two-level Planning
PRINCE® Project Board

Stakeholders – Identification and Communication

A stakeholder is anyone involved in or likely to be affected by a project or its outcome, or its failure to deliver the required outcome.

STAKEHOLDER IDENTIFICATION

Over the life of a project, you will find that there are many individuals and groups with an interest or involvement in activities and outcomes, or who will be affected by them. These interested parties are the 'stakeholders', and include those managing and working within the project, together with people or organizations directly or indirectly contributing to, or likely to be affected by, it. Your projects will always affect one or more stakeholders or groups – indeed, you initiate projects to do just that. During the life of a project, stakeholders may come and go, depending on the activities. However, key stakeholders, such as a Project Sponsor, will remain constant throughout.

Some stakeholders participate as advisers or in assurance roles; others will assess the realization of project benefits; yet others may have an audit perspective. There may be those who will be worse off because of the project. They may not be wholehearted supporters of your team's efforts, and may even lobby to prevent their success. If you are running a project to close down a company department, employees in that department may strongly disagree with the policy and your project's aims. If you owned a house in a valley that is about to be flooded as part of a hydro-electricity project, you are a stakeholder and your way of life is about to be submerged – would you be interested? Therefore, to manage stakeholders, you need to recognize that there will be those with both positive and negative positions. You may find that at the start of a project, there may be more 'antis' than 'pros'. As mentioned elsewhere, John Steinbeck referred to this when he wrote: 'It is the nature of man . . . to protest against change, particularly change for the better.'

Your stakeholders may include owners, shareholders, directors, operational managers or staff of:

- organizations sponsoring the project
- organizations and individuals affected by or involved in the project
- organizations supplying goods or services to the project
- organizations supplying goods or services to organizations affected by the project
- organizations and individuals that wish to block the project
- customers or consumers who will be affected for good or ill by the project, either as it is under way or when it has delivered its outputs
- internal and external auditors
- planning authorities
- security personnel
- trades unions or staff associations
- regulatory bodies
- the wider community in which the organization and people exist
- the project management team.

STAKEHOLDER ANALYSIS

You will find that each stakeholder has one or more specific interest areas, such as operational, financial, technical, regulatory or human resources. When identifying project stakeholders, it is important that you recognize their precise interests, to help you manage all their expectations more effectively. Try to create a Stakeholder Matrix, listing all those you have identified against each, and list those parts of the project in which you believe they have an interest (see the brief sample in Figure 80 that links stakeholders to the sections in a key document). You should find it a useful tool when identifying and planning project communications, and will add to its usefulness if you review it with the stakeholders to make sure you have represented their interests completely.

Internal Stakeholders	Sections in Document x of interest
Group Headquarters	All
Chief Executive	1, 3, 5, 10, 11, 12, 13, 14, 15, 16
Accountancy Department	1, 2, 3, 5, 6, 7, 8, 9, 11, 12, 13
Legal Department	1, 2, 3, 4, 5, 6, 7, 8, 9, 11, 12, 13, 14, 15, 16
Project Management Team	All
External Stakeholders	
Bank	1, 4, 5, 11, 12, 14, 15, 16
Investment Advisors	All
Participants in Invitation to Tender	1, 14
Other external interested parties	
Financial Services Authority	1, 2, 3, 4, 5, 6, 7, 8, 11

Figure 80   Sample Stakeholder Matrix

STAKEHOLDER COMMUNICATIONS

Achieving success in a project may involve trade-offs between one set of interests and another. Some will see themselves as winners, and some as losers. You may need to enlist the support of both groups at various stages, and as you may be closer to these groups than, say, your Project Sponsor, you will need to create a communications plan that keeps everyone in touch. You will need to set up and operate two-way communications between your team and those stakeholders whose co-operation the project needs, and those who object to what is being done. You should also have a similar approach for those 'internal' to your work – those managing and participating in the project – to keep them informed and motivated. Ignoring those who are your closest allies and supporters is not recommended. You will need to establish all stakeholder expectations, and manage them skilfully through all the twists and turns in your project's life.

You will need to:

- Keep awareness high to maintain commitment and a feeling of ownership.
- Ensure consistency in your communications in and around the project.
- Ensure that expectations stay in line with what you will deliver.
- Facilitate prompt and honest feedback from everyone involved in and affected by the project.

COMMUNICATIONS PLAN

Use your Stakeholder Matrix (see Figure 80) as a guide to who needs to know what about the project. Once you have established this, you will need to plan how (the medium) and when (the frequency) to communicate to each stakeholder individual or group. Do not lose sight of the milestones on your schedule, as at these points you usually have something significant to tell those stakeholders with a specific interest in that milestone, and something to tell stakeholders in general ('We have passed another major milestone').

Communication is central to any project process – the greater the amount of change or innovation, the greater the need for clear communication about reasons, benefits, plans and the intended effects. It is therefore important, that you define and implement your Communications Strategy as early as possible, and then maintain it adequately throughout the project.

You should maintain a key aim of communicating early successes, both to those directly concerned with the business operation and to other key audiences, especially where rapid progress in realizing benefits is required. These are often referred to as 'quick wins'. You should aim to secure commitment and build momentum. Thereafter, effective communications should enable you to transfer knowledge to project staff and into the business operations.

You should design your Communications Strategy with the following objectives:

- to raise awareness of the benefits
- to gain commitment from staff in those areas where you are introducing change, to help ensure long-term success
- to keep all staff informed of progress before, during and after implementation or delivery of project outcomes
- to demonstrate your commitment to meeting the requirements of those sponsoring the project
- to make communications work two ways, by actively encouraging stakeholders to provide feedback, and by ensuring they are informed about the use and value of their feedback in influencing the project and the way you are running it
- to ensure that all those responsible for projects have a common understanding of all the changes and innovations being introduced by the project
- to maximize the opportunity to gain the benefits of the outputs.

Your Communications Strategy should enable you to answer the following questions:

- 'What are the aims of your communications efforts?'
- 'What are your main messages?'
- 'Who are you trying to reach?'
- 'What sorts of information will you communicating?'
- 'When will information be disseminated?'
- 'How much information will be provided, and to what level of detail?'
- 'What mechanisms will be used to disseminate information?'
- 'How will feedback be collected, and what will be done with the feedback?'

The answers you give to these questions may differ for each of the stakeholder groups. You should identify such variations during the analysis of stakeholders, and document it alongside the Stakeholder Matrix.

ACHIEVING SUCCESSFUL COMMUNICATION

You should try to use four main elements in your communications:

1. Make sure your messages are clearly expressed and unambiguous.
2. Target your messages to the different stakeholder groups, so that each gets the information it needs.
3. Set up a method to encourage and collect feedback. Where possible, use this to assess the effectiveness of your communications process.
4. Choose the delivery system(s) with care.

COMMUNICATIONS CHANNELS

You have a wide choice of channels to achieve effective communications. You may use active approaches, such as seminars, workshops or presentations, or passive approaches, such as memos, newsletters, the noticeboard, or a website. Consult other Project Managers to find out which media perform best in your organization for each different need. Monitor your chosen approaches regularly, and do not hesitate to make changes to meet the requirements of your audiences.

Passive media

Internet/intranet

Many organizations host a corporate intranet, and this can be a useful communications tool provided you remain aware of its strengths and weaknesses:

- **Strengths:**
  - consistency
  - written
  - instant 'on-demand' access.
- **Weaknesses:**
  - publishing delays
  - people do not have to read it
  - may inform, but may not inspire.
- **Considerations:**
  - how will you also reach those without access?
  - keep it simple.

E-mail

- **Strengths:**
  - consistency
  - suitable for short messages or for longer attachments
  - written
  - can ensure it is addressed to all intended
  - can be published quickly for urgent outputs.
- **Weaknesses:**
  - people do not have to read it
  - may inform, but may not inspire.
- **Considerations:**
  - how will you also reach those without e-mail?
  - keep it simple
  - check it carefully if in a hurry.

Newsletters

You might use general or specific newsletters to provide updates on project progress and changes. Use general newsletters to keep all stakeholders up to date. Use specific versions to provide particular stakeholder(s) with precise information. Consider using a website, an intranet or e-mail if they are available to you and all the stakeholders you are trying to reach have access. Of course, it may also be appropriate to use paper, which people can read when commuting or at home.

ACTIVE MEDIA

Seminars, briefings, meetings and workshops

You might consider one of these face-to-face formats, if appropriate. If you use a passive approach such as a newsletter, you may put a lot of effort into writing and distributing your messages, but few people may take the time to read them carefully. You may believe that everyone now knows everything, but the reality may be that a few know a little. Again, there are strengths and weaknesses to a face-to-face approach:

- **Strengths:**
  - high impact and good motivator when well planned and presented
  - can help renew buy-in and ownership
  - can be targeted precisely (say, to enlist the help of a key group)
  - provides an opportunity to answer questions and concerns which you may not have recognized
  - shares knowledge across all stakeholders.
- **Weaknesses:**
  - negative impact if planned or presented poorly
  - people might forget quickly (unless you provide a handout)
  - provides an opportunity for an ambush.
- **Considerations:**
  - can be expensive (30 people in a room for one hour will cost one person-week of effort)
  - allow enough time for professional preparation
  - be clear on your precise aims (what do you need your audience to know/do when you have finished?).

Exhibits and roadshows

In some types of project, you may find it useful to set up a display that people can look at or even try. For example, when relocating or perhaps planning a call-centre, you might obtain space to create a 'model office', where people can see what their new environment and systems will look like. This can stimulate feedback and help you avoid expensive post-implementation changes.

OTHER MEDIA

Occasionally, you might consider using a video, a CD or a DVD to communicate with a large and distributed stakeholder audience. For example, if you are managing a project in a utility company and you want to tell your customers about a significant change to the way you supply or meter supplies, one of these might be ideal. Be aware that production costs are likely to be high and timescales likely to be long. You should also be aware that not everyone will use what you send, and you might need a back-up method.

SEE ALSO

Communications Plan

Starting a Project

There are many ways to start a project, but not all are to be recommended. For example, in some organizations you will be discouraged from doing anything that might cause a perceived delay, so any attempt to carry out detailed planning, estimating, risk analysis or any other 'fancy stuff' might be seriously frowned upon. Instead, you will be told the budget, and given a 'yesterday' deadline and a 'Just get on with it' instruction. This is the classic 'Fire, aim, ready!' approach.

An alternative lies at the opposite end of the spectrum, and is used in organizations that require so much reassurance on every aspect of a project that you will be exhausted, frustrated and late even before you get started. This is rather like someone unsure whether to mow the lawn for the first time in spring, who spends hours pondering the weather forecast, then retrieves the mower from underneath wherever it was buried, takes time out to tidy the shed, asks each neighbour's advice, worries about upsetting one of them because their advice conflicts, plucks up courage, shops around for the cheapest fuel, tries the engine, decides to go and buy a new spark plug, finally starts the engine, and then realizes that it is too dark to cut the grass.

Somewhere between these extremes lies a sensible balance between planning and action. Your organization will need to decide where this balance lies, but the options are similar to those faced in the old Sunday School hymn, between: 'The foolish man [who] builds his house upon the sand' and 'The wise man [who] builds his house upon the rock' (Matthew 7:24–27). Only 'when the tide came rolling in' did the differences suddenly become crucial. Sound but not over-engineered foundations are a worthwhile investment, whatever you set out to develop.

WHAT SHOULD HAVE HAPPENED BEFORE YOU START A PROJECT?

If we stay with the 'foundations' parable for a moment, you will see that before you reach this point, there are a number of prerequisites. You would need to know what you intended to build, and have at least outline planning permission. In addition, you would need to have an approach in mind, want to know that finance is available, know that you

301

can get the skills and materials when needed, be aware of any risks, and know that if building to sell, you can be confident of making a profit. Projects do not simply appear, but normally follow a number of important pre-project activities and decisions.

WHY DO PROJECTS FAIL?

You may already have seen, heard or experienced that projects are not universally successful. Some crash in spectacular fashion when the plug is pulled part-way through, while others wither through lack of interest. While some never reach fruition, others survive to deliver technically sound outputs which were never really needed or wanted, so are never likely to be operational successes, like London's Millennium Dome. Yet others become political battlegrounds, with one faction committed to success, and another equally determined to force a halt. It is no use discovering any of this when the project is well under way, which is why pre-project work is so important.

For a project to maximize its chances of success, it is vital for all the key stakeholders to 'buy in' to the objectives and scope, and to understand the constraints and assumptions right from the outset. If this is not immediately possible, it is really for the Project Champion to seek and establish this support, not the new Project Manager. Some organizations like to use a Project Kick-off Meeting to bring together the all main stakeholders and establish this shared understanding.

PRE-PROJECT

In order for your corporate decision-makers to finance and otherwise support a project, they will need to know answers to all the following questions:

- Why do we need this project? What problem(s) will it resolve, or what opportunities will it enable us to grasp?
- What must it deliver to give us what we need and what are its primary and secondary objectives ('musts' and 'oughts')? What 'solution' options exist and, if there are options, which appears to best meet our needs? Will there be any significant risks?
- How should we go about this? What optional approaches exist and, if there are options, which appears best fitted to our needs? Will there be any significant risks?
- How much will the options which best meet our needs cost?
- What return can we expect on our investment?
- When are project outputs needed? Are there any mandatory dates, such as to meet new legislation?
- What is our scope to be? What must be included, and what excluded?
- Who can create or deliver this? Do we have the skills to put this in place and make it work after it is established?

To get to this point, someone, or some part of the organization, must have had an idea, identified a problem or opportunity, and made some sort of project suggestion or proposal. However, for a project within a programme, this may not be the case, and the

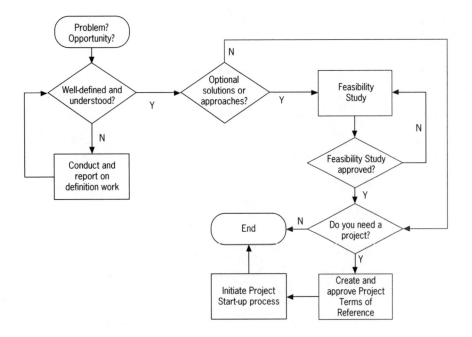

Figure 81   Possible project approval process

questions may already have been asked and answered at that level. If you use a formal project approval process, it may look similar to that in Figure 81.

To move forward from this point, you will first need to record answers to the questions above in a document such as Project Terms of Reference, or a Project Brief. If the situation is complex or you are likely to have to select from several optional solutions or routes, the next possible step might be to commission a Feasibility Study, which may be treated as a project in its own right, albeit one that will only deliver only management information. Its value should lie in helping the organization to reach a sound decision. You will need modest plans and a budget to conduct such a study, probably similar to those you would use for a small project, and of the 'plan it – do it', two-stage variety unless the study is large or complex.

However you have arrived at this launching point, still pre-project, you will need to be appointed to the Project Manager's role, probably by the individual who will be the chair or executive at the head of a future Project Board. You will then need to plan the start-up work by developing a plan and budget for the first initiation or start-up stage and gain authorization for their use. Though you may not yet have a Project Board or Steering Group in place, you will need it to be established in time to approve your outputs, the project and 'next-stage' plans and budgets (Project Initiation Document in a PRINCE® environment) once you have completed this start-up stage. A sample of such a document is shown in Figure 82.

1 Background
This should give general background to the project, including an explanation of why the project is required and answering the question: 'How did we get to where we need this project?'

2 Project Definition
This sets out what the project aims to achieve. The following elements should normally be included:

   2.1 Project Objectives
- What do we intend to achieve through this project?
- Which strategic aims will this project support?
- To which (if any) programme does this project belong?

   2.2 Project Approach
What method of approach will we follow? What standards and procedures are to be followed? For example:
- Will the output(s) be delivered by our own (internal) staff?
- Will an external supplier deliver any output(s)?
- Will any output(s) be delivered from other external organizations?
- Is an existing product or service being modified to meet changed needs?
- Is an 'off-the-shelf' output to be procured?

   2.3 Project Scope and Exclusions
What will be included in and excluded from the project? This should cover such aspects as business processes and departments.

   2.4 Project Deliverables and/or Desired Outcomes
Include here all main outputs, or outcomes that the project must deliver.

   2.5 Constraints
Define any 'limiting factors', confinements, limits, or other restrictions that may adversely affect your project. Include any limitations that may influence the project such as cost (limited budget), timescale (tight deadline) or resources (limited people skills, knowledge, experience or availability).

   2.6 Interfaces
Connection to or dependency on any other programmes, outputs, projects, business systems or processes.

3 Assumptions
Document any unresolved assumptions, including those related to planning, funding, and resourcing. You should also recommend when and by whom these assumptions should be resolved and the implications of not resolving them.

4 Initial Business Case
Outline the initial Business Case. Why are you doing this project? You should include such aspects as:
- how the project will support the strategic aims of the organization;
- justification for the project, by providing an outline of the benefits the project will realize and answering the 'What's in it for us?' question. Benefits might include forecasts of improved revenues and avoided costs, both of which will add to the corporate bottom line; comments on benefits realization, answering 'When might we recoup the investment?' Include first-pass estimates of costs and an investment appraisal.

5 Project Organization Structure
Who will make up the Project Management Team? How and to whom will this team report and who will direct their efforts, approve plans and authorize funding?

6 Communication Plan
You will need to:
- identify all the stakeholders with whom you will need to communicate through the project
- set up a matrix showing who needs to know what and when to maintain involvement, commitment and ownership
- maintain consistency in communications in and around your project
- enable feedback (two-way communications)

7 Initial Project Plan
How and when will the activities of the project occur? This is likely to include a high-level Gantt chart, with supporting text to explain and justify the stages and their proposed main outputs.

8 Quality Plan
This sets out the quality aims of the project, showing your understanding of your customers' quality expectations and any priorities. Outline the overall approach and standards to be used and identify initial estimates of resources needed for this work.

9 Project Controls
This explains the monitoring and reporting methods and reports that will be used, and their frequency.

10 Exception Handling
Exceptions are variations between 'plan' and 'actual' beyond a level deemed in advance as acceptable (fall outside agreed tolerance) and which thus need to be reported to management (escalated) for resolution. This section should cover such aspects as:
- What 'Tolerances' have been agreed – that is, at what points will any variances in timing or spending exceed the Project Manager's authority in these matters?
- How will any exceptions be communicated, and to whom?
- Who will make decisions on any exceptions?

11 Initial Risk Log
This should record specific identified risks, countermeasures, ownership and status.

12 Contingency Plans
These are usually major plans or measures that should be available in case particular circumstances arise that will have an effect on the entire project, rather than for specific risks that should be managed as set out in the Risk Log.

13 Project Filing Structure
This should describe rules and procedures for storage, retrieval, security and management of electronic and paper documents and products in any other medium used in, or output from, a project.

Figure 82   Suggested format for a PRINCE® PID (or other project start-up document)

Project start-up

At the end of this stage, you will need to deliver documentation that:

- fully defines the requirements the project must meet, confirms their justification, and sets out a scheme for their delivery; these will normally consist of a Project Start-up or Project Initiation Document (PRINCE®) and a Project Justification or Business Case

- provides a baseline, or yardstick, against which you as the Project Manager and the Project Board can monitor progress

- provides an agreed basis for a Post-Project Review.

Note that this is a significant piece of work that should not be underestimated in terms of both duration and importance. Rather than set out a format, which is likely to vary from one organization to another, or which is already defined in PRINCE® manuals if you are a user, typical work is shown in the sample Work Breakdown Structure in Figure 83 and a typical sequence, perhaps with some iteration, in the sample work flow diagram in Figure 84.

WHAT SHOULD YOU CHECK?

When you have been appointed Project Manager for a yet-to-be-started project, consider:

- Are your Terms of Reference clear? (You know your role and responsibilities to your full satisfaction, and there are no grey areas.)

- Do you understand the approvals and authorization procedures that will be used on your outputs from this stage, and do you know the required content, format, level of detail and style requirements?

- Have you planned/will you plan the planning work (plan the plan)?

- If you have a fixed deadline for planning, are you sure that you can meet the content, format, level of detail and style requirements? If not, what have you done about this? You should consider showing your decision-maker your plan immediately. Stress to her or him the importance of this 'foundation' work, and the risks of superficiality. If she/he insists, give it your best shot, but 24/7 working at this point will set a bad precedent.

- Will you encourage stakeholder participation in any planning workshops to confirm your understanding of their needs, priorities and acceptance criteria, and to gain their input to a Work Breakdown Structure, sequences and dependencies, risks, issues and constraints?

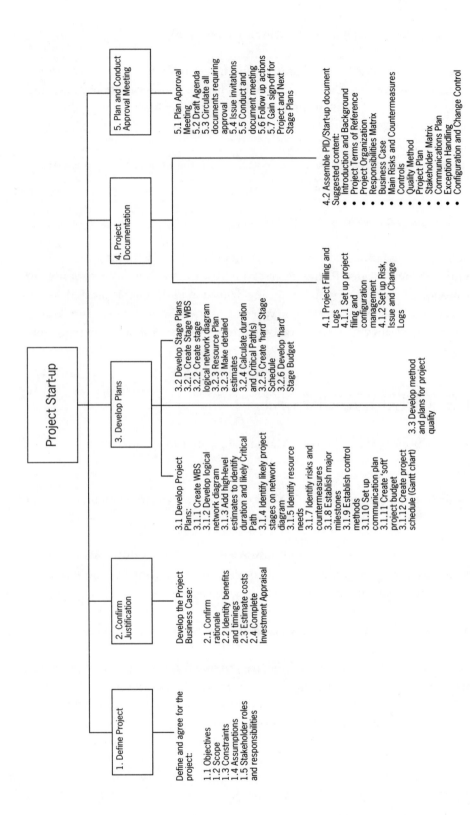

Figure 83   Sample WBS for project start-up

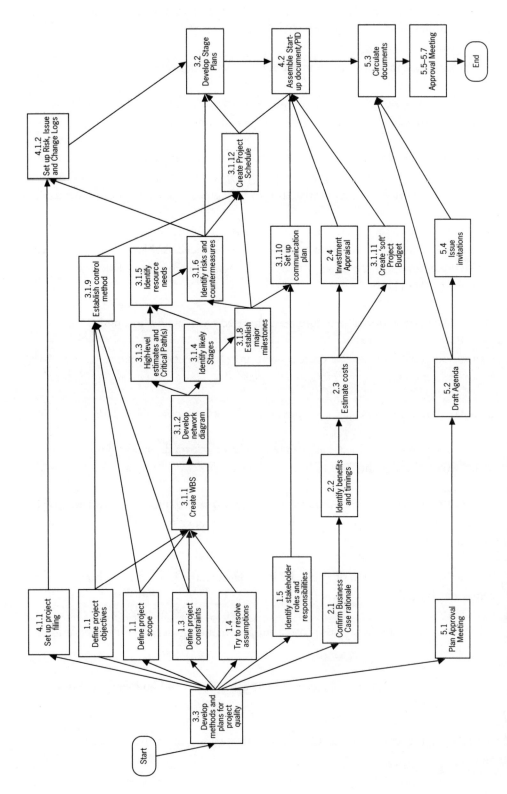

Figure 84 Sample work flow diagram for project start-up

- Have you thought of any other ways of stimulating stakeholder participation and buy-in to the planning?

- Have you identified any 'drop-dead' dates (milestone dates which are mandatory, not optional nor capable of being slipped)?

When you have got the project planning well under way, consider:

- Is the provisional Business Case standing up to critical review? Do you need to do anything to consolidate or advance it, or to identify any shortcomings?

- Does your project Work Breakdown Structure match the stakeholders' expression of their needs, priorities and acceptance criteria? Have you arranged an independent review of the Work Breakdown Structure, to help guard against 'errors of omission'?

- Have you created a logical network/flow diagram to illustrate sequence and dependencies and to see whether additional tasks are needed? Have you arranged an independent review of this, again to help guard against 'errors of omission' and to identify any flaws in the logic?

- Has the Work Breakdown Structure been updated with review findings?

- Can you identify likely logical project stages from your network diagram, particularly for work in the stage that will follow this one?

- Have you completed first-pass estimates for the tasks you have identified?

- Have you completed Critical Path Analysis to forecast overall project duration and to identify the critical path(s)?

- Does your estimate of overall duration meet any expressed duration requirements? If not, how and when will you draw this important variance to the attention of your management?

- Have you created an initial project schedule/Gantt chart? Does it show how you can achieve major milestones?

- Have you completed a first-pass project budget, including all costs for people and purchases?

- Do you have sufficient information to create a 'hard' plan and budget for the next stage?

When you are approaching the end of the Start-up Stage, consider the following questions:

- Have you planned the approval and authorization meeting and invited all the participants?

- Have you talked through key points in your documents with your project's key decision-maker (Project Board Chair/Executive) and reacted to any guidance from her or him?

- Have you created all the documentation needed to gain authorization for your Project Plan and budget and the Stage Plan and budget for the next stage?

- Have you organized or already experienced an independent review of all the principal documents, to ensure that they will meet requirements for content, format, level of detail and style? Note that this review should be 'internal', conducted by other Project Managers or Project Office staff against your organization's standards for such material.

- Will you be able to distribute all the documents for which you need approval plus an agenda to give sufficient time for participants to read them all thoroughly and prepare for the approval meeting?

- If you gain approval and authorization to proceed, are you ready to 'hit the ground running'?

SEE ALSO

Approval
Authorization
Budgets for Project Work
Business Case
Communications Plan
Controlling Against the Schedule
Filing and Document Management in Projects
Investment Appraisal for Projects
Issue Management
Milestones and Milestone Plans
Network Analysis and the Critical Path
Project
Project and Stage Plans
Project Life Cycles
Quality in Project Work
Reports in Projects and Programmes
Responsibility Matrix
Risk Management
Scheduling
Stage or Phase
Stakeholders – Identification and Communication
Statement of Work
Terms of Reference
Two-level Planning
Work Breakdown Structures

Statement of Work

A Statement of Work (SoW) sets out the objectives, scope, organization, roles and responsibilities of a project, and identifies the constraints it faces, in a similar manner to a Terms of Reference document or a PRINCE® Project Brief (see Figure 85 for typical content of a Project Brief).

Purpose of Document

A Project Brief is used to provide sound foundations for initiating a PRINCE® project.

Typical contents

Background to the need for a project
Project definition
Project objectives
Project scope and exclusions
Main project products/outputs/deliverables/outcomes
Constraints
Interfaces
Outline of the Business Case (project justification)
Project support needs
Reasons for selection of the solution and approach
Customer's quality expectations

Figure 85   PRINCE® Project Brief

WHY MIGHT IT BE USEFUL?

The SoW promotes a common understanding of a project at its outset, so that no stakeholder should be surprised by eventual outcomes, or the way the project pursues those outcomes. The value of such a document is usually gained during its development, when meetings and discussions resolve assumptions, secure agreement and develop ownership of a project, which the SoW then records as part of the communications effort, rather than as a quasi-legal document.

SUGGESTED 'TOP TEN' CONTENTS FOR A STATEMENT OF WORK

In addition to such standard features as document objectives and perhaps a management summary, a SoW might set out:

1. **The project rationale or justification**, to answer the question, 'Why do this?' – This will need to be substantiated and quantified in the Business Case.

2. **The project objectives**, to answer the question, 'What must this project achieve?' – These objectives need to be, as far as is possible, Specific, Measurable, Agreed, Realistic and Time-based (SMART).

3. **The project scope**, to answer the question, 'What must be included in and what must be excluded from this project?'

4. **The known constraints**, to answer the question, 'What do we know now that might put limits in or around our project?'

5. **The project's key outputs, outcomes or deliverables**, to answer the questions, 'What main outputs must the project deliver to whom (or to what function, department or customer), and what, if any, quantified performance requirements need to be fulfilled?'

6. **An outline project schedule**, to give a broad answer to the question, 'What is planned to be done, by when, to create and deliver the project outputs?'

7. **An outline project budget**, to give a high-level answer to the question, 'What order of direct and indirect costs is the project likely to incur, and roughly when?'

8. **The project organization**, probably a chart showing the roles and the reporting and authority lines, backed by an early draft matrix showing who owns main responsibilities and accountabilities, to answer questions such as 'Who will be responsible for what?', 'Where will the buck stop on this aspect?' and 'Who will own which decisions?'

9. **The first draft of a project communications plan**, listing all the known stakeholders and their likely communications needs, to answer the question, 'Who will need to know what and when as the project unfolds?'

10. **Any assumptions made**, to answer the question, 'What educated guesses have we made and treated as factually correct to enable the project to move forward, but which we still need to verify or discard?'

WHEN MIGHT YOU NEED IT?

A Statement of Work document should be made available to a Project Manager at the beginning of the Start-up or Initiation Stage. The work that then follows should develop and extend the project's foundations, delivering the plans and budgets that, once approved, will be used to manage the project.

HOW DO YOU USE IT?

You can add value by allowing some iteration when developing a SoW, by circulating draft versions and encouraging feedback, provided your Project Sponsor approves of this approach.

SEE ALSO

Starting a Project
Terms of Reference

Steering Group

As the name suggests, a Steering Group's main responsibility is to steer a project to a successful outcome. As in a PRINCE® Project Board, there needs to be an ultimate authority and decision-maker, who will normally be in the Chair for any Steering Group meetings and may nominate the members and appoint the Project Manager. In a PRINCE® project, this individual is known as the 'Executive'. Note that the terms 'Steering Group', 'Steering Committee' and 'Project Board' appear to be used synonymously. It is only in a PRINCE® environment that the name, organization and roles have very specific meanings.

WHY MIGHT IT BE USEFUL?

Where project scope crosses functional or organizational boundaries and is large and complex, it is widespread practice to use a group or committee approach, under the ultimate authority of the Sponsor. Some projects do not need this group organization to make decisions, particularly where the project is relatively small, straightforward and with limited scope. In these cases, the Sponsor, as customer-in chief, is probably the only authority needed.

WHEN MIGHT YOU NEED IT?

There are some important decision points in all projects, typically:

1. to approve the plans and budgets and authorize the project to start
2. to approve each stage's outputs, close that stage, and approve and authorize the plans and budgets from that point forward
3. to formally close the project.

It would be conventional for a Steering Group to participate in or be consulted about these approvals and authorizations at or before Steering Group meetings. The Steering Group should also:

- own the major Project Risks and Issues
- ensure that the best user resources are available when needed
- represent the project's interests in the wider organization.

WHAT TO AVOID

Some organizations find it difficult to run any part of their business without frequent and large-scale meetings. In a project environment, this can be counter-productive, as, if there are several participants who already need to attend all the other types of regular meetings, adding extra events to steer a project may be unwelcome and difficult to arrange. If this is the case, you need to propose use of a 'management by exception' approach as far as possible.

WHAT SHOULD YOU CHECK?

If you are the Project Manager, make sure that you know:

- the constitution of the Steering Group, the roles and authority of its members
- who holds the ultimate authority
- who you report to and take direction from
- whether and how the group will make decisions, particularly when those decisions may have cross-functional implications
- whether the group will operate on a 'management by exception' basis
- the information needs of the group, and their timing and format
- the frequency, purpose, information needs and standard agenda of any regular meetings.

SEE ALSO

Decisions in Projects
Exceptions (and Management by)
Sponsor
PRINCE® Project Board

Task Checklist

A task checklist is a list of the tasks to be completed during a stage, showing relevant important dates.

For each task on the Stage Plan, show and update:

- task identity by name and Work Breakdown Structure number
- planned delivery date/actual delivery date
- planned review date/actual review date
- planned approval date (complete and fit for purpose)/actual approval date.

This document can be produced using a word processor or spreadsheet. Its users might include:

- **The Steering Group**, to show what is planned at the start; to record advancement (or failure to advance) through progress or highlight reports; to enable stage completion to be recorded, when all task outputs are shown as approved, complete and fit for purpose

- **Any Stakeholders** you have identified on the Communications Plan as needing such information

- **The Project Team**, to show what has to be done, and when; note that on this version, you might also choose to show RACI information, those named individuals **R**esponsible for doing it, **A**ccountable for it being done, to be **C**onsulted about the task and its outputs, to be **I**nformed about the task and its outputs.

WHY MIGHT IT BE USEFUL?

The task checklist is a 'user-friendly' interpretation of the Stage Plan, which should eliminate any likelihood of daunting those unfamiliar with Gantt charts or the software used to create them. Note also that in many organizations, the majority of those who log on to a network may not have access to the planning software, but are almost certain to use both word processors and spreadsheets, so should not encounter any difficulties accessing the information.

WHEN MIGHT YOU NEED IT?

You should extract the checklist information once your Stage Plan has been approved and circulate it ready for the start of the next stage. You can use it as a basis for progress monitoring, communications and identifying issues throughout the stage. As the end of the stage approaches, you will use it for chasing completion of the final tasks and present it to summarize the end-of-stage status. You may also find it valuable when you update your Lessons Learned Report at the end of each stage.

HOW DO YOU USE IT?

Once you have determined the most helpful level of detail, create a matrix using a word processor table or a spreadsheet with all the tasks on one axis (probably down the page), with all the planned dates on the other axis (probably across the page), with interim blank columns to record 'actual' dates.

WHAT SHOULD YOU CHECK?

For all stages:

- Have you agreed the level of detail required with the Sponsor or Steering Group?
- Can you identify each task uniquely, to avoid any 'I thought that meant . . .' reactions? If you are using Work Breakdown Structure numbers, is this information known to all recipients of this checklist?
- Do you know which stakeholders need to know delivery dates?
- Have you included every task that needs to be included, and are the tasks and dates identical with those on the Stage Plan?
- Will those responsible for carrying out the tasks see this document?
- Have you included your main project management tasks?

At stage end:

- Is every task complete? If not, what impact will non-completion have? Have you agreed what needs to be done to resolve this with the Chair of your Steering Group or your Sponsor? If the agreed action is to deal with this in the next stage, does the plan and checklist for that stage now show this?

- Have you transferred information about any significant variances to the Lessons Learned Report and made a first-pass assessment of the reasons? For example, was a task genuinely late, or was the original estimate too ambitious?

SEE ALSO

Communications Plan
Lessons Learned
Steering Group
Responsibility Matrix
PRINCE® Product Checklist
PRINCE® Project Board

TASK
CHECKLIST

Terms of Reference

The label 'Terms of Reference' (ToRs) is applied to documents used in many organizations and circumstances to indicate the parameters of an assignment.

WHEN MIGHT THEY BE USEFUL?

Have you ever delivered an assignment in good faith, only to be told: 'This is not what I expected'? You are unlikely to forget such an unsettling experience. ToRs are valuable in reducing the likelihood of this happening to you and your team in the future.

Written Terms of Reference are important in defining and agreeing the expectations of those giving and receiving assignments, such as project roles. As a Project Manager, you should seek ToRs for your role, and give ToRs to those you appoint to key roles in your project team.

HOW DO YOU USE THEM?

It was Samuel Goldwyn who said: 'A verbal contract isn't worth the paper it's written on.' Although the founder of MGM died in 1974, this piece of wisdom still escapes many, who believe that they are always precise in what they say and that everyone who hears must share an identical understanding. The exchange between Lord Raglan and the Earl of Cardigan just before the Charge of the Light Brigade in 1854 is a classic example of misunderstood orders, still argued over today. At least these two military men can claim the noise and stress of battle as extenuating circumstances.

What do you do if you are given a role without ToRs? First, try asking whether there are or will be any. If there are, review and clarify them and ensure that any agreed changes are included in a revised version. If there are none, ask the person who wants you to take on the role whether they would object to you drafting your understanding of the ToRs for discussion. I have used this approach on every assignment for over twenty years as a freelance Project Manager, and not once has the offer been declined. It has always been received gratefully and positively.

Clearly, it will be impractical to write and agree ToRs for every task or product within a project, though you may, for example, use Product Descriptions to specify requirements for all Products in a PRINCE2® environment. ToRs are appropriate for more substantive and longer assignments, such as when appointing someone to a role, rather than just giving them a project task. Sample Terms of Reference are shown in Figure 86.

Draft Terms of Reference for PM's 'Cowil – CoAxial' assignment

Background
CoAxial Inc. will be the site of Cowil's first installation of its 'Silk' System in Atlantis. It is important to all of us at Cowil for this reason. It is also important to our partner, AWA, with whom we have a strategic alliance and for whom CoAxial Inc. is a key client in Atlantis.

Objectives
PM's objectives are to:

- Work with the existing team to enable delivery of the key business output, a Statement of Requirements (SOR) and to enable its use to analyse and identify the gaps between Silk's 'as is' functional and data capabilities and CoAxial Inc.'s SOR.

- Use the business outputs to develop and deliver the Management Products required from the Analysis Phase, principally a Project Initiation Document that sets out a scheme of work and a budget to bridge the gaps identified and enable implementation of the resulting solution in CoAxial Inc.

- Balance activity between managing progress and maintaining visibility and communications with CoAxial Inc. and AWA.

- Draw together subject matter experts to resolve Project Issues and to identify and estimate resource requirements for development work and installation.

- Review the existing plan and budget for Phase 1, and to recommend and implement any necessary changes after approval by the Cowil Project Board.

- Represent Cowil in all related project management matters.

Scope
Phase (1) of CoAxial Inc. Silk – requirements and gap analysis, and Project Initiation Document for any subsequent implementation project.

Constraints
Although initially described as a six-week assignment, it has since emerged that there is a 'drop-dead' date for delivery of the principal output, A, by dd/mm/yy, the last working day before the major holiday period in this part of Atlantis. As at dd/mm, this leaves only 22 working days, rather than the anticipated 30.

Assumptions

- Team members and CoAxial business specialists will all be 100 per cent available during Phase 1, and have the required skills for the tasks to be completed.

- Cowil will assemble a Project Board to steer the remaining work. It should consist of an Executive representing Cowil's business interests in the project, a user representative, probably from AWA, and John Doe to represent the Cowil 'supplier' view.

Reporting

- PM will report by noon on Friday of each week to members of the newly formed Project Board using a form with content in line with a PRINCE Highlight Report. PM will liaise with John Doe on day-to-day matters. Any forecast exception situations (anywhere delivery to CoAxial Inc. appears threatened) will be reported immediately to Project Board members.

- PM will also report on progress, Project Issues and Risks to the AWA Client Manager and to CoAxial Inc. management on an 'as required' basis.

Figure 86   Sample Terms of Reference

WHAT FORMAT SHOULD YOU USE?

Terms of Reference need to include:

- **O**bjectives — What has to be achieved?
- **S**cope — What is included in and excluded from the assignment?
- **C**onstraints — What might prevent you achieving everything?
- **A**ssumptions — What has been taken for granted to date, but may not be true?
- **R**eporting line(s) — Who needs to be kept up to date throughout the assignment?

You can see from this that you need an OSCAR format, or something that includes all the elements in a format appropriate to your organization. It will also make sense to have an initial paragraph setting out the background to an assignment (how did your organization, or your boss, or a potential Project Sponsor arrive at the point where the assignment was needed?). I learned this approach when working for the Hoskyns Group in the 1980s and have not started an assignment since without ensuring that ToRs are agreed first.

WHAT SHOULD YOU CHECK OR CONSIDER?

- Are all the main headings present and used?
- Are the objectives of the assignment or project unambiguous and SMART?
- Does the scope make the inclusions and exclusions clear?
- Are the constraints readily understandable?
- If there are any assumptions, how crucial are they, and is it clear what will be done, by whom, and by when to resolve them?
- Are the reporting lines clear, and can you see where the buck stops for important decisions?
- Is the whole document clear and precise, leaving no room for interpretation or guesswork?

'How many a dispute could have been deflated into a single paragraph if the disputants had dared to define their terms.'

Aristotle

SEE ALSO

Constraints
Objective(s)
Scope

Tolerance

The term 'Tolerance' is common to many project management environments, including PRINCE®. Tolerance can be set (a) for time and (b) for cost, to allow a Project Manager to make modest variations from plan or budget, which, as long as they stay within the pre-defined defined ranges (Tolerances), he or she can carry out without having to seek prior approval from a Sponsor. Note that you can also interpret the term 'sponsor' as the decision-maker or decision-makers for your project, such as your Steering Group or Project Board.

WHY MIGHT IT BE USEFUL?

Without some room for manoeuvre, a Project Manager would have to operate with one hand tied behind his or her back. Tolerance gives that flexibility. However good your plan, some tasks will run later than desired, some earlier. Some costs will be higher than budgeted, and some lower. Occasionally, a task will take exactly the time scheduled and cost exactly the amount budgeted. Even if the your Sponsor is a control freak, he or she will soon tire if you keep asking for approval for every minor overrun and overspend. However, we must not lose sight of one of project management's important realities: more projects founder because of the unchecked accumulation of modest problems than as the result of single catastrophic events. Use Tolerance to strike an appropriate balance between regulation and pragmatism.

HOW DO YOU USE IT?

You need to have a range of time and costs within which to operate, without the need for further permission. Corporate management or a Programme Board will normally set Tolerance to a Project Plan and Budget. The Sponsor will normally set Stage Tolerances, to enable conformance with those set for the project. This usually means that that once say a stage budget has been approved, you will not need to worry about variances, unless you forecast that the stage costs will fall outside the agreed Tolerance, normally expressed as plus or minus a percentage of the agreed budget. You could use say ± 10 or 15 per cent on costs, but your organization may choose to use different rates above and below the agreed budget, such as ± 10 per cent and −20 per cent. Once you have gained authorization to implement a plan, you should only need to report any variations when you forecast that the end date is likely to fall outside the agreed Tolerance of plus or minus so many days or weeks from the planned end date. For schedule variations, the stage Tolerance might be say ±10 working days, or +5 days and −10 days.

In Figure 87, provided that any variance stays within the range shown by the + and − Tolerance, a Project Manager should not need to seek any approvals from the Sponsor, who should also agree to accept that delivery of the outputs has been successful, when there is a within-Tolerance schedule overrun or overspend.

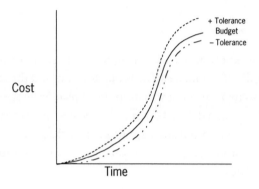

Figure 87   Cost Tolerance

You may ask why early completion and underspend ought to be subject to Tolerance, but if resources, financial and otherwise, are in short supply, it can be of great value to an organization to know that they will not be needed, in time for them to be used elsewhere.

WHEN MIGHT YOU NEED IT?

You will be aware of trends throughout a project stage, and should monitor them carefully. As soon as you forecast that a Tolerance might be exceeded, you should alert your Sponsor. The Sponsor may choose to extend the Tolerance, or to request an Exception Report.

WHAT SHOULD YOU CHECK?

- Do you have agreed Tolerances for your Project? Are they realistic? If not, what are you doing to rectify this?
- Do you have agreed Tolerance for your current and next stage? Are they realistic, given the Tolerances on the Project?
- Do you have Tolerance on stage and project end dates?
- Do you have Tolerance on stage and project budgets?
- Are the Tolerances you know expressed as ranges, usually + and −?

- Are the units in the Tolerances usable? For example, is a range expressed as a percentage of any practical use when applied to dates?

SEE ALSO

Exceptions (and Management By)
Sponsor
Steering Group
PRINCE® Project Board

Tranche (of a Programme)

A Programme Tranche is usually a group of projects within a programme that will deliver distinct outcomes, capabilities or benefits. It is perfectly possible to deliver a programme without tranches, and much depends on how your business needs to organize, execute and manage its programmes, and how it wishes to optimize the use of perhaps scarce resources.

HOW DO YOU USE IT?

Creating Tranches is perhaps more an 'art' than a 'science', and choices could be based, for example, on projects that are related by function, or on projects related by time or location. For instance, in an office relocation programme, you could set up three Tranches consisting of all the projects related to:

1. accommodation, equipment and furnishing
2. human resources, such as relocation, recruitment, training and outplacement/redundancy of those not wishing to move
3. procuring all the supplies and services for the new location and for winding down those at the existing location.

These are illustrated in Figure 88.

Alternatively, you could decide that groupings of projects into Tranches based on distinct and logical timings might help you more, such as:

1. pre-relocation
2. relocation
3. post-relocation.

These are illustrated in Figure 89.

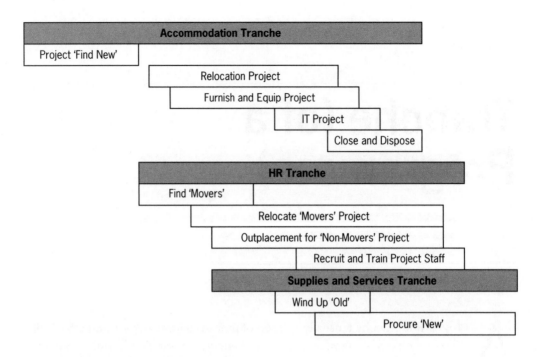

Figure 88 Tranches based on function

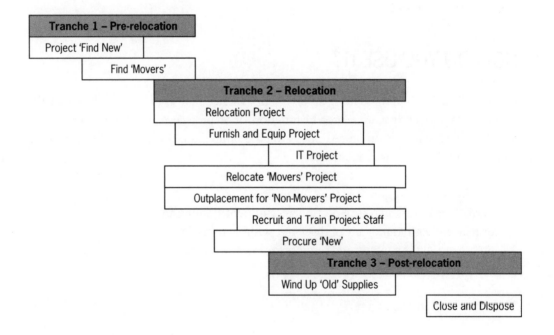

Figure 89 Tranches based on timings

You will note from a comparison of the examples in Figures 88 and 89 that one appears to have a more even distribution of projects between Tranches (Tranche 2 in Figure 89 is very large, and probably complex). There are other alternatives for creating Tranches within a programme, such as by location (one Tranche of projects to move from, close down and dispose of the 'old' location, and another to set up, staff, furnish and equip the 'new' location. You can also divide some programmes into Tranches, to ensure that you make best use of scarce resources, whether in the execution or management of your portfolio.

You will also note from the examples that you do not have to complete one Tranche before starting another, and can arrange the flow of project activity to meet your organization's needs.

WHAT SHOULD YOU CONSIDER?

- Do you need to deliver a project portfolio through a formalized 'programme' approach?

- Would it help you to manage more effectively if you spread the portfolio across a number of Tranches?

- Can you identify useful groupings of projects that might give you a basis for creating Tranches? For example, can you see groupings that are linked by location, function (discipline), delivery of distinct capabilities or benefits, or that enable you to avoid serious resource shortfalls?

FURTHER READING

CCTA (1999), *Managing Successful Programmes*, London: The Stationery Office.

Reiss, Geoff (1996), *Programme Management Demystified: Managing Multiple Projects Successfully*, London: Spon.

SEE ALSO

Programme or Project?

Tuning or Scaling a Project

The important concept of scaling, or tuning, a project approach ought to be self-evident, but experience suggests that this may not always be so. Projects can be as much endangered at one end of the scale by an over-bureaucratic approach, as by one that is over-casual and indifferent to its circumstances at the other end. An over-bureaucratic approach can demoralize the team, who may feel that all they do is complete forms and reports, with no time left to complete any 'real' project work and deliver it to the customers. At the other end of the spectrum, projects attempted with inadequate plans and controls can founder without warning. Projects of differing size, complexity and risk need different approaches to their organization (who is responsible for what?), structure (how many stages are needed?), planning (how many plans are needed, and at what level of detail?), risk and issue management, change and configuration control procedures, and so on.

WHY MIGHT IT BE USEFUL?

If you use identical approaches on large complex projects and small simple ones, you run the risk of either falling dangerously short on the former, creating unreasonable overheads for the latter, or falling somewhere between the needs of both. Scaling is the process of putting appropriate factors in place for each project, according to its importance, size, complexity and risk. Figures 90 and 91 show approaches for projects of different sizes.

In the example in Figure 90, the organizational needs should be satisfied by a Sponsor, who will justify the work and who holds the budget for the area in which it will take place, plus a Project Manager, who may also be the only resource. The single plan should be brief and simple, showing what has to be done, when, and by whom, and what the outputs will be. It could sometimes be as simple as a 'to do' list with completion dates. Use it to create and justify the small budget and to review progress. In these circumstances, the Sponsor and Project Manager are likely to see each other frequently, so the need for scheduled formal meetings should be minimal. Project Risks are unlikely to be high for the business area, but should be identified and monitored. Any Project Issues are likely to

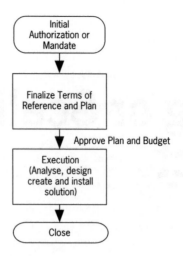

Figure 90   Typical 'small' project structure

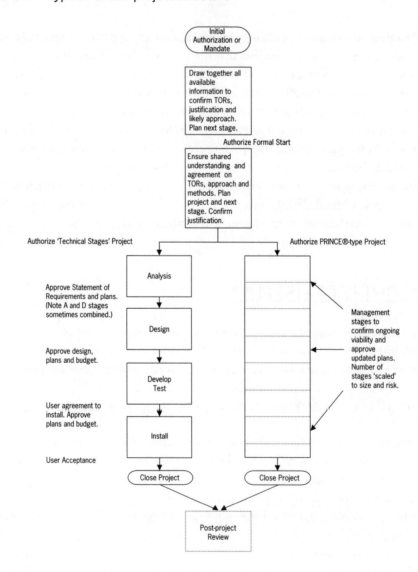

Figure 91   Typical 'larger' project structure, showing non-PRINCE® and PRINCE®
options

be owned by the Sponsor, who can also consider and approve any changes without undue delay.

For larger projects you are likely to need a formal organization, such as a Steering Group or Project Board, headed by a Sponsor or Chair. The decision-maker(s) should appoint a Project Manager and assist her or him to create a team appropriate to the needs. There should be a formal Start-up, with a Business Case, a plan for the project and each succeeding stage, logs for Project Risks and Issues, Change Control procedures, and regular formal reporting. The timing and number of stages should be appropriate to the size, complexity and risks, so that the Project can be managed effectively. If you are running a non-PRINCE® project, you need to consider whether it will be prudent to use intermediate Management Reviews by setting milestones part-way through long technical stages.

WHAT PROCEDURES SHOULD YOU CONSIDER 'SCALING'?

If you work in a project-based organization, or one that runs a reasonable number of projects, you may have project models or templates to help you reach early and consistent decisions on whether your project fits a standard project approach. If so, use it to make decisions on the level and detail of plans, controls, risks, issue and change management matters, documentation, and decision-making needs and timings. You should have no need to re-invent any wheels: just fine-tune and use it. If you just have a standard 'large' project model, consider scaling it up or down to suit your project's characteristics.

If you use PRINCE®, your Project Board should define how many stages will be used, or perhaps the time interval between each. Your expertise might be called upon to advise these decision-makers, so analyse the size, complexity and risks, and make appropriate and justified recommendations.

SEE ALSO

Approval
Authorization
Budgets for Project Work
Business Case
Change Control
Decisions in Projects
Handover options
Issue Management
Milestones and Milestone Plans
Project Life Cycle
Risk Management
Small Project
Sponsor
Starting a Project

Steering Group
Terms of Reference
PRINCE®
PRINCE® Project Board
PRINCE® Project Initiation

Two-level Planning

If you use detailed plans for project work that will take place within a relatively close horizon, such as a current stage, and an outline, less detailed plan for work beyond that horizon, such as the project beyond the current stage, you are already using two-level planning. You may know this better as 'hard' and 'soft' planning, but whatever you call it, it provides a pragmatic approach, with a detailed plan for each stage, and an outline for the remaining stages in the project. As you approach the end of each stage, you can plan the next stage in detail and firm up the Project Plan. This approach is also known as 'Rolling Wave Planning'.

WHY MIGHT IT BE USEFUL?

Early in any project, you face many uncertainties. Things may go exactly to plan, but this would be rare. Variations may be positive or negative, with things going better or worse than planned. As you move through any project, you need to reduce the uncertainties. Figure 92 shows a hypothetical range of uncertainties you usually can face at the start of a project.

At the end of each stage, you will know more, and will modify your plan to reflect this

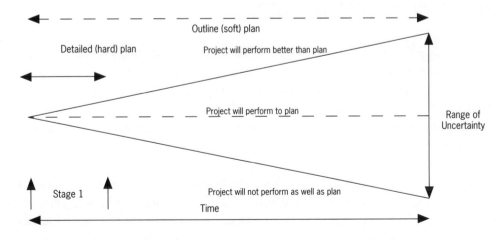

Figure 92   Range of uncertainty

new knowledge. Your planning horizon should have moved, and you can plan now for the next stage and refine the Project Plan (see Figures 93 and 94).

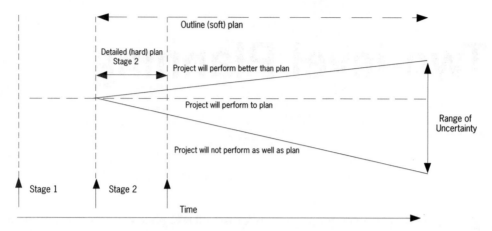

Figure 93   Reducing the range of uncertainty

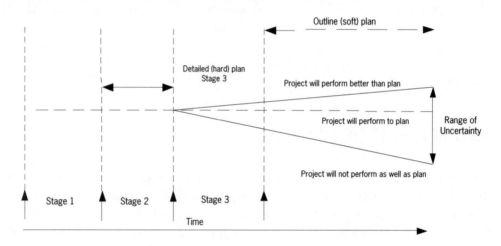

Figure 94   A two-level plan later in the project

WHEN MIGHT YOU NEED IT?

The shortest projects are sometimes accomplished in two stages: Stage 1 – plan it; Stage 2 – do it. Even for such a relatively modest undertaking, someone will ask, 'How long will it take?' If you reply, 'I can tell you when I have finished the plan', they may well ask, 'When will that be?' If you can produce a detailed plan for the planning work and give a broad indication of the overall duration, you will be able to refine the broad indication as soon as the planning is complete.

This principle of planning your next work in detail and subsequent work in outline is a common-sense approach used in many walks of life. For example, while the captain of your aircraft will file a flight plan, he or she will revise and refine the plan as the journey progresses, taking account of such factors as weather and air traffic, and will agree a detailed landing plan with air traffic control only as the destination draws closer.

HOW DO YOU USE IT?

To gain approval for project work, you will need a project plan and budget for the whole endeavour, and to gain approval and authorization for both. However, at such an early point you will face many unknowns, so many organizations will give conditional authorization to proceed by releasing funds for the first stage, based on a detailed plan and budget for that work. When you complete the stage, you will know more about the whole initiative and be able to refine the overall plan and produce a detailed plan and budget for the next stage. This gives your Steering Group the chance to manage the risks inherent in projects, particularly when your work early in the project finds that the challenges are much greater than originally perceived. When this happens and your plan and budget double in size, they might choose to opt out, or re-start with a different scope and objectives.

Note that if you use a prescribed method for routine and repeated projects, you may know well in advance many of the 'Hows?' and 'Whats?' of the project – those standard tasks you perform each time. You will know much less about answers to questions such as 'When?', 'Where?', 'Who?', 'How big?' and 'How much?'. In these circumstances, you may be able to create a Work Breakdown Structure relatively early, but will still need to review and update it, allocate available resources, estimate effort and duration and so on, until you are ready to create a detailed plan.

HOW MIGHT YOU PROCEED?

1. Develop a Project Work Breakdown Structure, say down to Level 3.
2. Convert the Project Work Breakdown Structure into a logical network diagram showing sequence and dependencies.
3. Identify stage boundaries on the network diagram, to show which tasks belong in which stages.
4. Develop a Stage Work Breakdown Structure to the required lowest levels of detail, to develop a detailed (hard) plan for the next stage.
5. Use the remaining Project Work Breakdown Structure to develop or refine an outline (soft) plan for the rest of the project.
6. Review steps 1–3 and repeat steps 4 and 5 as you approach the end of each stage.

SEE ALSO

Estimating
Network Analysis and the Critical Path
Project and Stage Plans
Project Life Cycle
Scheduling
Stages – Start and End Procedures
Work Breakdown Structure
PRINCE® Product Breakdown Structure

Web Projects

These hints and tips may help you if you are planning and managing a project where a simple website, or web pages on the Internet or intranet, are included somewhere among your deliverables. You might also have decided to use web communications for your project, particularly where your stakeholders are widely scattered. If so, you would create this as one of your earliest deliverables, enabling you to maximize the sharing of plans and information throughout.

WHAT DOES ALL THE WEB JARGON MEAN?

The following list contains a brief selection of common web terms and acronyms, but is not intended to be exhaustive (feel free to skip the list if you are already familiar with basic web terminology).

- **Browser** – Software used to access the Internet and intranets. The two most widely used are Netscape Communicator® and Microsoft Internet Explorer®.

- **Firewall** – Security software to protect sites from intrusions and from theft of and interference with your data.

- **FTP** – File Transfer Protocol, which provides software and method for moving files around the Internet. Most commonly, you will need to use such a product to move your web pages, in HTML format and probably with graphics in Graphic Interchange Format (GIF) or Joint Photographic Experts Group (JPEG) format , from wherever you have created them to the server from which the world will be able to access them.

- **Home Page** – Your 'front' page, which should have a 'contents list' and signposts to all the other pages on your site. This is the first page that visitors see when they come to your URL address from a search engine or from information you have published elsewhere, so it needs to look good.

- **HTML** – Hyper Text Mark-up Language – a programming language widely used for publishing on the web, developed by Tim Berners-Lee, the founding father of the

World Wide Web. It combines normal word processor documentation with the addition of 'tags', which are those letters or symbols surrounded thus <>. Note that you do not have to know HTML to create web pages, as many word processors will translate into HTML for you. For example if you write 'Use Microsoft Word® to build a simple web page!' and view the HTML version, this is what you might find hidden among all the other HTML that has been automatically generated:

<p class=MsoNormal><span lang=EN-GB style='mso-bidi-font-size:11.0pt; mso-bidi-font-family:Arial'>Use <b style='mso-bidi-font-weight:normal'>Microsoft Word®</b> to build a simple Web page!<o:p></o:p></span></p>

You will notice many tags giving instructions, such as the ® which puts the 'registered' sign in superscript.

- **Internet** – A world wide network of computers that hosts domains such as the World Wide Web.

- **Intranet** – A private, internal version of the Internet, normally published within and normally only accessible to an organization, and possibly its customers and suppliers.

- **Net (The Net)** – The Internet.

- **Search engine** – Software tools that allow you to search billions of web pages for sites related to keywords you choose. You can use HTML tags called Meta Tags (<META>), so that you can list all the keywords you think potential customers might use when searching for products or services such as yours. Such search engines include Lycos, Infoseek, Webcrawler, Excite, Yahoo!, Google, Altavista and many more.

- **Server** – Any computer that 'serves' information to others.

- **Tags** – HTML instructions and information. For example, HTML <B>Jargon!</B> would put the word **Jargon!** on your site in bold type. <B> Gives the instruction to display what follows in bold type until the instruction is terminated by </B>, when type reverts to normal.

- **TCP/IP** – Transmission Control Protocol/Internet Protocol provides the fundamental technology for Internet and intranet use, but is not something with which you should need to become too closely involved!

- **URL** – Universal Resource Locator, the unique address of an Internet page. Your site's URL address might look like <http://www.yourownsite.co.uk>.

- **Web** – The World Wide Web, part of the Internet.

CREATING PAGES OR SITES

Putting simple pages and graphics online is something that many computer-literate people are able to do, after a short familiarization process with the technology and with little or no knowledge of project management. However, if you manage a project that puts pages on the web that are poorly designed, slow to load, hyperactive when loaded, inaccurate, badly written or impossible to find, you might seem to have achieved your project plan, but success will be empty as your hit-counter remains almost static and those who do find your site find few reasons to linger.

Do not be swayed by views that the only person capable of managing a web project is a technical guru. The old saying that 'the more technical a project, the less it needs a technician to manage it' remains valid. Clearly, it is useful to understand the terminology, the approach and problems, but if you get too close, you risk being drawn into a technician's role, leaving the project to stumble along by itself.

WHY MIGHT KNOWING THE BASICS BE USEFUL?

There have been many occasions in the history of projects where technicians have been able to manage, or manipulate, Project Managers from behind a technical smokescreen. Provided you have project management experience, a broad understanding of the technology, identify some very specific deliverables and build in some sensible monitoring measures, you should be able to deliver successful web-based outputs. The great thing about web pages and sites is that they are tangible. Tangibles are great for Project Managers – either the page or pages exist, containing all they are supposed to, in the colours, fonts and formats agreed, with logos, pictures and animations and working links, or they do not. You don't need to be a guru to check this. However, if your organization is implementing a corporate e-commerce strategy, you might need the support of a Technical Project Manager to manage the technicians and to be accountable to you.

WHAT STAGES MIGHT YOUR PROJECT GO THROUGH?

Given that your project has sound justification and is seen to be desirable, technically feasible and affordable, you may need to go through technical stages such as:

1. **Requirements Definition** - Establish a precise customer and user specification and any prioritization ('must', 'ought to' and 'nice to haves').

2. **Design Part A** – 'Build' the site on a storyboard using flipcharts, which you review frequently with customers and users. You can establish a contents list for each page and work out links to other pages on this site and elsewhere. If you need graphics, such as corporate logos and any pictures, you can sketch these too. You might follow this with **Design Part B**, where you create simple mock-ups or prototypes of the pages, so that your customers and users see what they will look like, and be happy that the 'look' is right. From this, you can finalize the specification, the design and the infrastructure that your customer will sign up to. You can now use this as the basis for your Project Plan and budget. Work with a Technical Team Leader designate, if appropriate, to create a detailed plan and budget for the 'build' stage. Identify

milestones wherever significant outputs should be available. Present your Project and Stage Plans to gain authorization for the remainder of the project. This is the major 'go'/'no go' decision point, where the customers know the design and the likely costs and duration.

3. **Build** – Establish the technical team, and build the outputs. Make sure you have online access to the outputs, so that you and the customers can stay very close to what is being created, and influence it if appropriate. Stick to the milestones, and make sure the Team Leader tracks and reports progress in a manner and at a frequency that satisfies your requirements. Conduct reviews with the stakeholders and developers regularly.

4. **Test exhaustively in conditions as close to reality as it is possible to get** – Remember that tests on web pages on a standalone PC or your corporate network may produce very different results from tests conducted on the Internet! Test your FTP server for uploading the finished pages. Check page loading speeds, links, buttons, dropdown menus, feedback forms, order forms, credit card checking and transactions, interfaces with your database, search facilities, text clarity, and make sure there are no blind alleys where users might find themselves unable to navigate properly. You should have already worked out where your site visitors will come from and updated corporate stationery with your new web site address if appropriate. This will keep your existing contacts informed. You may also advertise in trade journals or other selected media, to attract new contacts. Note that if you set and publish a launch date using any of these methods, you have a self-imposed constraint, and will need to stick to it.

5. **Implement** – Load your pages and prime your selected search engines so that other new contacts can find you. Have your technical team stand by in case of the unexpected, and track both 'hits' on your site, which may just reflect curiosity, and transactions that complete as you hoped, such as by completed orders. Do not close the project or disband the team until you are satisfied that presentation and performance are satisfactory.

WHAT MIGHT YOU CHECK?

For any website, keep a close eye on the following:

● Keep page size manageable and navigable. You do not want a site visitor to get lost on one page and not know whether up or down is the best way to go. Build your home page like a town centre, with information about the main attractions, and how to find them. Try to stick to a core topic for each page so that once there, a visitor should be able to find everything on that topic.

● Make sure your text serves you well and presents the image that you seek. Spelling, grammar and punctuation should be accurate and help to ensure that the visitor reads what you intended, not something that is capable of misinterpretation. If your pages are accessible worldwide, be careful not to use words or symbols which may not mean what you intended in another country, particularly if you are trying to find customers there.

- While a picture may be worth a thousand words, many used on websites are worthless decorations. Too many or large pictures slow the page loading process. Invite visitors interested in seeing an enlarged picture to click on a thumbnail version, which will have loaded quickly. If you have an online catalogue, you will probably need to use this thumbnail method or risk browsers falling asleep while waiting for the images to load. Animated graphics should be used sparingly, but can be superbly eye-catching for something you need to highlight.

- You may have walked into a room and felt unease because everything clashed with everything else. Conversely, you may have had a different experience in a room where everything blended and felt harmonious and comfortable. The style of your pages is under your control, and should support the message you are trying to get across. Choice of colours and fonts are important to your image, so choose with care. Only use wacky text and colours if this is the impression you want your site to create – say, if you sell jokes and novelties.

- Help visitors find their way around, back and out by providing excellent links and easy-to-follow guidance and instructions. If you would like them to contact you, make sure directions are clear and accurate.

SEE ALSO

Communications Plan
Project and Stage Plans
Project Life Cycle

Work Breakdown Structure

A Work Breakdown Structure (WBS) is a planning structure, usually a list or chart, that shows how the work to deliver a given project is to be broken down into the tasks and sub-tasks that are likely to be required. Samples of list and chart formats are shown in Figures 95 and 96.

BS6079 describes a project as 'a unique set of co-ordinated activities, with definite start and finishing points, undertaken by an individual or organisation to meet specific objectives within defined schedule, cost and performance parameters'. In project work, you will normally be dealing with sets of activities and you are likely to apply the WBS technique to this part of your planning work.

In his book *A Survival Guide for Project Managers* (Amacom, 1998), James Taylor describes the Work Breakdown Structure as 'perhaps the most useful technique of project management'. In their book *Project Management, System Development and Productivity* (Daniel Spencer Publisher, 1985), Stephanou and Obradovitch state: 'The project WBS is the heart … the framework on which the project is built.'

Once your management has defined and issued a Statement of Work or Terms of Reference for a project, (perhaps called a Project Brief or something similar), you will need to start planning. Your first steps are likely to be those of identifying and documenting what has to be done. You should find a top-down method helpful, where you can start with a high-level statement of objectives and scope, and finish with a detailed understanding of all the tasks you will need to plan and execute. You will need to include tasks to create the outputs you will eventually deliver to your customers as well as those interim tasks you will need to plan and steer the project to a successful conclusion. All will consume effort, time and money. You might develop a table or chart showing how you have broken down your project, possibly starting at the level of major sub-systems, or perhaps Project Stages. Once you have done this, you can then break each of these down into lower levels of detail, eventually showing all the necessary tasks and sub-tasks.

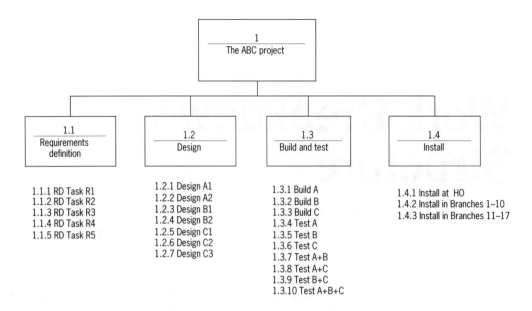

Figure 95 Graphical Work Breakdown Structure with lists: a combination of the diagram and structural list approaches

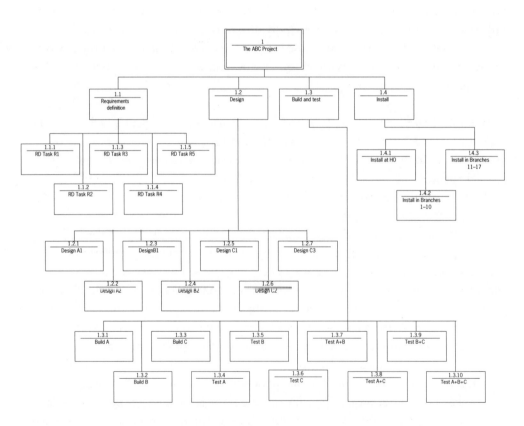

Figure 96 Graphical Work Breakdown Structure

You should find the Work Breakdown Structure a useful technique for this crucial work. You can produce your WBS as a diagram similar in form to an organization chart (Figure 95), or as a structured list (Figure 96), or as a combination of these two approaches, perhaps the most common form (Figure 97), showing everything that will need to be done. If your organization uses the Work Breakdown Structure and has existing standards, you should use these and seek any help you need from experienced practitioners. If you have a software package, so much the better later on, but you might find that the brainpower you can harness in a workshop and a supply of Post-it® notes will get you off to a flying start.

1	**The ABC Project**	
1.1	*Requirements Definition*	
	1.1.1	RD Task R1
	1.1.2	RD Task R2
	1.1.3	RD Task R3
	1.1.4	RD Task R4
	1.1.5	RD Task R5
1.2	*Design*	
	1.2.1	Design A1
	1.2.2	Design A2
	1.2.3	Design B1
	1.2.4	Design B2
	1.2.5	Design C1
	1.2.6	Design C2
	1.2.7	Design C3
1.3	*Build and Test*	
	1.3.1	Build A
	1.3.2	Build B
	1.3.3	Build C
	1.3.4	Test A
	1.3.5	Test B
	1.3.6	Test C
	1.3.7	Test A+B
	1.3.8	Test A+C
	1.3.9	Test B+C
	1.3.10	Test A+B+C
1.4	*Install*	
	1.4.1	Install at HO
	1.4.2	Install in Branches 1–10
	1.4.3	Install in Branches 11–17

Figure 97   Indented List Work Breakdown Structure

REFERENCE NUMBERS

You will note that the samples use numbering conventions that provide unique and permanent reference numbers for every task in your project. You will see also that these identify the level (1 is a project – Level 1; 1.1 is at Level 2; 1.1.1 is at Level 3 and so on). It is conventional to show the project name with the number 1. Numbering conventions do vary from one organization to another, so don't worry if yours doesn't match this example. However, the level of a piece of work on a WBS diagram should also be apparent from the number, with perhaps one digit at Level 1, two at Level 2 and so on. You may find that your organization allocates a unique reference to every new project, which may also appear as part of the identifier for every task and sub-task, making each rather long, but unique in your project and accounting history. If your project is part of a programme, you will need to conform to the programme's conventions.

KNOWING WHERE TO START

Where and how might you start a Work Breakdown Structure? Let's look at two examples of projects and options for the first steps in each breakdown. First, let's consider a project to turn a large plot of land surrounding a new house into a garden. You have been asked to create a Work Breakdown Structure for 'The New Garden Project'. Your customer has already agreed the design, but wants you to plan the work to implement the design, so from this point on, you, as the Project Manager, have to decide how to break the project down into all the likely tasks, and sub-tasks where appropriate. Where should you start? What are the main task groupings? Well, you might choose:

1.   The New Garden Project
     1.1   Clearance and site preparation
     1.2   Vegetable garden
     1.3   Fruit trees
     1.4   Ornamental trees
     1.5   Shrubs
     1.6   Lawns
     1.7   Flower beds
     1.8   Water features
     1.9   Paths
     1.10 Patios and paving
     1.11 Storage
     1.12 Seating
     1.13 Greenhouses
     1.14 Statues and features.

The next level of breakdown for, say, 'Statues and features' would be numbered 1.14.1, 1.14.2 and so on.

You might choose to break it down a different way:

1.   The New Garden Project
     1.1   Front garden
     1.2   Back garden
     1.3   Side garden (east)
     1.4   Side garden (west).

Or you might decide on yet another approach:

1   The New Garden Project
    1.1   Earthmoving
    1.2   Drainage
    1.3   Heavy construction
    1.4   Light construction
    1.5   Turfing and groundwork
    1.6   Planting
    1.7   Features
    1.8   Buildings.

Take another example of, say, a marketing campaign. You might break the campaign down into Direct Mail, Website Development, Radio Advertising, Sports Sponsorship and Free Seminars, then decompose each of these into their component tasks. Or you might decide to break the campaign down by socio-economic groups, or alternatively into age-ranges, or something completely different. Don't get hung up on 'rights' and 'wrongs' – think more about approaches that might be helpful or unhelpful, easily understood or confusing to your customers, or natural or unnatural, when being used on your project. Which best suits your purpose or fits your organization's approach? Do not forget that a WBS does not attempt to indicate sequence, which you will identify later, in a network diagram. What is important is that whichever option you choose, you will eventually identify the same tasks to implement the design and create the garden. If you are unsure, experiment with more than one approach, and run with the one that then feels best-suited to the project you are working on.

KNOWING WHERE TO STOP

Once you have started breaking the major parts down (known as 'decomposing' or 'decomposition'), where do you stop? Stop at the level where the work is actually going to be done, effort applied and costs incurred. You will probably describe this level using an active verb and an object. For example, refer to any one of Figures 94–96. If, for example, Task 1.4.1 – 'Install at HO' was to deliver a new accounting system, you would probably need another (fourth) level, numbered 1.4.1.1 to 1.4.1.n, including such tasks as 'Install new terminals', 'Install software', 'Deliver user training', and so on.

Rules of thumb:

●   It is unusual to find more than five levels in a WBS, unless the project is very large and very complex, or the person developing the WBS has missed something important in the technique. Note that your organization's standards may define how many levels you should use, and what ought to appear at each of those levels.

●   Not every part of a WBS will decompose to the same level, so do not struggle to achieve this.

- A task should be a cohesive piece of work capable of being measured on its own.

- Avoid going into micro-detail level on a Work Breakdown Structure, which should define work that has to be done, not how to do it. At the same time, avoid leaving potentially very large pieces of work undivided. For example, on a small project you could decide that it is not worth sub-dividing any piece of work that you believe should be completed within one day. For larger or more complex projects, you might decide that lowest-level tasks might take five days, or maybe even ten (but perhaps no larger if you want to control progress effectively).

- The WBS does not seek to express or imply sequence, other than when you use project stage names at Level 2.

- Don't forget that project and quality management tasks are work, so need to be included on your Work Breakdown Structure. If not, how will you remember to include them in the plans and budgets?

If the WBS is so useful, why do we not find one at the core of every project? Here are some answers:

- Standards and conventions vary considerably, even though the underlying principles remain common.

- Experienced Project Managers who have never been trained in the use of the WBS will use their own approaches to identify tasks. The WBS approach may never have appeared in their organizational standards, so you may well experience an 'If it ain't broke, don't fix it' response.

- Many Project Managers produce lists of things to be done to deliver the project, but perhaps do not structure them in any way, and simply add 'hindsight tasks' to the bottom of the list.

- In projects where there is great uncertainty, it may be claimed that no useful purpose will be served in creating a WBS that will be out of date very quickly.

Once you have examined the samples in Figures 95–97) and perhaps tried a few dry runs on parts of a familiar project, you may quickly appreciate, and soon be able to use and demonstrate, the strengths of the Work Breakdown Structure in getting project planning under way.

PRINCE®

Note that if you use PRINCE®, you will probably create a hierarchical chart called a Product Breakdown Structure (PBS). This has a similar valuable role, but shows products (deliverables) rather than tasks, and is fully described in the OCG's *Managing Successful Projects with PRINCE* (The Stationery Office, 2002).

SEE ALSO

PRINCE® Product Breakdown Structure

Work Distribution Model

A Work Distribution Model is a high-level estimating model based on the historical distribution of work across past projects, used most often in organizations that:

- repeat projects broadly similar in characteristics and structure
- maintain project histories recording the effort and duration of projects and their stages.

This approach is also known as 'comparative estimating'.

When projects deliver regular outputs such as software-based business systems to their customers, whether internal or external, each project is likely to follow some form of 'System Development Method' (SDM), with pre-defined stages that will include similar tasks each time they are used. In such cases, it becomes sensible to record 'actuals' against plans, and to store this information in order to help and improve future estimating. Once an organization has been through this cycle several times, project or Project Office staff will be able to analyse the records and establish patterns of such things as relative effort and durations of stages. These can then be expressed as heuristics, which are assumptions based on past experience, perhaps more commonly known as 'rules of thumb'. Your organization may choose to express these as percentages, which will give a guide to the broad distribution of work or duration of project stages over a typical project. For example, if you have a six-stage system development method, your findings might be:

Stage	Typical Effort
Initiation	5%
Requirements Definition	13%
Design and Specification	20%
Development and Testing	35%
Implementation	25%
Close down	2%

Note that these are hypothetical figures for illustration purposes only. You will need to analyse your organization's project histories to develop figures relevant to your typical projects. Note also that the above figures are based on situations where any Feasibility Study would have been conducted pre-project.

WHY MIGHT IT BE USEFUL?

If your organization regularly runs projects that have similar characteristics, keeps adequate records of 'actuals', and records and studies 'lessons learned', you should be able to create your own model, reflecting typical projects and stages. You may find that you will come up with more reliable and useful figures on the 'effort' consumed by a project and its stages, which you can record in person-days, weeks, or months. Actual durations are subject to many variables, such as when a particular project stage coincides with a holiday period. In such circumstances, it might take 50 per cent longer, but still consume the same effort.

WHEN WOULD YOU NEED IT?

One of the more useful applications of this 'rule of thumb' approach is in validating estimates made using different approaches or at different points in an evolving project. For example, if a pre-project Feasibility Study has made a high-level estimate of the possible effort needed to deliver the recommended solution and approach, this will need to be investigated and verified, or refuted. If you are conducting a project start-up or initiation stage, to deliver plans and budgets for the coming project and you have reasonable confidence in the typical effort consumed during this work, you can apply the percentage provided to effort actually expended on the start-up and calculate possible overall project effort. You can then use this to cross-check the validity of your detailed estimates and the Feasibility Study's global estimates. The effort (person-months) figures you will need will be those you developed during the start-up work, probably based on a Work Breakdown Structure and supported by some bottom-up estimating techniques. If this varies significantly when cross-checked against what typically happens on such projects in your organization, this variance ought to be checked.

COST ESTIMATES

You may be able to extend your analysis to include typical costs and model these too, though the profile might be different. For example, Figure 98 shows a sample cost profile for bespoke business system development. Different types of projects can have similar profiles. For example, if you were to design and build a house on a plot you already owned, the profile could look similar.

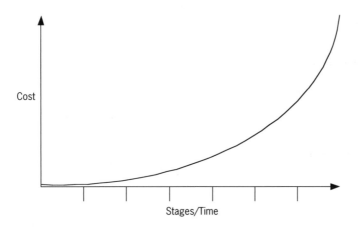

Figure 98 Sample project cost profile

WHAT SHOULD YOU CHECK?

If you do not have existing work distribution 'rules of thumb':

- Do you have 'actual' figures readily available for projects similar to your own?

- If so, can you determine and quantify how the effort was distributed across project stages?

- Is this distribution such that you could assign a typical percentage effort to each stage?

- Don't forget that if you experiment with this, you will need to keep recording actuals and tuning the figures.

If you do have existing work distribution 'rules of thumb':

- Apply them to actual effort consumed during your project start-up work and cross-check your detailed estimates and any global estimate produced pre-project.

- If your detailed estimates vary significantly, investigate before using them. If you are still confident after the investigation, use them, record actuals, and apply any lessons learned to future project and stage estimating.

- Also cross-check any global estimates produced pre-project, such as in a Feasibility Study. The project will have been justified on these global estimates, so if your cross-check brings them into serious doubt and this is supported by your detailed estimates, you may be starting a project for which the justification is flawed. Your role is simply to report your findings. Your Sponsor or Steering Group will need to consider what action to take once they have received this information.

SEE ALSO

Budgets for Project Work
Estimating
Lessons Learned
Sponsor
Steering Group
Work Breakdown Structure

Work Package

A work package is a group of work activities in a Stage Plan, supported by an information set, normally relating to a key deliverable, with a named individual accountable for its delivery.

'A set of information about one or more required products collated by the Project Manager used to pass responsibility for work or delivery to a Team Manager or team member.'

The term 'Work Package' has a specific meaning in PRINCE® terminology: The term has been adopted for a similar purpose within other project approaches. When you break down (decompose) a project into its constituent work elements, a typical hierarchy might be Project, Stage, Work Package, Activity and Task. Note that the terms 'Task' and 'Activity' seem to be used interchangeably, and are not universally used in the sequence shown above.

'Work Packages' are specified clusters of work within a stage, to produce the main deliverables, products or outputs of that stage. For example, let us assume that you were planning a Feasibility Study, and that within the study you need an investment appraisal for each solution and approach that looks politically, operationally and technically feasible. It might make very good sense to set up an Investment Appraisal Work Package and allocate it to an individual with the special skills, knowledge and experience. This 'deliverable' orientation means that each Work Package can usually be delegated to an individual, who will become accountable for its 'on time and to budget' delivery and its conformance with specification. This individual may be a Team Leader assisted by others, each of whom may be given responsibility for delivering one or more parts of the Work Package.

You may identify your Work Packages at Level 3 in a Product or Work Breakdown Structure diagram (perhaps below 'Project' at Level 1 and 'Stage', 'Phase' or major deliverable name at Level 2) – see Figure 99. You may decompose each into its supporting Activities and Tasks at Levels 4 or 5, but beware – this terminology and usage varies between organizations and authors.

If your organization uses a 'Work Package' approach, consult your standards to see what information needs to be made available to the accountable recipient, so that he or she has

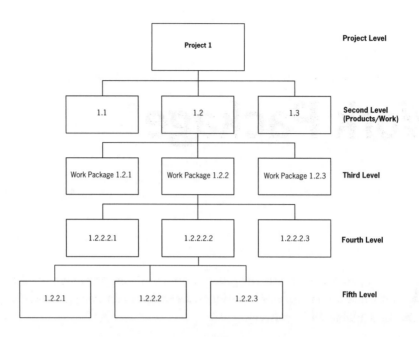

Figure 99 Example of a possible Work Package structure

a full and clear understanding of what is required. If the recipient of a Work Package is a third-party supplier, there is likely to be a contractual imperative for a clear, detailed written specification when such work is allocated.

WHAT SHOULD YOU CHECK?

- Have you conducted product and/or work decomposition and identified major tasks and deliverables – that is, have you broken down large pieces into smaller component parts, either through creating a Product Breakdown Structure (PRINCE® Project) or a Work Breakdown Structure?

- Can you readily identify Work Packages – logical groups of activities to produce each major deliverable?

- Are the Work Packages identified on the schedule?

- Do you have a format and procedure for documenting such a Work Package, to enable it to be delegated to a named and accountable individual?

- Have all the Work Packages in the current stage been documented, allocated, estimated and budgeted?

- Is each component of the deliverable specified?

- Is it clear how progress will be monitored and reported?

- Have you confirmed your detailed estimates and budget after consulting the accountable individual to whom the Work Package has been/will be delegated?

- Does the Work Package documentation specify how quality and completeness will be assessed, and by whom?

- Does the documentation identify who should be consulted or communicated with as the deliverable is created?

- Are interfaces with and dependencies on other Work Packages identified?

- Is reference made to all project constraints, risks and issues that may affect the Work Package?

POSSIBLE CONTENT OF A WORK PACKAGE ALLOCATION DOCUMENT

Note that in smaller projects, Work Package allocation may be relatively informal, though you may still wish to include:

- the individual accountable for the Work Package
- date allocated
- date required
- Work Package narrative, outlining the requirements
- Product Descriptions or specifications, to add necessary detail
- tools, techniques, procedures and standards to be used
- interfaces to be maintained during and fulfilled after the Work Package is completed
- quality method that will be used to check output
- schedule information from the Stage Plan
- any other relevant/helpful information, such as risks or issues that exist, contacts and stakeholders.

SEE ALSO

Quality Reviews and Product Descriptions
Work Breakdown Structure
PRINCE® Product Breakdown Structure

Zero Tolerance

A CAUTIONARY NOTE FOR PROJECT SPONSORS

One objective when deciding on a suitable title for any non-fiction work is to describe the book and its purpose succinctly. When Jonathan Norman at Gower Publishing suggested 'A to Z' as part of the title of this book, it was a wise recommendation. After all, the topics in the book are arranged in alphabetic sequence. This approach to the name was so obvious that it had been overlooked entirely. Were there likely to be any drawbacks? At the front of the book, you will find the topics 'Approval' and 'Authorization' that satisfy the 'A' requirement. At the end of the text, I only got as far 'W', for such topics as 'Work Breakdown Structures' and 'Work Packages'. Alas – no 'Z'! At first there was no obvious 'Z' candidate, but perhaps 'Zero Tolerance' is worth a few words, of value to those readers who oversee, direct, sponsor or steer projects and programmes.

WHAT IS 'TOLERANCE'?

'Tolerance' is the term for ranges within which variations from a project or stage plans and budgets can be made by the Project or Stage Manager without the need to seek prior approval from whatever higher authority is in place, such as from a Steering Group. Many project practitioners have a good understanding of this concept. However, experience suggests that this does not always mean they make good use of their knowledge. At Sponsor level, rather than seeing the judicious use of 'Tolerance' as a project management 'best practice', many perceive it as a threat to control. When used as intended, Tolerance provides a simple mechanism for empowering Project Managers and liberating the Sponsor. It should enable them to run projects smoothly and flexibly, without the Project Manager having to seek approval for corrective measures whenever unexceptional variances in plans and budgets occur, which they do regularly in the nature of projects. Sponsors can use Tolerance to stay in control, but with a 'hands-off' approach. All they need to do is agree a range of Tolerances, plus and minus for time and money, within which the Project Manager has freedom to act. Only when the Project Manager forewarns the Sponsor that variances are likely to exceed this range should that individual need to act.

WHAT IS ZERO TOLERANCE?

Zero Tolerance is best known as a policing philosophy, applied in hotbeds of criminal and anti-social behaviour, with the aim of making them fine places – anyone who deviates beyond the letter of the law faces a fine, or worse. While very often strikingly effective in these circumstances, a 'Zero Tolerance' approach to project management is not recommended for the following reasons:

● It can demonstrate a serious lack of trust.

● Project problems often demand full-time attention and prompt decisions, which they will not get from many Sponsors, who normally have other significant demands on their time. The Project Manager usually knows what needs to be done, but may be prohibited from taking action.

Nothing above should be seen as a suggestion that tight control of time and budget is not important. Very few project practitioners would argue with the saying 'Take care of the pennies and the pounds will take care of themselves', or with Fred Brook's famous answer, 'One day at a time' to the question 'How does a project get to be a year late?' Sound control is crucial to project success. The questions are how, when, where and by whom control is first exercised. Clearly, Sponsors may be tempted not to use Tolerance for projects managed by new and less experienced Project Managers. Before they select this option, they may do well to consider coaching, mentoring or training the newcomer in the identification and handling of variances. Sponsors can set tighter tolerances until they become more comfortable and confident in the Project Managers' abilities, at which point Tolerances can be set to normal ranges.

SEE ALSO

Tolerance

Appendix: PRINCE®

This Appendix contains brief introductions to some of the important processes and products in PRINCE®, the United Kingdom government's project management method for information systems. PRINCE® is also now used in industry and commerce, in fields far beyond both information systems and government. Although PRINCE® has a systems pedigree, its concentration on project management rather than technical activities makes its application universal. The definitive text on PRINCE® is:

> Office of Government Commerce (2002), *Managing Successful Projects with PRINCE2*, London: The Stationery Office.

The author has used PRINCE® in both its original and PRINCE 2® versions for almost ten years and became a PRINCE 2® Practitioner in 1999. He was introduced to PRINCE® by Chris Ferguson, then of Duhig Berry Limited, whose directors and consultants made a major contribution to its development. Chris is now Managing Director of Novare Consulting Limited (<http://www.novareconsulting.com>), and contributed enthusiastically to this Appendix by reviewing the text and using his experience and knowledge to suggest improvements.

This manual does not advocate PRINCE® as the best or only way of managing projects successfully. Critics of PRINCE® believe that it can be bureaucratic, and that some organizations appear to apply it in such a manner that the means is more important than the ends, with the real outputs of their projects seeming of secondary importance. Like all methods, its success depends on how well, how sensibly, and how pragmatically it is implemented and managed.

PRINCE®: Introduction

PRINCE® is a project management method widely used in government, commerce and industry. It has become the standard project management approach in many organizations in the United Kingdom. The acronym stands for **PR**ojects **IN** Controlled **E**nvironments. PRINCE® was established in 1989 by the Central Computer and Telecommunications Agency for UK Government projects and is currently owned by the Office for Government Commerce (OGC). Because it concentrates on project management 'best practice', it is widely used across many different types of projects. PRINCE® is a registered trademark and all references to PRINCE® throughout this manual acknowledge this trademark. At the time of writing this manual, PRINCE 2® is the current version.

PRINCE® is made up of components, processes and techniques:

- **Components**
  - Organization
  - Plans
  - Business Case
  - Controls
  - Risk Management
  - Quality
  - Configuration Management
  - Change Control

- **Processes**
  - Starting Up a Project (SU) – purpose: approval for commencement
  - Initiating a Project (IP) – purpose: developing the PID, a project 'contract'
  - Directing a Project (DP) – purpose: overall control and 'steering' decisions
  - Controlling a Stage (CS) – purpose: day-to-day management
  - Managing Product Delivery (MP) – purpose: interfacing with suppliers
  - Managing Stage Boundaries (SB) – purpose: inter-stage review of ongoing viability
  - Closing a Project (CP) – purpose: formal project closure
  - Planning (PL) – purpose: recurring process to maintain effective approach.

- **Techniques**
  - Product-based planning
  - Change Control
  - Quality Reviews
  - Project filing

WHY MIGHT KNOWING ABOUT PRINCE® BE USEFUL?

PRINCE® is the project management method of choice in many organizations, and is based on 'best practice' over many years. It is an open, public-domain product, founded on the need to justify projects properly, put an appropriate project management structure in place, break the project into a suitable number of stages, and tune its use in accordance with project size, complexity and risk.

HOW DO YOU USE PRINCE®?

PRINCE® differs from many other methods because of its orientation is towards project management, irrespective of the technical nature of the project. This means that it can support your project aims, whether in information technology, business change, procurement, training development, or any combination of innovation or change. Other methods have grown from very specific needs, such as those used to develop and implement computer-based systems. These have tended to follow technical phases or stages, rather than being derived in a structured way from the needs and expectations of customers and users. The crucial difference between PRINCE® and many other approaches is that PRINCE® is product-based, whereas many alternatives are activity-based with the activities often being technique-specific, such as those used when developing IT systems. In PRINCE®, some of your earliest planning work will be centred on identifying and defining the products you will eventually deliver, which could include almost anything. The strength of PRINCE® is its universal applicability.

The publication, *Managing Successful Projects with PRINCE2* (The Stationery Office, 2002) is the main reference work for PRINCE users. Many organizations have based their approach and standards on its contents. PRINCE® users also work to pass the PRINCE 2 Practitioners' Examination in order to become registered PRINCE 2® Practitioners and demonstrate their understanding of its application.

SEE ALSO

Ten particularly important or useful PRINCE® topics have been included in this Appendix. Note that the topics are in alphabetical order and are not intended to be read in their physical sequence. Use of *Managing Successful Projects with PRINCE 2* is highly recommended, as this definitive publication covers the entire range of components, processes and techniques for PRINCE® projects in great detail.

- PRINCE® and Planning Software Tools which covers the use of PRINCE® in partnership with activity-based software planning tools, such as Microsoft Project®
- PRINCE® 'Off Specification'
- PRINCE® Product Breakdown Structure
- PRINCE® Product Checklist
- PRINCE® Product Description
- PRINCE® Product Flow Diagram
- PRINCE® Products
- PRINCE® Project Board
- PRINCE® Project Initiation
- PRINCE® Tolerance

PRINCE® and Planning Software Tools

While the PRINCE® project management method is 'product' based, many planning tools, such as Microsoft Project® are 'task'-based. Note that Microsoft Project examples are used throughout this topic. If you are a user of PRINCE® or such planning software, you may recognize their individual strengths and potential. If you are a user of both, you may wonder how best to reconcile this seemingly fundamental difference and combine the strengths of the method and the tool in a productive partnership. It can be done earlier in the planning process than you might think. How might you carry out the necessary transition from 'product' to 'task' and make it work well for you?

Those familiar with PRINCE® will know that the recommended first step in the planning process is to develop a Product Breakdown Structure (PBS), in which one attempts to identify all the needed products. The resulting diagram should look something like an organization chart with 'The Project' at the head of the hierarchy rather than 'The Organization'. The main products (deliverables) can then be broken down into their components in a similar way to an organization chart's division into Departments, Sections and Roles. The approach is logically quite close to that in Work Breakdown Structures (WBSs) described elsewhere in this manual, though the second level in a PBS usually breaks down into the same three products – Management Products (to plan and manage the project), Quality Products (to support the management of the project) and Specialist Products (those items that the project has to deliver to its customers – the real reasons for doing the project). A 'specialist product'-oriented analogy could be that of some of the information in a 'Bill of Materials', where, for example, all the parts of motor vehicle may be identified under major headings such as Engine, Transmission, Bodywork or Suspension. Each of these can be described by Assemblies, Sub-assemblies, Components, and so on. For example, replacement parts for a diesel engine might include piston assemblies, each with a piston, compression rings, oil control rings, a gudgeon pin and circlips, within a cylinder liner, all packed ready for distribution. You could initially show the components on a PBS as in Figure 100.

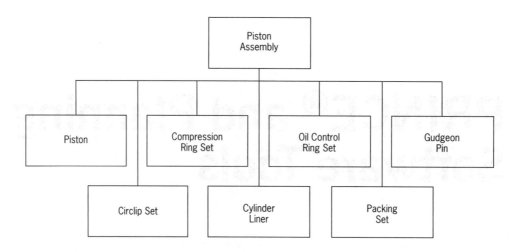

Figure 100   Sample product Breakdown Structure (PBS)

Then you could use Product Flow Diagram to show an assembly and packing sequence as in Figure 101.

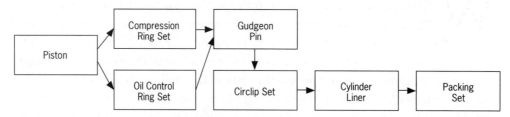

Figure 101   Sample Product Flow Diagram

WHAT SHOULD YOU DO OR CHECK WHEN PLANNING PROJECT WORK?

1. Create a Product Breakdown Structure, as you would normally do when using PRINCE® as in Figure 102, where the example will be a procurement project.

2. Input your products via the Gantt entry screen as in Figure 103.

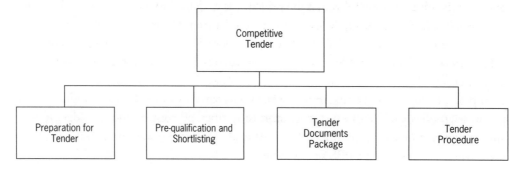

Figure 102   Product Breakdown Structure: Levels 1 and 2 only

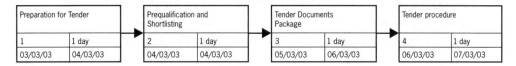

Figure 103   The four products, now on a Gantt chart

3. When Gantt input is completed, change to the PERT screen, and create a Product Flow Diagram directly. You can move any box by highlighting it, holding the Control key and using the keyboard's directional arrows, or by using the 'drag and drop' method.

4. Once the boxes are roughly in position, create the logic flows. Click on a 'predecessor' box, then drag an arrow to a 'successor' box. Continue through the diagram to show the logical sequence and dependencies, as in Figure 104.

Preparation for Tender		Prequalification and Shortlisting		Tender Documents Package		Tender procedure	
1	1 day	2	1 day	3	1 day	4	1 day
03/03/03	04/03/03	04/03/03	04/03/03	05/03/03	06/03/03	06/03/03	07/03/03

Figure 104   The four main products in 'delivery' sequence: a basic Product Flow Diagram

5. Adjust the box size depending on the size and complexity of your PFD. (In PERT view – Format/Box Styles/Boxes – Small, Medium or Large ('Smallest' is no good for this, as it only shows an I/D number).

6. At this stage, the only information you probably need for each PFD box is the name of the Deliverable/Product. Click on 'Format/Box Styles/Boxes'. Dropdown menu 1, the top of five boxes, defaults to 'Name' in any case, so leave this unchanged. Select the **blank** entry at the top of each dropdown menu (2–5). You will then end up with an undivided box for each product containing just its name. See Figure 104.

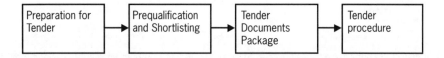

Figure 105   Reformatted version of the Product Flow Diagram in Figure 104

If the full name does not show, either consider making the box size larger as described in (5) above, or make the text size smaller. Use 'Format/Text Styles/Size to select a point size that you can read, but which also allows you to see the full Product name. (Note that although the dropdown menu shows 8 point as the smallest size, you can enter a point size as small as 4.) You should now have a draft PFD.

7. If you are planning a project and are already aware of the likely project stages, you can also arrange the diagram to show the stage in which you intend to deliver each

PRINCE® AND
PLANNING
SOFTWARE
TOOLS

product. To do this, try treating each stage as a separate page. Page divisions show as broken lines on the PERT view. Using 'drag and drop', move the boxes to the appropriate page and arrange them to show the time flow from left to right – that is, the products early in the stage to the left, and the later ones towards the right. Once they appear to be in the appropriate place, enter 'File/Page set-up' and click the 'Footer' tab. Where it shows 'Page &[page]', change this to 'Stage &[page]'. This will work simply, provided your first stage is Stage 1. If you then change to the 'Header' tab, you can then add a title for your Product Flow Diagram, which will appear above each page/stage.

8. As is always the case, some third-party review will be beneficial at this time, to check for flawed logic and missing dependencies. Your planning software will not have permitted you to create any 'loops' (circular dependencies).

9. From now on, you should keep each of the Products in the Product Flow Diagram as a 'Summary Task', as you develop from logical plan to schedule. Back in Gantt Entry mode, you can then identify the one or more activities to create each product, without affecting the sequence of the Product Flow Diagram, as in Figure 106.

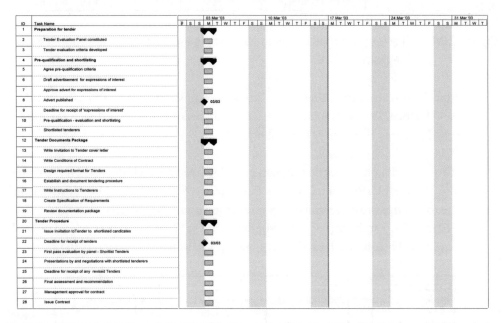

Note: The diamond shapes are 'milestones' that mark significant points in time such as deadlines, but do not use up time or any of your other project resources.

Figure 106   The four products, now showing as 'Summary Tasks' and containing the tasks needed to create them

10. Next, you will need to work out the sequence and any dependencies between the tasks. Estimate the duration of each, based on the size of each task and the skill level(s) of the resources available to do the work (see Figure 107). Note that for most software planning tools the default for dependencies is 'Finish to Start', and this is implied on a Product Flow Diagram. Once you have drafted the Gantt chart, you may need to check whether 'Start to Start', 'Finish to Finish' or 'Start to Finish' might be more appropriate for some aspects of your plan and adjust it accordingly.

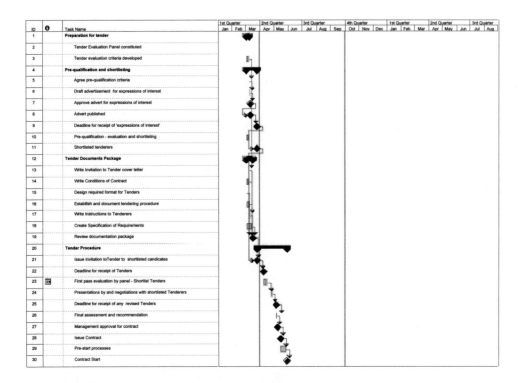

Figure 107   The four products, showing as 'Summary Tasks' containing the tasks needed to create them, and now showing durations, sequence and dependencies

Now, you will have a schedule derived directly from your PRINCE® Product Flow Diagram, with each product at 'Summary Task' level, and each showing all the required tasks. You will probably already have experienced the potential for iteration as you do similar work, so check to guard against errors of omission. This may help you to identify 'new' or 'forgotten' tasks and may make you re-think some products. For example, in the planning above, you may decide that you need a new product, 'Contract'. If this is the case, you would need to add it to your PBS, then to the PFD with revised high-level dependencies, and finally to the Gantt chart, showing all the contract development tasks and their dependencies.

SEE ALSO

Estimating
Milestones and Milestone Plans
Scheduling
Work Breakdown Structures
All PRINCE® topics

PRINCE® 'Off Specification'

‘Off Specification’ is a PRINCE® term used to describe a product that does not or is forecast not to match its specification, or that should have been but has not been produced and is not forecast to be produced. In a PRINCE® project, all such occurrences should be captured and recorded as Project Issues. Where PRINCE® is not being used, the term ‘non-conformance’ may be applied.

WHY MIGHT IT BE USEFUL?

If you or any of your stakeholders have identified the need for a product, which has then been recorded on a Product Breakdown Structure, you should also have identified the work needed to produce it, allocated resources and funding and scheduled its development. If, for whatever reason, you do not deliver the product, or if you deliver it other than as specified, there may be cause for concern. Such concerns need to be investigated and resolved.

WHEN MIGHT YOU NEED IT?

The technique could be useful any time a project stakeholder raises a concern about an apparently flawed or absent product.

HOW DO YOU USE IT?

1. Someone identifies a concern.

2. Check the Issues Log to make sure it has not already been raised and examined.

3. Help the individual check whether there is a simple explanation, such as a wrong Product name, or a misunderstanding of a plan or Product Description. If no simple explanation, ask them to raise a Project Issue in the Issues Log.

4. Use normal methods for examining any Project Issue, and if appropriate, treat this as an 'Off Specification'. Note that where any of your outputs is flawed or forgotten, you, not your customer, will normally need to meet the cost of any remedial work.

5. If the concern turns out to mean that a customer wants to change something that had originally been agreed and planned, this is still a Project Issue, but may lead to a Request for Change, which your customer is likely to need to pay for, if the change is accepted and included.

6. If the decision is to bring the off-specification product up to scratch, then any rework should be planned and delivered – it may be at the supplier's expense. Otherwise the product may be accepted as substandard, if agreed by those who will use it next.

WHAT SHOULD YOU CHECK?

If there is a stakeholder concern about a product of the 'flawed' or 'forgotten' variety:

●   Does any originally planned product appear to be missing, or not forecast to be delivered?

●   Does any product, whether still under development or seemingly completed, appear to be flawed in any way?

●   Is there a simple explanation? If so, explain this to the stakeholder, then record and close a Project Issue with the explanation, to avoid anyone else having to raise the same concern. If not, raise a Project Issue and action it as appropriate. If there is an 'Off Specification', record this in the Project Issues Log.

SEE ALSO

Change Control
Issue Management
Request for Change
PRINCE® Product Description

PRINCE® Product Breakdown Structure

For those using PRINCE®, a PBS provides you with an outcome similar to the Work Breakdown Structure – a hierarchy that shows how you intend to decompose large products into their smaller component products. In the WBS, you break large pieces of work down into smaller component pieces of work (Tasks).

WHEN MIGHT IT BE USEFUL?

Producing a PBS is an essential prerequisite for, and input to, the rest of the planning process, for which creating Product Descriptions (PDs) and a Product Flow Diagram (PFD) are subsequent steps.

HOW DO YOU USE IT?

Under the PRINCE® Planning Process, there is a sub-process, 'Defining and Analysing Products' (acronym PL2) which you will use to define your plan by identifying the products it will deliver. Note that you use this approach whether working on a Project Plan or a Stage Plan – the principles and practice are identical.

Under PRINCE®, there are three pre-established product types:

1. **Specialist Products** – those outputs the organization is running a project to deliver to the customer(s), for ongoing use after the project has been completed.

2. **Management Products** – those outputs that you use to start, manage and close down the project under management control; this category includes such items as plans and reports.

3. **Quality Products** – those outputs used to help establish that products satisfy stated requirements; Quality Products include such items as Quality Plans, Product Descriptions and Quality Logs showing authorizations and sign-offs.

Your first steps are likely to be those of identifying and documenting everything that you have to produce. You should find a top-down method helpful, where you can start with a high-level statement of objectives and scope, and finish with a detailed understanding of all the products you will need to plan for and deliver. You will need to include both the outputs you will eventually deliver to your customers, and those interim products you will need to plan and steer the project or stage to a successful conclusion. Both will consume effort, time and money. You will start with a very simple hierarchy, as in Figure 108.

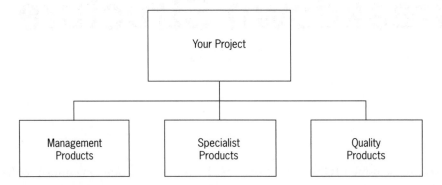

Figure 108   Initial PBS

Once you have done this, you can then break each of these down into lower levels of detail, eventually showing all the necessary products and sub-products. Note also that where your project needs 'external' or existing products – that is, items that you will not create, but acquire or refer to – you should show these using a clearly recognizable format, such as an ellipse or circle, rather than a box. Such products might include items like mandatory standards, existing infrastructure that you need to use, or reference to an existing database, such as an address list or catalogue. Check your organization's standards to see how you should show such products.

You can produce your PBS as a diagram similar in form to an organization chart, as in Figure 107 above, but may also find a structured list, or a combination of these two approaches helpful. It is common practice to use a diagram for the top levels, with lists of products below each main product-type as in Figure 109.

If your organization requires Product Breakdown Structures, use existing standards and seek any help you need from experienced practitioners. If you have a software package, so much the better later on, but you might find that the brain power you can harness in a workshop and a supply of Post-it® notes will get you off to a flying start.

WHAT SHOULD YOU CHECK?

● Have you included all the products, at the levels you intended?
● Have you identified and included any required external or existing products?
● Have you verified completeness by transferring the products to a Product Flow Diagram and to Product Descriptions? Has this helped you confirm that the products you have identified are complete and will satisfy all dependencies?

● Have you identified the products needed to deliver the Business Case and manage the risks?

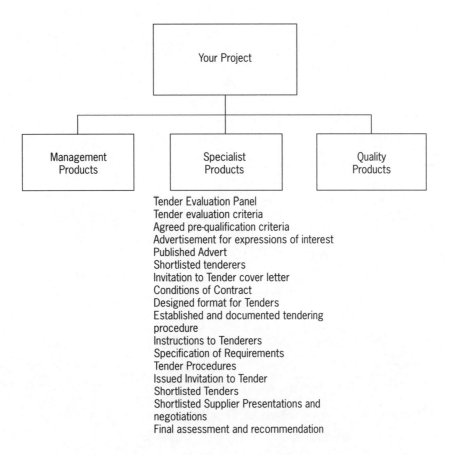

Figure 109   Combination of diagram and lists (specialist products only)

SEE ALSO

PRINCE® Product
PRINCE® Product Breakdown Structure
PRINCE® Product Description
PRINCE® Product Flow Diagram

PRINCE® Product Checklist

The PRINCE® Product Checklist is a list of the products to be delivered during a Stage Plan, showing relevant important dates.

For each product on the Stage Plan, it should include:

- Product identity/name
- Planned delivery date/Actual delivery date
- Planned review date/Actual review date
- Planned approval date (complete and fit for purpose)/Actual approval date.

This document can be produced using a word processor or spreadsheet. Its users should include:

- the Project Board or Steering Committee, to show what is planned at the start; to record advancement (or failure to advance) through highlight reports, and to enable stage completion to be recorded, when all products are shown as approved, complete and fit for purpose

- any stakeholders on the Communications Plan who you have identified as needing such information

- the Project Team, to show what has to be done and when; note that on this version, you might also choose to show RACI information – those named individuals:
  - **R**esponsible for creating the product
  - **A**ccountable for it being delivered
  - those to be **C**onsulted about the product
  - those to be **I**nformed about the product.

WHY MIGHT IT BE USEFUL?

This is a 'user-friendly' interpretation of the Stage Plan, which should minimize the risk of daunting those unfamiliar with Gantt charts and the software used to create them. Note also that, in many organizations, the majority of those who log on to a network may not have the planning software, but are almost certain to use both word processors and spreadsheets, so will not encounter any difficulties accessing the information.

WHEN MIGHT YOU NEED IT?

You should extract the checklist information once your Stage Plan has been approved and circulate it ready for the start of the next stage. You can use it as a basis for progress monitoring, communications and identifying issues throughout the stage. As the end of the stage approaches, you will use it for chasing completion of the products and present it to summarize the End of Stage status. You may also find it valuable when you update your Lessons Learned Report at the end of each stage.

HOW DO YOU USE IT?

Once you have determined the most helpful level of detail, create a matrix using a word processor table or a spreadsheet with all the products on one axis (probably down the page), with all the planned dates on the other axis (probably across the page), with interim blank columns to record 'actual' dates.

WHAT SHOULD YOU CHECK?

For all stages:

- Have you agreed the level of detail required with the Project Board?

- Can you identify each product uniquely to avoid any 'I thought that meant . . .' reactions? If you are using product identification numbers, is this information known to all recipients of this checklist?

- Do you know which stakeholders need to know delivery dates?

- Have you included every product that needs to be included, and are the products and dates identical with those on the Stage Plan?

- Will those responsible for creating the product see this document?

- Have you included your main project management products?

At stage ends:

- Is every product complete?

- If not, what impact will non-completion have? Have you agreed what needs to be done to resolve this with the Chair of your Project Board or your Sponsor? If the agreed action is to deal with this in the next stage, does the plan and checklist for that stage now show this?

- Have you transferred information about any significant variances to the Lessons Learned Report and made a first-pass assessment of the reasons? For example, was a product genuinely late, or was the original estimate too ambitious?

SEE ALSO

Communications Plan
Lessons Learned
Reports in Projects and Programmes
Responsibility Matrix
PRINCE® Project Board

PRINCE® Product Description

Product Description (PD) is a PRINCE® term for the document that describes a product's 'purpose, composition, derivation and quality criteria'. You produce Product Descriptions during the planning process.

WHY MIGHT IT BE USEFUL?

A product description serves a number of valuable purposes:

- It makes you iterate when planning, and helps guard against sins of omission by requiring derivation information ('What needs to be completed to provide the inputs to this product?').

- It provides a clear and unambiguous specification, names the person or team who will be responsible for creating a product, and tells them how and against what criteria it will be reviewed to determine whether it is fit for purpose and thus complete.

- It creates a framework for those responsible for reviewing it, and provides the quality criteria.

- It is easy to replicate for standard products, such as Highlight Reports, Stage Plans and even Product Descriptions.

WHEN MIGHT YOU NEED IT?

Note that many organizations that use PRINCE® sensibly do not require you to create a PD for every product you identify on your Product Breakdown Structure. This pragmatism avoids situations where you might spend as much time producing a Product Description as you will spend on creating the product. Some organizations also have standard PDs for routine Management and Quality products such as, for example, a

Highlight Report. In these organizations, you should have criteria to help determine which product types need a PD, often described as 'major' or 'key' products, alongside other perhaps more simple checklists for the balance. Common sense should be the arbiter.

WHAT SHOULD YOU CHECK, AND HOW MIGHT YOU FORMAT A PRODUCT DESCRIPTION?

- **Coverage** – Have you created a PD for every product on the Product Breakdown Structure for which a PD is required?

- **Name** – Have you given a descriptive, meaningful, and unique name to the product? Have you considered showing the unique Product Breakdown Structure reference number to avoid any ambiguity?

- **Purpose** – Have you explained the purpose that the product will serve?

- **Components** – Have you listed all the components that must be present to complete the product?

- **Derivation** – Have you identified the prerequisite products that will need to be completed, so that all the information required to create this product will be found ready for use? Have you included products from outside the project?

- **Format** – Have you specified the format or template to be applied and what medium the product must be created on, including software to be used if any?

- **Quality Criteria** – Have you specified what quality evidence will indicate completeness and fitness for purpose?

- **Quality Method** – Does the PD describe how the quality of the product will be reviewed and by whom? Note that such a review aims to ensure that a product satisfies what has been specified in the Product Description ('Does it meet the Quality Criteria?').

- **Assigned to** – Have you named someone who will be responsible for creating the product? (Optional.)

- **Skills Required** – These are sometimes added to specify skill levels that will be needed to create the product. (Optional, but sometimes important.)

SEE ALSO

Quality Reviews and Product Descriptions
All PRINCE® topics

PRINCE® Product Flow Diagram

I f you are a PRINCE® user, you are likely to create a PFD to show the sequence and dependencies of stage or project products that you have identified and documented on a Product Breakdown Structure (PBS) diagram. This step marks a transition from establishing what you have to produce to working out the sequence of that production. In a task-based approach, you may have first identified tasks on a Work Breakdown Structure diagram, and then represented dependencies on a work flow diagram. In both cases, you will also need to create Product Descriptions for your PRINCE® products, or specifications for your deliverables (non-PRINCE®).

WHY MIGHT IT BE USEFUL?

When planning, you always need to establish what you are going to produce and in what sequence. As part of this process, there are three important steps you should take. First you should create a PBS, followed by a PFD, and then by as many Product Descriptions (PDs) as are needed. When you write a Product Description, you need to identify any prerequisite products, those that it will be derived from and upon which it will be dependent. For example, when drawing a PFD showing the flow and sequence for the production of your Management Products, a PBS is will appear before a PFD and any PDs. See Figure 110.

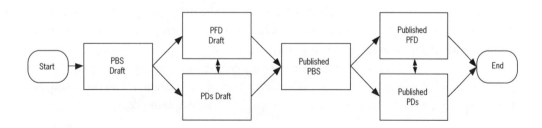

Figure 110   Sample Product Flow Diagram

This is not a diagram for PRINCE® purists, but an illustration of what tends to happen during this part of the planning process. The diagram represents the likely iteration during this work, particularly when you need to complete the 'derivation' information on a PD and find that, without adding a 'new' product to both the PBS and the PFD, you might not have the right information or basis to be able to create the product you are describing in the PD. The double-ended arrows in the diagram are not technically correct, but are used to show the necessary iteration between the two document types, as derivations (dependencies) are worked out. Note also that the three 'draft' documents would not need unique Product Descriptions as they are working versions only and you would normally only arrange Quality Reviews using Product Descriptions, for those to be baselined, published and used.

WHEN MIGHT YOU USE A PRODUCT FLOW DIAGRAM?

You will need to work on PFDs during the planning process for both Project and Stage Plans, and on Exception Plans if you encounter serious difficulties on a stage. In PRINCE® terminology, this work will be part of process PL2, 'Defining and Analysing Products'. You should also review the PFD to help you assess the potential impact of any significant changes proposed during the project's life cycle.

HOW DO YOU CREATE ONE?

You should find that in a PRINCE® environment, some templates might already exist for Management and Quality Products for Project and Stage Planning, such as PBS elements and their typical flows, so you may not need much original thinking here. If you have no templates, you might consider creating them as a by-product when conducting a planning process next time. You will need original thinking when working on the Specialist Products – those products that any project is established to deliver to an organization. Such projects could vary in complexity and scale: for example, from providing refurbished accommodation and office services for a small number of staff to creating a satellite-based battlefield communications system for the combined services. The good news is that symbols used in PFDs do not come any simpler – you use boxes containing words, linked by arrows, except for products provided externally, for which you use an ellipse.

You will find that if you have conducted a planning workshop to identify Specialist Products, any sticky Post-it® notes you may have used to develop a PBS can, once you have documented this accurately elsewhere, be re-used by the same group of people to draft a 'Specialist' PFD. Use whiteboards or wide sheets of brown paper stuck on the walls. You will find this approach valuable not only because you can 'pick the brains' of the participants to gain a clear understanding of requirements and constraints, but also because you can identify 'new' products and resolve differences about dependencies there and then, building a valuable feeling of shared ownership of subsequent plans.

You will need to avoid mixing different levels when creating a PFD. For example, at the top of a PBS you will find a box with a project or stage name, and below that you should find three boxes, one each for Management, Specialist and Quality Products. These are group headings only, and need not appear on your PFD. If below this you have two more levels, use one or the other, not both, on the same diagram, depending on the level of detail you require. Note that for detailed planning, you will tend to use the lowest-level breakdown, while for outline planning you may choose to use the next level up.

Here are some hints

- Try working backwards from final products and asking workshop participants 'What do we need in place before we can create this?'

- Add any Management and Quality Products later, avoiding unnecessary complexity during a workshop or during the initial work on developing the plan.

- Remember that on a Product Breakdown Structure, not all breakdowns will end at the same level. Many are likely to stop at Levels 3 and 4, possibly even Level 5 for large and complex projects and products. When developing your PFD, it is quite possible for these levels to be mixed – say, for example, where a Level 5 product is derived from one at Level 4, and one at Level 3.

WHAT SHOULD YOU CHECK?

- Have you included all the specialist products, at the levels you intended?
- Have any required external or existing products been identified and included?
- Have you checked the derivations (dependencies) to make sure they are logical and will work?
- Have you created Product Descriptions where required? Do the derivation sections reflect your PFD accurately?
- Have you revised your Product Breakdown Structure to include 'new' products identified during the development of the Product Flow Diagram and the Product Descriptions?
- Have you added Management and Quality Products as required?
- Have you arranged for a Quality Review?

SEE ALSO

PRINCE® Product Breakdown Structure
PRINCE® Product Description

PRINCE® Products

PRINCE® uses a product-based approach to planning, so if you work in a PRINCE®-based environment, you will need to be familiar with the terminology. In PRINCE®, the word 'product' has a specific meaning, being the generic name for every project and stage input, deliverable, output or outcome. PRINCE® differs from other project management approaches in its initial concentration on products rather than activities. Products are of three main types:

- **Management products** – These are normally documents, which are inputs to and outputs from the management of the project and include such items as the Business Case, a Risk Log, schedules, budgets and project management reports.

- **Quality products** – Again, normally documents, these are used to support the process of managing the quality of project and stage products and include such items as Project and Stage Quality Plans, Product Descriptions, a Quality Log, Quality Review inputs and outputs, a Project Issues Log, Requests for Change and 'Off Specification' documentation.

- **Specialist products** – These are the project's 'technical' deliverables, including products to be delivered during the project, as well as those which comprise those ultimate items or outcomes that you will deliver to your customers. A project's Specialist Products could be just about anything; some will be tangible, such as the report recording the findings and recommendations of a major study, or a workforce relocated to a new building whereas some will be intangible, such as an empowered workforce, or a new teamwork culture.

Note that not all products are outputs from project work. For example, a Project Mandate (a Management Product) might come from a programme to your project as an input; the standards that you use will already exist, but will provide essential prerequisite information. Note that some products are essential inputs from a project's customer: say, for example, an existing database. This customer product would consume no time or effort at the outset, and might appear on your Product Breakdown Structure (PBS) and Product Flow Diagram (PFD) as 'Customer Database'. However, if your project team need to analyse the database, you will consume time, effort and costs. The database will then need to appear on the PBS and PFD with two different names and statuses:

1. Customer Database
2. Analysed Customer Database.

Although the analysis will not change the database in any physical sense, it will change in the logical sense. You knew nothing about it before, but everything you need to know afterwards, so for planning purposes it is two different products. You will need to plan and budget for the work to achieve the 'new' product status.

You should also include key deliverables from external suppliers. PRINCE® provides a robust management process, 'Managing Product Delivery' (acronym MP), for handling the specification and receipt of such products.

HOW DO YOU USE PRODUCTS WITH PRINCE®?

Most project products will be outputs, used for the purposes described above. To deliver each of these, you will use resources such as time, effort, equipment and facilities, so all must appear on both plans and budgets. At the start of each planning process you undertake at project and stage level, you will have an opportunity to identify all the products and then the effort and other resources you will need to deliver them. When you work on the PRINCE® planning process, you will use one of its lower-level processes, PL2 'Defining and Analysing Products'. One of the main outputs from this will be a Product Breakdown Structure, which then becomes an important input to the remaining lower-level processes (PL3–PL7) that deal with dependencies, estimating, scheduling, risk analysis and completing the plan, so a Product Breakdown Structure and its contents are of fundamental importance.

The optimum way to plan products is first to identify for them a Product Breakdown Structure. Then try to describe the key products using the Product Descriptions. Then attempt your first pass at a Product Flow Diagram. As you spot things you have missed and as descriptions and purposes become clearer, you will need to repeat these iteratively to derive a definitive set of schedulable products for your project.

WHAT SHOULD YOU CHECK?

● Are you clear which products are Management, Quality and Specialist?
● Have you identified supplier and customer-supplied products?
● Do your estimates, budgets and schedules show all the work needed to deliver all the Products other than those supplied externally?
● Has each supplier provided a plan showing the schedule and cost for delivery of their products?
● Have you developed a Product Breakdown Structure?
● Have you developed a Product Flow Diagram?
● Have you developed Product Descriptions for all the main products? Is this in line with the requirements of your Quality Plan?

SEE ALSO

PRINCE® Product Breakdown Structure
PRINCE® Product Checklist
PRINCE® Product Description

PRINCE®
PRODUCTS

PRINCE® Project Board

The Project Board in a PRINCE® environment has well-defined roles and responsibilities so that its members can represent the managerial interests of the:

- **business** – ensuring there is a business need to satisfy and that the project will, and eventually does, satisfy it and provide value for money
- **users** – who represents the ultimate users of the final product in one way or another, who perhaps need the product to achieve a Key Performance Indicator or objective
- **supplier** – who is responsible for creating and/or delivering the final product and who may be internal or external

HOW IS A PROJECT BOARD NORMALLY ORGANIZED?

There are three principal roles on a Project Board:

- **The Executive** – with whom accountability for the success of the project lies, and who must ensure that the Business Case is and remains viable, and eventually that it has been satisfied

- **The Senior User** – who is accountable for user inputs and resources and who needs to ensure that products satisfy user requirements

- **The Senior Supplier** – who is accountable for delivering the products and satisfying the Business Case and user requirements.

Notes

1. In almost all cases, the people fulfilling these roles will have other business and departmental duties to perform, and they will only be expected to be available on a part-time basis. For this reason, PRINCE® uses the concept of Tolerance to avoid the

need for a Project Manager to seek daily decisions and authorizations from a Project Board.

2. Sometimes it is possible to combine the roles, but never to eliminate them, perhaps on smaller or relatively straightforward projects. It is not recommended that you ever combine the roles of Senior User and Senior Supplier because of the potential for conflicts of interest.

3. Sometimes roles are split, such as when a project will deliver products to more than one user area and may need more than one Senior User. You might then have too many Senior Users, so it may be better for users to meet at another place and time and nominate the Chair of those meetings as Senior User on the Project Board.

4. The relationship between the Project Board and the Executive should be a democratic one. The Executive should always consult the members, but as he or she holds ultimate accountability for the project, will have to make the tough decisions.

5. Beware Project Board meetings with 'casts of thousands'. Some organizations (mis)use such meetings for large-scale, wide-area communications. If your project needs to run a major briefing, run a major briefing. Avoid trying to use the Project Board to make committee decisions which belong with the Executive.

6. The normal means of communications from Project Manager to Project Board should be a Highlight Report, at intervals determined by the Project Board, typically every week or two. It makes sense to supply an updated Product Checklist at the same times, so that progress can be tracked simply.

SEE ALSO

Steering Group
All PRINCE® topics

PRINCE® Project Initiation

At the end of the PRINCE® process 'Initiating a Project' (IP), you will need to have drafted a vital product (document) known as a Project Initiation Document, invariably referred to as 'the PID', which will form the foundations on which you will gain authorization to develop and manage the remainder of the project. This section provides an overview of a complex and important process that leads towards approval of a PID. Because you create all the foundations for future success during Project Initiation, you might consider deploying your most experienced Project Managers, either to conduct the work, or as mentors. Alongside PID approval, you will also need to seek approval of your detailed pan for the next stage and authorization to proceed with that.

WHEN MIGHT YOU USE IT?

Following the PRINCE® process 'Starting Up a Project' (SU), you should receive a Project Brief, an initial Risk Log, and information on the selected Project Approach, the structure of the Project Management Team and any relevant job definitions, and a plan for the work needed to produce the PID. These are important inputs to what is perhaps the most significant process in any PRINCE® project. You will eventually submit the draft PID, along with the plan for the next stage to your decision-maker(s), who may be the Project Executive or the Project Board, so that the project can be formally authorized.

HOW DO YOU USE IT?

It might be useful to identify the information needs of those who will use a PID, and work backwards from there to identify what you are likely to need to do during Project Initiation. Consult your own standards first, but typically a PID might contain:

1. a description of the background to the project, answering the question, 'How did we get to where we are today?'

2. a definition of the project's:
   - objectives including the required outputs and/or outcomes
   - scope (inclusions and exclusions)
   - constraints
   - approach (how the project should go about delivering the outputs)
   - interfaces (both during the project's life cycle and what its outputs will need to co-exist with).

3. any significant assumptions that have been made to permit progress, but which remain in need of resolution, to answer the question, 'What have we treated as facts but know not to be?'

4. the Business Case, to answer the questions, 'Why are we doing this?' and 'How much is it likely to cost and what benefits will we gain?'

5. the organization and membership of the Project Management Team, to answer the question, 'Who will be accountable and responsible for this project in what roles?'

6. a stakeholder matrix and initial communications plan, to answer the question, 'Who needs to know or be consulted about what as we progress?'

7. a Project Plan, including schedule and budget, to answer the question, 'What needs to be done when and how much is it likely to cost?' and describing the key project products

8. a description of controls, monitoring and reporting, to be used to answer the question, 'How will we keep everything under control?'

9. a Project Quality Plan, describing quality criteria and the control and audit processes that should be used to answer the question, 'How will we ensure that products are fit for purpose and complete?'

10. the process that will be used if any Exceptions occur, to answer the question, 'What will we do if a stage or the project is forecast to be outside the agreed Tolerance?'

11. initial Risk and Issues Logs, and any Contingency Plans to be used if Risks happen, to answer the questions, 'What might go wrong or not happen when we need it and what should we do the?' and 'What Issues do we know to exist, and how, when and by whom should they be resolved?'

12. document management and filing provisions, to answer the question, 'Where should we keep stuff so that we can access it when we need to?'

To create and deliver the information outlined above in a PID, you have six PRINCE® lower-level processes available to you. Using PRINCE® names and acronyms, these are:

- **IP1, Planning Quality** – Here you will use your existing quality standards, the Project Brief and the Project Approach to document how the project will manage quality to achieve the customers' quality expectations in a Project Quality Plan (PQP).

- **IP2, Planning a Project** – In this process, you will use the Project Brief, Project Approach, PQP (from IP1) and Risk Log, to document the timings and resource needs for the project and update the Risk Log.

- **IP3, Refining Business Case and Risks** – Use the Project Brief, Project Approach and the Project Plan (from IP2) to develop the Business Case and Risk Log for the project.

- **IP4, Setting up Controls** – Use the PQP from IP1, the Project Plan and Risk Log from IP2 to develop Project Controls and a Communications Plan and to update the Risk Log if needed.

- **IP5, Setting up Project Files** – Use the PQP from IP1 and the Project Plan from IP2 to set up a Project Filing Structure, Issues Log, Quality Log and a framework Lessons Learned Report.

- **IP6, Assembling the PID** – Draw from all the earlier initiation processes and from some of the earlier Start-up (SU) processes and documents to create the Project Initiation Document.

WHAT SHOULD YOU CHECK?

- Is there now a Project Initiation Document?

- Does it comply with PRINCE® standards (or your organization's standards, if different)?

- Is it clear and unambiguous?

- Does it appear to include all the information needed for decision-making?

- Has the PID been quality reviewed, and have follow-up actions been completed?

- Are the Project's Business Case, objectives, scope, constraints, approach, organization, plan, Quality Plan, Communications Plan, controls, interfaces, risks, Contingency Plans and issues included and complete or appropriately updated at this point?

- Does the PID appear to create a sound basis for approval for the coming project?

- Is the PID accompanied by a Stage Plan for the following stage?

Note that, after approval, you will need to baseline the PID and use it as the standard for assessing progress. If circumstances change significantly and you need to change the PID to reflect the new situation, you will need to undertake this change formally, subject to impact analysis and change control procedures, then re-approval and reauthorization by your Project Executive or Project Board. In practice this is only likely be done for major changes or restructuring.

SEE ALSO

Impact Analysis
All PRINCE® topics

PRINCE® Tolerance

The term 'Tolerance' is found in PRINCE® and non-PRINCE® environments, and is used for a similar purpose. Tolerance can be set (a) for time and (b) for cost, to allow modest variations from the plan or budget and within the Tolerance range defined, without the Project Manager having to seek prior approval from a Project Board.

WHY MIGHT IT BE USEFUL?

Without some room for manoeuvre, a Project Manager would have to operate with one hand tied behind his or her back. Tolerance gives that room. However good your plan, some tasks will run later than desired, some earlier. Some costs will be higher than budgeted, and some lower. Occasionally, a task will take exactly the time scheduled and cost exactly the amount budgeted. Even if the Chair of your Project Board is a control freak, he or she will soon tire if you keep asking for approval for every minor overrun and overspend. However, we must not lose sight of one of project management's important realities that more projects founder because of the unchecked accumulation of modest problems, than as the result of single catastrophic events. Use Tolerance to strike an appropriate balance between control and pragmatism.

HOW DO YOU USE IT?

You need to have a range of time and costs within which to operate, without the need for further permission. Corporate management or a Programme Board will normally set Tolerance to a Project Plan and Budget. The Project Board will normally set Stage Tolerances, to enable conformance with those set for the project. This usually means that once, say, a Stage Budget has been approved, you will not need to worry about variances, unless you forecast that the stage costs will fall outside the agreed Tolerance, normally expressed as plus or minus a percentage of the agreed budget. You could use, say, ±10 or 15 per cent on costs, but your organization may choose to use different rates above and below the agreed budget, such as +10 per cent and −20 per cent. Once a Stage Plan and schedule have been approved, you should only need to report any variations when you forecast that the Stage End date is likely to fall outside the agreed tolerance of plus or minus so many days or weeks from the planned end date. For schedule variations, the Stage Tolerance might be say ±10 working days, or +5 days and −10 days.

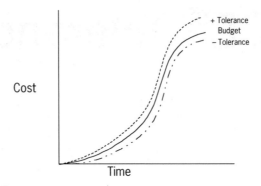

Figure 111   Cost Tolerance

In Figure 111, provided any variance stays within the range shown by the + and − Tolerance, a Project Manager should not need to seek any approvals from the Project Board, which should also agree to accept that delivery of the outputs has been successful when there is a within Tolerance schedule overrun or overspend.

You may ask why early completion and underspend ought to be subject to Tolerance, but if resources, financial and otherwise, are in short supply, it can be of great value to an organization to know that they will not be needed, in time for them to be used elsewhere.

WHEN MIGHT YOU NEED IT?

You will be aware of trends throughout a project stage, and should monitor them carefully. As soon as you forecast that a Tolerance might be reached, you should alert the Project Board. The Project Board may choose to extend the Tolerance, or to request an Exception Report.

WHAT SHOULD YOU CHECK?

- Do you have agreed Tolerances for your project? Are they realistic? If not, what are you doing to rectify this?
- Do you have agreed Tolerances for your current and next stages? Are they realistic, given the Tolerances on the project?
- Do you have Tolerance on stage and project end dates?
- Do you have Tolerance on Stage and Project Budgets?
- Are the Tolerances you know expressed as ranges, usually + and −?
- Are the units in the Tolerances usable? For example, is a range expressed as a percentage of any practical use when applied to dates?

SEE ALSO

Exceptions (and Management By)
Steering Group (references to a PRINCE® Project Board)

Bibliography

Andersen, Erling S., Grude, Kristoffer V. and Haug, Tor (1995), *Goal Directed Project Management* (2nd edn), London: Kogan Page.

Baker, Sunny and Baker, Kim (2000), *The Complete Idiot's Guide to Project Management*, London: Alpha Books.

British Standards Institute (1996), *BS6079: Guide to Project Management*, London: British Standards Publishing.

Brooks Jr, Frederick P. (1975), *The Mythical Man Month: Essays on Software Engineering, 20th Anniversary Edition*, London: Addison-Wesley.

Buttrick, Robert (2000), *The Project Workout: A Toolkit for Reaping the Rewards from All Your Busines Projects* (2nd edn), London: Prentice-Hall.

CCTA (1999), *Managing Successful Programmes*, London: The Stationery Office.

Chapman, Chris and Ward, Stephen (1997), *Project Risk Management: Processes, Techniques and Insights*, Chichester: John Wiley.

Frame, J. Davidson (1995), *Managing Projects in Organizations*, San Francisco, CA: Jossey-Bass.

Gane, Chris P. and Sarson, Trish (1979), *Structured Systems Analysis: Tools and Techniques*, Upper Saddle River, NJ: Prentice-Hall.

Lientz, Bennet P. and Rea, Kathryn (2001), *Project Management for the 21st Century*, London: Academic Press.

Maslow, Abraham H., Frager, Robert and Fadiman, James (1987), *Motivation and Personality* (3rd edn) (first published 1954), Boston, MA: Addison-Wesley.

Office of Government Commerce (2002), *Managing Successful Projects with PRINCE2*, London: The Stationery Office.

Project Management Institute (2000), *A Guide to the Project Management Body of Knowledge* (PMBOK), Philadelphia, PA: Project Management Institute.

Stephanou, S. E. and Obradovitch, M. M. (1985), *Project Management, Systems Development and Productivity*, Malibu, CA: Daniel Spencer Publisher.

Taylor, James (1998), *A Survival Guide for Project Managers*, New York, NY: Amacom.

Wilson, Terry (1994), *A Manual for Change*, Aldershot: Gower.

Young, Trevor (1996), *How to Be a Better Project Manager*, London: Kogan Page.

Young, Trevor (2000), *Successful Project Management*, London: Kogan Page.

Index

(Page references to detailed treatment of a topic are in **bold**)